# LET ME FINISH

More musings on walking, Wetherspoon pubs, football grounds and travelling the world.

Alan Forbes

**A&A Travels**

Copyright © 2024 ALAN FORBES

All rights reserved

No part of this book may be reproduced, or stored in a retrieval system, or transmitted in any form or by any means, electronic, mechanical, photocopying, recording, or otherwise, without express written permission of the publisher.

ISBN: 9798326944412

*IN MEMORY OF BOGUSIA & COLIN*

*Gone far too soon and missed terribly.*

# INTRODUCTION

Welcome back! Do any of us have the faintest notion of where our journey in life will take us or where we want it to take us? When Pete Irwin unwittingly compelled me to start "collecting" airports over 40 years ago could I have imagined that this would, in turn, lead my wife, Agnieszka to &"invite" me to visit every Wetherspoon pub and walk over 2,600 miles in our beautiful island?

Of course not, but what I did know back then was that I loved travelling. Whatever the excuse I was addicted to being on the move and still am.

Roughly 3 million miles later, I'm not "hanging up my boots" but if we could finish what we started then who knows how exciting the next chapter of our lives will be?

# PREFACE

For those of you who managed to avoid "But I digress" let me explain the purpose of this, eagerly anticipated follow up "Let me finish!". I am an addict to collections/collecting. My wife (I've finally managed to stop calling her my girlfriend after nearly a year of marriage) Agnieszka, Aggers, Agi not only joined me on 1 of my existing collections but added 2 more. I collect football league grounds. I was also collecting airports/airfields/aerodromes. We now collect those together along with Wetherspoon pubs and the National Trails in England and Wales.

When I finished "But I digress" I had visited 87 out of the current 92 football league grounds and was on 149 overall. That included new grounds and clubs not currently in the football league in case you non-football folk were just ever so slightly interested how I had visited 149 of 92. I was on 931 airports etc and Agi 411. We had completed 13 1/2 of the 15 National Trails and visited 681 Wetherspoons out of a total of roughly 875.

This book details our efforts to complete the National Trails, visit the remaining unvisited Wetherspoons and for me to get back to 92/92 football league grounds. The bulk of it, though, describes in some detail, the travels we enjoyed on our journey to reach the retirement totals we set ourselves in order to control our airport collecting obsession.

There are lots of serious collectors out there, of stuff way weirder than us: roundabout enthusiasts, pillbox collectors, Tesco collector (I'm sure there isn't more than one of those), all kinds of transport associated collections, to name but a few. Many of these know they are addicted to their collections and will go to extraordinary lengths to increase their collection.

I hope there will be some amusing anecdotes along the way and I will try to offer some recommendations on where our travels have taken us. So, this is it. Will we get there and, if so, will we know what the hell to do with ourselves next?

# ACKNOWLEDGEMENTS

Agnieszka the (wonderful) wife, the travel companion extraordinaire, the inspiration of 2 collections and now, the publisher. I'm not sure if either book would have made it into print without her.

Charlotte, our wonderful daughter-in-law, thank you so much for saving us the grief of coming up with a title for this book!

And the rest is pretty much the same as those in But I Digress, but there was one glaring admission: Tim Martin, now Sir Tim Martin. For those still not in the know, the founder of J D Wetherspoon. Whilst Brexit has recently proved an enormous inconvenience for me personally, we will be forever grateful that he ruddy well did know how to run a pub....and some!

Mr Davies and Mr Newman are not my parents, as I realise it may look in But I Digress. I will always be indebted to the founders of Dan (Davies and Newman) Air Services or as it originally said on the aircraft, Dan Air London. I loved Dan Air London and loved being in their employment for 14 years and the opportunities they gave me to travel the world for next to nothing. I reckon I can count around 100 airports attributable to Dan Air.

Finally to those folk kind enough to buy and read But I Digress and particularly to the 4 who left a nice review! You erased the tiny doubt of whether to continue my career as an author!

# CHAPTER 1

So, what have we been up to I hear you asking? Well, more interestingly, to me, what had (Sweaty) Pete been up to? Peter, recently retired and, after a mystery illness, appeared to be back to top form. We met him in our local Spoon in Oxted and were delighted to learn that, earlier in the week, he had spent 2 1/2 hours discussing with a fellow "enthusiast" when a litter bin had been removed from a bus stop! Of course, this was on his favourite route the number 64, currently running from New Addington to Thornton Heath. In fact, he was trying to narrow down when the dedicated bus stop with bin was replaced by a lamp post with a bus stop sign attached but no bin. Fascinating stuff, eh? Seriously, to me. I think that my admiration for his attention to detail and his memory has yet to peak.

I think he said he had narrowed it down to a 2 week period some time in 1973. To be honest, my brain was so busy trying to digest the basic information that he would spend so much time on this little snippet that I don't remember the exact result he achieved. He arrived at this 2 week window by virtue of when some of his 12,000+ bus photos showed the bin and when they didn't. Peter knows some very interesting people through his interest in rail and bus travel. Maybe the people themselves aren't that interesting but their collections are, if, like me, this subject fascinates you.

Having finished my first book (and finally published it some 18 months later, i.e. not long before this one was almost done) on our journey home from Colombia we now find ourselves back in South America. During a couple of weeks back home we managed a much needed if brief, 2-day Spoons tour. As usual, this took us to towns and a city, that we previously had not visited. We added 10 to our total, rising from 681 to 691. We headed off to Birmingham early for breakfast in The Black Horse before enjoying the usual coffee refills in the relatively newly-opened Navigation Inn. Thankfully with Covid restrictions finally lifted a brief visit to Lichfield to watch my youngest daughter, Molly, pass out from her medics' training in the army followed and had been, believe me or not, the primary motivation for this mini tour. Yes, for the Spoons aficionados, we had already visited The Acorn in Lichfield, actually as far back as October 2016, in our very early Spoon collecting days. Pub number 43 seeing as you asked. In fact during Molly's time in Lichfield we arranged to meet in Rugeley, some 535 pubs later, and Cannock, with another 101 pubs in our collection. After some early resistance I think she has finally accepted Spoons as our natural first choice meeting venue.

My son, Callum is a regular, particularly, well probably specifically on sports related trips but I wouldn't say it would be uppermost in his mind when planning a night out with his wife, Charlotte. Although, if I'm not mistaken, she has expressed a certain partiality towards Spoons, which surprised me; she's quite posh by Forbes' standards. Maybe this has something to do with our nearest Spoons being very much towards the relegation zone; so unimpressed was I by East Grinstead's offering, on pre-Aggers visits, that I held off until almost a year into the collecting before treating her. The Oxted Inn, our only pub within realistic walking distance is better, but not by much. The reason they would both get low marks (if we gave pubs marks, which we don't) is because they're within relatively modern buildings so lack any character. At least the Oxted Inn educated us that Oxted sits on the Greenwich Meridian; the selection of clocks above the bar, with different time zones alluding to this interesting fact. Actually maybe I'm being a bit harsh on Oxted; it has some good history and cozy booths and the train station is next door if we don't fancy the walk uphill home. As for Jordan (eldest daughter) let's just say that her lovely dog, Dudley, provides ample excuse! A work in progress. I think it's fair to say that Callum is the only one who is in any way impressed by the number of pubs we've notched.

Maybe Molly is but keeps it to herself. I think Jordan still wonders what's wrong with us.

We may have been tempted to agree with her after the lengths we went to in order to visit one of the least interesting Spoons on the circuit. The NEC near Birmingham has 2 Wetherspoons, as you may know if a) you've read But I Digress or b) you've become or were already a Spoons collector. A few years ago Aggers had flown back from Germany to Birmingham in order to add that airport to her collection. It made reasonable sense as we were off to walk some of the Cotswolds Way that weekend and planned to spend the evening visiting some Brummy Spoons. Before we did we headed to the NEC in search of both Spoons. A kind chap agreed not to charge us the £12 parking fee involved in attending the Weddings and Honeymoons event that was being held. Probably something to do with it ending in the next hour. We dashed off to The Atrium for a quick half and the obligatory carpet photo. We learned that the unimaginatively named Wetherspoon was closed as they, understandably, only opened when an event was on in that area.

I knew nothing about the NEC having never been there before but Agnes was an old hand with her visits for the dive show. She knew there were 2 halls so expected that one Spoon may be closed. We had put off our visit to the remaining pub for a few years but, having called ahead to see if Wetherspoon was open, it was time to bite the bullet. Once again we were lucky with another friendly parking attendant. On this occasion we wouldn't have minded a nose around the Caravanning and Camping exhibition to salivate over some brand new campervans/motorhomes but Spoons were our mission and we needed to get off to Great Malvern via Redditch.

Crikey, what a long walk to get to Wetherspoon from our free parking. I questioned our sanity, not for the first time. A very small, busy, nonentity of a pub awaited us. Still, it was done. What wasn't done was Birmingham Airport Wetherspoon. It is not the only airport we will need to revisit as the pub is airside and can only be visited when departing, not on landing.

ALAN FORBES

Bit of a nuisance, but, if we are serious, which we are, about visiting every Wetherspoon, it will have to be done. I was going to say that we eagerly await the reopening of the Wetherspoon Express at Stansted airport. However, maybe the opposite is true. Unless one has a flight departing from the area of the airport in which it is situated it is a complicated process.

Many years ago I made a schoolboy error with a couple of friends at Stansted. We mistakenly boarded the train which takes you to the gates where the Spoon is located. In order to get to the correct gate where our flight was departing we had to go back through arrivals and then security again, very nearly missing our flight, rather than being allowed to return by the same train to the departure lounge. I'm sure we are not the only people to be so dumb. Knowing that we would have to go through this process, unless we were lucky enough to have a flight leaving from that area, makes me feel that I wouldn't shed a tear if it closed permanently.

After a brief stop in both Redditch pubs, neither the town or pubs being particularly memorable, The Foley Arms Hotel in Great Malvern was a significantly more worthwhile addition; a lovely example of a Wetherspoon hotel with decent beers, fish and chips and a very comfortable bed after a long day. Suitably refreshed we headed over to Ross on Wye for breakfast, Gloucester for coffees and beer (2 pubs) and another beer in Stroud. Both towns and the city of Gloucester were all worthy of a short visit, once again, thanks to Spoons for increasing our knowledge of Blighty.

I also managed to add one more footy ground. Okay it was only an Under 23 match but it did involve Leeds and was at the new Tottenham stadium. They all count. Inside it is a fine stadium, obviously virtually deserted for this game. Outside it is just another example of how soulless new footy grounds are, in my humble opinion. So that's 88/92 footy grounds and 691 Spoons for those of you keeping count. We weren't back long enough to do any walking. Had the weather been similar to that of the first March lockdown we may have been tempted to stay in UK and walk. It wasn't, so we weren't.

For a couple of indecisives like us a relatively blank sheet presents a bit of a quandary. We decided to narrow it down to a destination not requiring us to take a covid test. That narrowed it down too much really but we were almost decided on Botswana. An interesting and fairly cheap route with Ethiopian Airlines via Addis Ababa and Victoria Falls to Gaborone would allow Aggers to catch me up by 2 more. I'm determined to make it a joint celebration of 500/1000. There could be 3 more airports in Botswana to add. We have never been on safari together. While I pondered over whether we would be able to do this on our budget, a quick check on the weather forecast sent me back to Senegal, our original choice.

I wasn't convinced about this one either. We toyed with Sri Lanka, but domestic flights weren't due to return until May. I couldn't quite bring myself to venture off for a month without collecting a new airport. Aggers also had Colombo in her locker, although she was keen to visit the country. I could say that the worsening economic situation shelved Sri Lanka but who would I be trying to kid? We decided to ditch the no test requirement and, bob's your uncle, up pops a cheeky little £250 fare to Buenos Aires from Madrid.

It seemed remarkably cheap for such an imminent departure. We could have even gone in 2 days' time, rather than the 5 we plumped for. The reason we left it for 5 days was because I couldn't find a direct flight from London to Madrid for much under £150. Well, if you've read any of my previous blurb, you'll know I'm all about percentages. No way am I paying £150 to fly 2 hours when I'm only paying £250 to fly 13! OK, so I know I have to take it on the chin when we pay more to get from home to lousy Luton or shitty Stansted than we ever pay for the flight to Poland or wherever but this? Nope.

I'm all about turning a negative into a positive. I'm going to create a shortcut, just in case. I think it's an acronym but can't be sure. IYRBID = If You Read 'But I Digress'. So, IYRBID, you'll know that. IYRBID you'll know about my dear friend Colin in Dublin and his health issue. Gatwick - Dublin - Madrid, £23 each. Good old Ryanair. No trek to LTN or STN. I'm thinking of getting you into airport 3 letter codes. I'll explain why a bit later. Colin was in week 5 of his treatment so I checked with his wife, Kelly, as to whether she thought it would be appropriate to visit and if so, should we do a surprise? Yes, but best not to.

I've done a few surprises in my time. I've done a few digressions too. I'll stick to the surprises involving new airports, or maybe just airports. It started way back in 1978, shortly after I joined Dan Air. Jackie, first wife to be, already had a flight booked with her parents and a friend to Menorca before we started courting. I think I had been at Dan Air about 3 weeks when she was due to return. I wasn't yet keeping a diary or counting airports so forgive any inaccuracies. Not that, unless you're Jackie, you have any way of verifying the dates. Anyway as luck would have it she was flying on Dan Air. We had only been courting 3 months but I thought it was going pretty well. I decided I couldn't wait for her to come back so took the flight down to Mahon on which she would return. It just so happened that the captain was the same guy, who had taken me on my first ever flight deck trip to Bergen a few weeks earlier. The flight from Gatwick was full so he kindly allowed me to sit in the flight deck again. I didn't tell him the purpose of my journey.

Once we arrived in Mahon I started to feel a little apprehensive. Looking back now it was a bit silly but Jackie was my first proper girlfriend. I liked her a lot and had pined for her for 2 weeks. What if she had met a geezer on holiday and he just happened to be going home on the same flight? I'm not a jealous type and this was probably only a fleeting, irrational thought. Not that she may have had a holiday romance but that the dude in question would be on the flight, boarding the plane with her arm in arm. I watched the passengers board from the safety of the flight deck, out of her view. No bloke in tow, just her, her parents and her friend, Louise.

Safely in the cruise I told Captain Hughes I needed the toilet. No, I didn't actually. I asked him, if I could go to the toilet. Maybe I thought I was still a school boy. I really was so shy back then. I couldn't bring myself to tell him the true reason for me joining him again. I wandered down the cabin and Jackie, deep in conversation, didn't notice me until I said hello. I can't remember how surprised she was but don't recall a yelp or any other outpouring of emotion, but she did tell me that she was rather shocked that she had missed me while she'd been away. It just so happened that the only spare seat on the 89 seater BAC1-11/300 was next to her. I've only thrown that bit of information in about the aircraft type to show off my memory, and for all those aviation enthusiasts who may be reading. I did pop back to the flight deck to explain to Captain Hughes what I had been up to and to ask if he minded if I spent the rest of the flight next to my girlfriend. He thought it quite amusing.

My parents were holidaying in the Algarve in late 1980. Airlines used to, and I believe still do, occasionally operate what Dan Air referred to as W patterns. In this instance the aircraft operated Gatwick - Faro - Manchester - Faro - Gatwick. This would give Jackie and me a few hours to spring a surprise on my mum and dad while the plane went to Manchester and back. Luckily my parents were in their hotel grounds that day. We'd figured they wouldn't stray too far from the hotel or beach. I don't recall either of them being overexcited about our unexpected visit but I wasn't permanently put off.

It was to be almost 4 years before I tried again. I'm not sure if there had been any obvious opportunities in the meantime, if I did one and have forgotten or if I was otherwise occupied. The summer of 1984, school holidays, Los Angeles Olympics. What would be the chances of travelling standby to Vancouver at such a time? Pretty darn good actually if you put a bit of time into research. I was well into counting airports by now. Vancouver was out of the question. All the flights were showing full and, even though the purpose of the trip was to surprise my parents and family, I certainly wanted a few airports on the way.

It was always worth a punt to try an airline which Dan Air didn't have a self-ticketing agreement with for staff travel. In my experience they would often offer a free ticket, standby, of course. Not only did Northwest Orient (long since gone, but not before they changed their name, at least on their planes, to NWA -well I found it amusing, if inappropriate) offer me a free ticket, they offered me a free First Class ticket. The rather obnoxious (at the time, she did mellow towards me once our paths crossed in later life. I think she just didn't like the frequency and success of my ad hoc requests) staff travel manager blatantly accused me of making a direct approach to the airline for a ticket. This was a no no and could result in one losing their travel concessions if found out. She couldn't understand why NWA would offer a lowly Assistant Operations Controller a First Class ticket. Such privileges were normally only afforded to senior managers or sales staff.

Not only was I potentially going to experience my first First Class travel I would also add 4 new airports to my slowly increasing total on my way to Seattle and back. There was probably only about 8 First Class seats in the nose of the old (Classic according to Virgin) B747 but, as luck would have it, there was only a couple of passengers booked so I was off to Minneapolis/St Paul in what was for me, at the time, unadulterated luxury. I'd never had caviar before! My connecting flight via Spokane to Seattle also allowed me to stretch my legs.

I've often experienced slumming it after travelling in luxury since but this was my first taste of it. It would seem I hadn't really thought the last part of the journey through. There wasn't a Greyhound bus to Vancouver until 0330. I was properly knackered by the time I arrived in Vancouver, 30 hours after I'd left Gatwick, the First Class luxury becoming a distant memory. I still had another hour to get to Abbotsford where one of my cousins lived and was informed there was a bus strike. Clearly taxis were cheap back then, not that I had another option. Finally I arrived in Abbotsford around 9.30 in the morning.

I think it is worth recalling how the surprise unfolded. My cousins in Abbotsford are older than me. They were out but fortunately their 3 kids were home. Lesley, the oldest, probably about 16 at the time, answered the door. As you can imagine she was pretty surprised to see her 2nd cousin from England standing there. I plonked myself on their sofa until their parents, my cousins came home. When they did, it's fair to say they were slightly taken aback, in a positive manner. As luck would have it, they would be driving to my uncle and aunt's in the afternoon where my parents were staying. Then we would all go to my other cousin's place for a barbecue.

My uncle answered the door to their apartment with a look of disbelief when he saw me. Momentarily, I was worried he was going to have a heart attack. I motioned to him to keep quiet and proceeded to the living room. My mother was not prone to displaying emotion or affection but, such was her shock, and joy, at seeing me she overdosed on both. I'm afraid her response to my totally unexpected appearance has obliterated any memory I may have had of my dear father's reaction.

On to my cousin Doug's. I hid in the boot of my cousin Eileen's car just before we arrived. Everybody managed to keep the secret as they arrived and Doug was dispatched to get the beers from the boot. "What the fuck!" he rightly and fairly exclaimed on popping the trunk (as they do in North America). This surprise had gone as well as its predecessor back in '78. I was chuffed to bits and buzzing on pretty much no sleep for 48 hours by the end of the day.

Whilst on Canada surprises, my parents were making a round the world trip winter '86/87. I had called my mum on Xmas day to wish them festive greetings whilst they were in New Zealand. I had difficulty convincing her I was not in a callbox round the corner from them in deepest South Island NZ. This prompted me to hatch a plan for another Vancouver surprise in the New Year when they would be passing through. I arrived at Vancouver airport a couple of hours before they did from Hawaii. Enough time to greet my cousins. Shock and surprise were still in abundance even though they figured they should have guessed I may turn up. Similar reaction to that of my parents when they realised I was amongst their welcoming party.

There are quite a few more of these little events I could recall but, even for me, this digression is long enough and becoming a tad too self-indulgent. I will conclude with one more, as it did involve 2 new airports, if I may. My parents had gone to Zell am See in Austria for Christmas 1985 with my aunt and cousins. So, after working the festive period off I popped to Innsbruck; a quick hello for a couple of days then off to Salzburg for my return flight. It was a lot of fun again, to see my parents' and aunt's reaction. I had let my cousins in on the plan as I felt I needed some inside help, on this occasion, to ensure the plan went smoothly.

Right. Sorry about that. Where was I? Ah yes, Kelly had suggested no surprise element on this occasion. Colin was delighted that we would visit and, it just so happened that our arrival time and his treatment timing enabled us to pop up to nearby Swords to add one more Spoon to the total before we would meet up. Bingo! We will be back when, God willing, Colin will be in better health and hopefully join us on a tour of the remaining Ireland Spoons.

Whilst the weather was naturally of no importance on this first leg of our journey to Buenos Aires, given the magnitude of what our dear friend was going through I'm still going to mention it. Why? Because (yes, I'm still allowing myself some grammatical no no's) of the gradual change we experienced. It was blowing a gale and threatening to pee down on arrival in Dublin. Luckily the rain held off long enough for our pub visit, and a quick tour of Colin's less than humble land mass on arrival - the mini goats were hilarious. After that, the rain barely relented.

After successfully filling in all the necessary forms on previous covid times' travels my right index finger, or rather my brain let me down badly this time. I'm going to blame it on the lateness of the hour and that I was on form 6 of 6. The fact of the matter was that when I submitted Aggers' form for admittance to Argentina I was horrified to receive a red alert reply saying that she would need to quarantine on arrival for 14 days!! What had I done differently to my own form allowing me to wander freely on arrival!!?

As per IYRBID let me remind you all things in perspective as always, but this was not in the plan and was an in perspective cock up. On closer inspection I realised that, what I had done, or more correctly, not done, on Agi's form was untick the box that said she had not been vaccinated. That was it. Simple as that. Surely I could not be alone in making such a simple error? Surely logic would dictate that having a vaccination certificate to show on arrival, or, equally as important, to show to the airline on departure, would override that tick being in the wrong box? We all know that logic has been in very short supply during covid.

We tried, with no success, to resubmit a new form. Agi was remarkably more understanding of my error than I was. She was sure it could be remedied in the morning. I wasn't. She was right as usual. After a quick call to the Argentine embassy in Dublin, not much help but friendly nonetheless, and a more productive call to Agi's friend in Buenos Aires (B.A from now) we found a way to delete the dud form and resubmit a new one with all the ticks in the right boxes. Phew!! We were off to Madrid, at least.

It felt quite odd going back there so soon. We would not be going into the city centre this time. For some reason hotel prices were particularly high to go with the London - Madrid flight prices. We found a not unpleasant little establishment in nearby Barajas - the recognised name of Madrid airport before Adolfo Suarez got in on the act - which was just a 30 minute stroll away, yet a quiet and pleasing suburb to spend the remainder of the evening and the next morning.

The weather was a vast improvement on Dublin and a gradual step towards what we hoped we would, and did, experience in B.A.

Before heading back to the airport and off on our latest adventure I'm going to share a little something with you. I have noticed recently that whenever writing, reading about, planning travel in or watching a programme based in a different country to the one we currently find ourselves in I forget where I am. I am transported to the country of writing, planning, reading or watching. This went into total overdrive when we were in Dublin airport. I kept thinking we were already in Madrid. Where was I going to think I was on arrival in Spain? B.A? Of course. Fortunately this feeling doesn't last for too long but I find it quite amusing and even a tad unnerving at times.

Having landed in B.A Ezeiza airport (a newbie for Agnieszka) at the rather unsociable hour of 0320 we were off on a new, and, as usual, unplanned adventure, and it was warm, very nice and warm.

# CHAPTER 2

What a charmingly bonkers country Argentina is. Once we had settled in for a few hours' wait in a deserted area of one of Madrid's terminals we decided we should start reading up on what awaited us. I mention this for one other bonkers reason. There was quite literally nobody else within 500 metres of where we had plonked ourselves. That's why we chose to sit there, plus they were very comfy seats, almost beds. The occasional worker would pass by, at least 20 metres away from us, the other side of the travelators. Then this one dude on an e-scooter passed by. I knew as soon as he passed us and reached the end of the travelators that he would come back to us as we weren't wearing masks.

He didn't disappoint. Unbelievable. As he approached us and started to remonstrate, I picked up my empty coffee cup and pretended to drink. He made a U-turn and went on his merry way. I wonder if he had been without electrical power if he would have bothered to make the diversion. Maybe he would just have shouted at us from afar. Either way, utterly bonkers. I like that word. Quite an old-fashioned one really but aptly describes Argentina and mask wearing. I've noticed it becoming increasingly popular to use, since I first wrote that, but I reckon I was using it first! It will most likely have faded again by the time you read this anyway.

I'm not going to bang on about the latter but suffice to say that bonkers examples of mask wearing continued in Argentina as they had in Colombia. It's not that either of us are blasé about covid. There most likely are times and places where mask wearing makes sense - isolated in Madrid airport is not one of them.

Before I tell you why Argentina is bonkers, I would just like to sing the praises of Aerolineas Argentinas. I do not ever recall being offered a large can of beer, I'm talking 500ml minimum, on any flight I have taken. Of course, they gave us wine too but when I got into conversation with one of the cabin crew about the God named Marcelo Bielsa, he immediately offered us a couple more large cans of Argentinian lager. Aggers didn't know why but she had a vision that Aerolineas Argentinas would be on a par with Cubana. It would be difficult to damn an airline with a worse comparison. Imagine how pleasantly surprised she was once on board.

Just before we boarded in Madrid, we began to discover the bonkers nature of Argentina. I'm not going to overuse my new favourite word, promise. It is pretty much all economy related, the bonkersness - I know that's not a word and pushing it a bit but it'll do for now. As I write, we have been in Argentina a little over 3 weeks so I think we can justify our opinion on the state of play here. Fortunately, Aggers has a couple of friends in Buenos Aires. They had both mentioned to her to bring some US Dollars for the "Blue market". I figured that blue market was the new politically correct term for "Black market". We hadn't paid too much attention to this advice but, thankfully, as we were making our way to the gate in Madrid, I asked Agnes to contact her friend again and check on the money situation.

Luckily for us she responded immediately. Basically, the official rate of exchange for Argentinian pesos to pounds was currently 140=£1. The blue market rate was 250!! Now that's roughly 80% difference!! Obviously, Argentinians want dollars not UK pounds. We hastily diverted to a nearby Travelex. Neither of us were comfortable carrying wads of cash but settled on $800. Even though we were losing around £50 on the conversion of pounds to euros to dollars at a money exchange it would still be a major saving.

When we landed in Buenos Aires the fun started in my head about how much a taxi would cost. Did I convert at 140 or 250? Seeing as we had no pesos and, if we exchanged dollars at the airport, we would only get the official rate we decided to pay in euros. Every traveller knows that taxis from big international airports are invariably a rip off but, it was 4am and Agnes' friend Jenny had insisted it was no problem to arrive at their downtown apartment at an ungodly hour so we bit the bullet. The next bus wasn't until 6 am so we took a cab for 30 euros.

Before we left the airport I had a fleeting moment of extreme excitement. Fellow Leeds supporter, Jim the pilot, had become quite good friends with Marcelo Bielsa. I texted him from Madrid to let him know we were heading to one of his favourite cities. On arrival in B.A I had a text from him telling me that he'd just arranged Marcelo's flights to leave UK that evening. We were definitely the first flight from Europe to arrive that morning. I told Aggers we were going to wait for Marcelo to arrive, so I could finally put right my wrong of not saying hello to Don Revie, almost 40 years earlier, when the opportunity presented itself. She didn't protest. My excitement was short-lived. Jim's response to my enquiry as to which flight Marcelo was on put paid to any brief hello I had in mind. Marcelo wasn't going home to Argentina. He was going on holiday to Brazil. Gutted. Never assume, eh?

So, off we went to Jenny's. After an hour or so sleep we awoke to a perfect morning - a totally cloudless sky. I had very fond memories of my previous 2 visits to B.A. It's a majestic, charming, buzzing city. Considering it has no natural beauty to its setting like Rio, Vancouver or Cape Town for example it is still one of my favourite cities. We set off with Jenny to change our dollars with her uncle on the blue market. We learnt that the black market still exists but that it is seen as the unofficial, unofficial market, whereas the blue market is the official unofficial market. Got it? There's also the white market but we won't get into that as I can't remember it.

We now had wads of pesos. Luckily in this instance, mainly 1,000- and 500-pesos denominations. For people like us who now live in a predominantly cashless society this was an interesting situation. Where were we going to keep all this money? Certainly not in my wallet. For a start, it literally would not fit and, with my recent penchant for losing stuff it would be a rather silly option. Jenny was happy to, no, insisted on keeping it in her small backpack until we returned home. Fair enough but I didn't fancy the awkward conversation if she got robbed or just happened to misplace her bag. Neither of which happened.

Whilst admiring the architecture of the buildings and general niceness of the main, wide streets and charm of the not so wide streets on our private tour with Jenny, we learnt of the difficulties with their economy. Why so many Argentinians were leaving for Uruguay or Europe because of it. Inflation is currently running at 60%. I was busy trying to work out whether I should be converting at 140 or 250 still. $800 wouldn't last long and if we bought anything on line or by card it would be 140 anyway. You may think I'm labouring the point here. When you travel on a budget for any length of time money is obviously important. When you travel full time, more so.

We bought lunch at a very pleasant dockside development. A not unreasonable £25 at 250 but a pretty pricey £45 at 140 for budget travellers. I thought I may get the whole money malarkey out of the way in one go but there's too many examples to list in one hit so, forgive me, but I'll be back on this subject from time to time, mainly from an amusement perspective. Let's get back to the real reason why we are here - airports! Now IYRBID you'll know I'm only kidding or, maybe you've decided I'm not. Either way I had some serious planning to do. There's a lot of airports in this country. Unfortunately, even more so than Colombia they tend to operate, in the main, from 2 or 3 bases. Sadly, no air pass this time. More worryingly, even though I'd had a quick glance at Skyscanner before we left there seemed a distinct lack of cheap flights. Maybe my glance had been too quick. Perhaps I was overexcited by the sheer volume of potential airport opportunities.

The other problem was that we were having such a nice time with Jenny and her husband, Luciano, that I was having difficulty setting aside time to plan. If we wanted to see some of the 8th largest country in the world, I needed to get my shit together. After one evening set aside to do just that I finally settled on a flight to Bariloche, followed by a flight from Neuquén to Salta 5 days later. After that I was buggered. Every time I thought I had a plan I was thwarted by some ridiculous price at some point on the itinerary I worked on. The low-cost airline bubble that was inflating in Argentina had been well and truly burst by covid. Norwegian had disappeared completely and Jetsmart's prices bore no resemblance to those we had enjoyed in Chile. FlyBondi, low cost? I don't think so.

It wasn't like we could bin off air travel. Pretty unlikely for a couple of airport collecting addicts anyway but, having all but scrapped the entire network of railway lines the Brits had lovingly created for them, and with a coach/bus network that wasn't cheap either, our options were non-existent. The distances involved, 24 hours by bus from B.A to Bariloche, for example, were not appealing, let alone the price.

Whilst I was beginning to fret about how we were going to increase our airport totals (made a change from worrying about the weather affecting them in Colombia), Aggers was busy increasing her knowledge, once more, by joining local Facebook groups. Through this she learnt that we could potentially obtain more blue market money through Western Union. I'd seen Western Union signs all over the world but neither knew what they really did nor had had cause to find out and use them. If it was true though, which it proved to be, this meant if we went to airline offices and paid for flights in cash, they would be up to 80% cheaper than on line. Result! Off we trotted to Aerolineas Argentinas to book some flights. There was a bit of a queue but hey ho, needs must. We enquired if we needed to take a ticket. "Do you have an appointment?"
"Err, no."
"Well, you need an appointment"
"OK, can we make an appointment?"
"Yes, we have a few available on Thursday"

It was Monday! Told you this country is bonkers. Back to square one. We were not disheartened. Just a little frustrated. We had enjoyed a marvellous 5 days in B.A. Apart from Jenny and Luciano's hospitality we had met up with a couple of Agnes's other friends and took ourselves off around the city and its suburbs. It's a must-see city in my humble opinion but do check on the currency exchange situation. If it hadn't had been for Jenny, we would have been blissfully unaware. We were working from Lonely Planet 2017 for our information. No blue or white markets back then, only a black one which didn't offer much difference.

We had 3 airports to add, well, 4 for Aggers. Whilst not walking distance like Medellín's city airport, Aeroparque in B.A is much more conveniently located than the main international airport, Ezieza, and was another new one for my wife. I did say I would explain why I may teach those of you who are not in the know about airport 3 letter codes. Well, that's because Jenny, on learning of our collections, came clean on hers. She collects airport 3 letter codes. More specifically the bag tags for checked in luggage. Why you may ask? Why not? I used to play footy with a bloke who collected airline sick bags. I was able to help him grow his collection before airlines got boring and many used a nameless white bag. Jenny was collecting the tags in order to make a poem out of the 3 letter codes. Way more intellectual than any of my/our stuff wouldn't you say? Just so you can see how this will or won't work I'll give you some examples along the way. As we travel hand luggage only, we won't be able to help Jenny. We considered waiting for other people's bags and asking if we could have their labels but that would be a bit weird, wouldn't it?

Jenny was off to Montevideo MVD for work whilst we had a rather early flight from Aeroparque AEP to Bariloche BRC. Not sure how you make a word out of any of those, but we were off on our Argentinian adventure.

# CHAPTER 3

Seeing as we left Argentina for Brazil 4 days ago it feels a tad fraudulent to write a diary of our time there. I know there's no law against writing a diary retrospectively and it wasn't really my intention to do that anyway when I first started writing. Argentina was just too much fun and too bloody beautiful to bury my head in my iPad/phone for any longer than my daily addictions. IYRBID you may remember what they are. If not I'm sure you won't die wondering.

I also said I had no intention of writing a travel book. I slipped into that when writing about India and Colombia in particular. However, maybe for my own benefit, as well as recounting how our airport collections increased, I'm going to give a brief resume of our time in Argentina and add a few thoughts along the way.

I doubt this book will ever be read by an Argentinian so I think I'm fairly safe to say, without repercussions, "No they are not! Get over it!" It's everywhere. "Las Malvinas son Argentinas". Every town we visited made some claim or other. The airport in Rosario was called Aeropuerto Las Malvinas.... We found a bus company called Las Malvinas, an hotel, let alone all the streets and parks. Now, whilst I may retain a little more patriotism than is fashionable in UK, I really don't mind who owns/controls the Falkland Islands. Surely it is down to the people who live there? Simple as that in my little world.

What we did learn from the few people we spoke to about this obsession (it's still a touchy subject according to LP 40 years later) is that the Argentinians blame their regime for the deaths of their military in the conflict, rather than the Brits. We happened to be flying on the public holiday they have commemorating the war and Aerolineas Argentinas had placed headrest covers with "Malvinas nos une" on every seat! They are not yours. No country in the world recognises them as Argentinian except Argentina to my knowledge. It started out as amusing but by then it became a little tiny bit irritating. Not much, just a wee puckle as my old man would say.

Bariloche was a bit of a shock to the system after Buenos Aires. In fact it was bloody freezing but also very beautiful. It's very touristy but a must see if you go to Argentina, which you really should, and which I didn't on my 2 previous visits. So who I am to say you should. We hired a car and drove to San Martin de Los Andes. The scenery was, to coin an oft overused phrase, breathtaking. In this instance it was justified. Before we left I had a first since 1977. I hope I wasn't as irritating as back then but I went to a travel agent after a 45 year absence.

In 1977 I made a solo trip to Canada, flying to Montreal Mirabel, taking a Greyhound bus to Vancouver (for those of you not in the know, that's about 3000 miles on a bus) and flying back. I enlisted the help of the local travel agent in Shirley, Croydon to book my flights and bus. I was 16 when I booked it, and barely 17 when I travelled. Now I know it's not up there with those clever sods who've flown themselves solo around the world before their 18th birthday but I was excited. I found any excuse I could to pop in after school to, most likely, the infuriation of the agent.

On the subject of Montreal it had/has two airports. Back then Mirabel handled the international flights and Dorval the domestics. Aggers and I went via Montreal to Costa Rica a few years ago. I assumed Trudeau airport was just a new name for Mirabel. Imagine my delight when I stumbled upon the fact that they had moved international flights to Dorval some years back and used the president's name, potentially denying me one more to my total. I believe this is the reason why I now check Wikipedia for airport history just in case. No such luck on this trip with the previous airports I had on my list. Apologies for the repetition IYRBID!

Having failed to secure an appointment with Aerolineas

Argentinas in B.A we were not surprised to find that their office in Bariloche was permanently closed. Credit to Aggers for coming up with the travel agent idea. We found Haylands Travel hiding up on the 6th floor of an office block. Luciano (not Jenny's husband or Luciano Becchio) was more than happy to help us. I felt it prudent to come clean on our addiction so that he didn't think us odd. Obviously he probably thought we were very odd when I proposed some routings to him. He took it in his stride and accepted the challenge. When Agnieszka, giggling like a 5-year-old, informed him that the only reason we wanted to fly to Jujuy was because it meant willie in Polish, in the most obscene form (think prick etc I guess) he was putty in our hands.

I gave him around 8 itinerary options to add 8 airports to the 3 I had already booked. I must say I was mightily impressed with his speed, all the time muttering Jujuy to himself. He managed to add 7 but was stuck on the vital 8th. I then remembered that I could book flights on line with JetSmart, albeit at the shitty official rate. I matched an 8th with his 7 and breathed, not a metaphorical, but a literal sigh of relief. Luciano had managed to achieve an average and very acceptable flight price of £30 per sector. I happily parted with the majority of our wad of 70,000 pesos.

Whilst in B.A I had looked at how we were going to return to UK. It's all very well when you can fly to Argentina for £250 but not really in our budget to pay £6-700 to fly back, particularly with no new airports along the way. Unlike returning from Colombia or Dominican Republic, where our BA points had enabled us to get home for a ridiculous 50 odd quid each, this option did not exist. Neither from Argentina nor Brazil. So...... I found an airport collector's dream ticket and a normal person's nightmare route home. Florianopolis - Brasilia - São Paulo Congonhas - bus trip across São Paulo with a few hours sightseeing and lunch - São Paulo Guaralhos - Heathrow. 3 new airports for me, and 4 for 'er indoors (who is clearly not indoors any more than I am). An 0540 departure from Florianopolis was a little daunting as was the 30 hour journey time but the price was right and one ain't gonna get to 1000 airports if one passes up this kind of opportunity.

Quite why LATAM would choose to give us a couple of domestic flights and charge us less than if we had just flown from São Paulo to London is just another quirk of aviation life. I mention this now because it meant we could go ahead and book our last flight in Argentina to Iguazu. I was chuffed to learn that there was an Iguazu airport on the Argentinian side of one of nature's greatest spectacles. Many years back I had flown from Rio to Iguazu on the Brazilian side. The Varig pilot had been kind enough to make 2 flypasts so that both sides of the plane got a spectacular view.

I spent many an hour searching to add 2 more airports to our journey from Iguazu to Florianopolis to no avail. Flying in Brazil is not cheap. Actually it is ludicrously expensive. No word of a lie. I found flights of 2 hours duration or less for anything between £2-400. Just to clarify that is £200-400, not £2.00-4.00. We were paying less to get home! It looked like we would have no option but to suck it up and take the 17 hour bus ride. Aggers may have flinched internally but, externally she stoically accepted this probability.

After returning our car to Bariloche we embarked on a 5 hour bus ride to Neuquén from where we would fly to Salta. The bus journey was equally as spectacular as our 3 days in the car. Instead of numerous lakes we followed the most gorgeous river for the best part of the journey. Neuquén was fairly unremarkable but we did encounter yet another weird anomaly with the money situation. The hotel we had booked on Booking.com required us to pay an extra 21% tax if we paid in cash. If we paid by card we would pay the price Booking.com had quoted. We're not talking a whole lot of money here. It was a very nice apartment for a very acceptable price but what was this all about? The night receptionist was adamant that we had to pay it, to the point he suggested we could look elsewhere. He diffused the situation by saying we could pay in the morning. His colleague the next morning was equally insistent. We paid the extra 21%, rather than the extra 80% it would have cost us to pay by card. We really didn't understand it though.

Both staff members insisted that it was out of their control. Funny that we had paid in cash for the 3 hotels we stayed in during our lakes tour without such penalty. That was a mere inconvenience in comparison to the hotel we booked in Salta. On arrival the room looked nothing like Booking.com's pictures. Apparently the room we had booked had a problem. The owner, who was only contactable by phone, knew this, contacted Booking.com who suggested he offer us an alternative. It's very rare for us to walk away when shown a room but this was a hovel. We went off for some delicious local delicacies of the liquid and solid variety before finding ourselves a suitable alternative. Neither Booking.com nor the owner had proven capable of this.

Argentina did absolutely nothing to encourage us in restricting our alcoholic intake. It was difficult to pay much more than £1 for a bloody nice beer. Not only that, a decent bottle of wine could accompany a meal for a couple of quid. We weren't walking much in general. Coupled with the irresistible dulce du leche and some of the best ice cream I've ever been lucky enough to enjoy, Argentina, whilst incredibly healthy on the wallet with the blue pesos bulging, wasn't so kind on the physical health. We were only there for a jot over 3 weeks. We could exercise more control once we left. Warm weather, tasty alcohol and food, great settings. Life's too short not to, even if it may ultimately make it shorter.

Our flight from Jujuy took us briefly to Córdoba, another pretty decent city before a 6 hour bus ride took us to the home of Leeds United's saviour, none other than Marcelo Bielsa himself. It just so happened that one of Agnes's friends in B.A had a friend in Rosario whose partner used to work for Newell's Old Boys. We only had our own private tour of the Marcelo Bielsa stadium! This was the next best thing to seeing a game there or meeting the legend himself. Marcelo is rightly revered throughout Argentina and Chile. I'm not going to say it was one of the highlights of our trip but it was a lot of fun.

The previous evening when we arrived in Rosario it was blowing a right old gale. Enough to take quite a few trees down. We didn't wish to venture too far from the bus station for a hotel. We found one and secured a discount for sharing the Bielsa love of 80 pence. The next morning we received a further discount of £2 by virtue of having got stuck in the lift for the best part of half an hour.

After our stadium and city tour in Rosario we enjoyed a short flight back to B.A with splendid views of the city. More great food, drink and company was enjoyed with a much more sociable afternoon departure than that of 0620 to Bariloche. We landed in Rio Hondo, a curious place which, likely, only Moto GP fans would be familiar with. We hotfooted it on a bus to Tucumán that evening in readiness for our next car tour the next morning. The only problem was that the Moto GP was taking place the following weekend and Tucumán had already shipped 1000 hire cars down the road (1 hour by bus) in preparation for the event. I mention this mainly because of the next money adventure it caused us.

We struggled to find a car at all until the kind man at the tourist office, miraculously open on a Sunday morning, located one with Alamo at the airport for 33,000 pesos. We had enough cash so jumped in a cab to the airport only to be told they had made a mistake and it would be 52,000 pesos. It wasn't just the fact that they'd hiked the price that was inconvenient but the fact that we didn't have 52,000 pesos. Even if we did this would leave us very short of cash for the next 3 days where Western Unions were sparse. Fortunately the agent allowed us to leave without paying. We could do so on our return.

After enjoying what can only be described as scenery where one runs out of superlatives, overnighting in delightful Cafayate and Cachi we were back to Tucumán with a flight to catch and nowhere near 52,000 pesos.

Tucumán is Argentina's 5th largest city. Around one million folk I believe. We had no need to go into the city as the airport was on our way back. I was sore enough paying £70 a day for a brand new Chevrolet, instead of £40 quoted. If we didn't want to pay £125 a day we needed cash, and fast. We tried 5 Western Unions before we finally found one with enough pesos for us. Job done, just. Hopefully we would waste less time when we got to Mendoza.

At the risk of repeating myself, we like clear blue skies (to be fair, I am repeating myself because my iPad failed to save my last few paragraphs, yet again). Temperature is not so important. Just as well. It was 2 degrees when we arrived in Mendoza at 8 am, but it was gloriously sunny yet again. Apart from some very UK style grey skies in Rosario we had been blessed throughout our time in Argentina. I'm sorry but it makes so much difference. Maybe it shouldn't, but, to us it does. After finding ourselves a delightful old hostel in downtown - well the building was old, but the hostel anything but - we headed off to breakfast in a sunny courtyard and then took a bus to rent bikes to visit some vineyards. What an extremely desirable experience. We're by no means wine connoisseurs so tasting for us is really just drinking slowly.

We only visited a couple of vineyards that afternoon but it was a fabulous experience and we clocked up a few miles on the bikes. The next day we not only wine tasted, but beer, chocolate and ice cream tasted too. Not a bad way to waste a day. Before we left we needed more pesos. We skipped over to the Western Union opposite us. "Do you have 60,000 pesos for us, por favor?" No problem. What the young lady failed to mention was that she had 60,000 pesos for us in 100 peso notes. That's £240 in 40p notes. That's 600 notes. It could have been worse. They have 10 peso notes!! Can you believe a 4p note!? This was not practical. The kind owner of the hostel offered to try and change the 100 peso notes for us so we left him with 500 of them and headed off with a much more manageable wad. We no longer looked like drug dealers with our ill-gotten gains.

When we came back that evening we were happy to be down to a totally acceptable 50 notes. Revolut clearly knew what was going on in Argentina. They emailed saying they'd noticed I hadn't used my card lately. What was up? How caring of them! You may very well be thinking that this bloke, me that is, doesn't half harp on about money. I can't deny it. It's fundamental though when travelling endlessly on a budget. It also interests us how locals manage. It's very, very cheap to eat and drink well in Argentina but car hire and flights are very expensive in comparison. We struggled to hire a car on three occasions. Flights were invariably full. Yet, apparently the average monthly salary in Argentina is $300-350.

Moving on, as we did, we took a bus down to San Rafael. The journey there was average but the landscapes the next day? Another day of wows. This time we drove down into and through a canyon. It was simply stunning. We headed back from another charming airport back to B.A for the final time. We kind of regretted eating and drinking until 1.30 am when we awoke at 4.30 for another 6.20 flight from Aeroparque, but only momentarily. We were off to Iguazu Falls. I quote from Lonely Planet:
"No matter the number of waterfalls you've checked off your bucket list, no matter how many times you have thought you'd be just fine never seeing another waterfall again, Iguazu Falls will stomp all over your idea of water trickling over the edge of a cliff. The thunderous roar of 275 falls crashing across the Brazil and Argentina border floors even the most jaded traveller. Loud, angry, unstoppable and impossibly gorgeous, Iguazu will leave you stunned and slack-jawed at the absolute power of Mother Nature."

I couldn't have put it better myself, which is why I haven't. What LP didn't tell us was that the Falls were closed on the Brazilian side on a Monday. Fortunately we hadn't booked any onward travel to Florianopolis. Fortunately it was a Monday because it hammered it down all morning. They did us a favour as it happened. Fortunately Aggers, clearly secretly determined to avoid that overnight bus journey had stepped away from her accommodation researching duties and found us an affordable flight from the Brazilian Iguazu airport to Curitiba. She'd even researched the bus on from Curitiba to Florianopolis.

After a day of doing pretty much jack, apart from a

painless border crossing, saying farewell Argentina and alright Brazil(?), we left early for our Brazilian Falls experience, thus avoiding the crowds to come and almost having the place to ourselves. Our only complaint about the Brazil experience is that they have tried to go down the Disney route on the entrance. Like Argentina though they have failed in any attempts to bastardise what is so well described above. It was a shame that our cheap flight left at 0545 the next morning thus robbing us of an aerial view on departure.

We saw nothing of Curitiba. I had done a double check on which airports I had visited in Brazil previously as I had a vague recollection that my flight from Rio to Iguazu had made a stop. Sadly it was in Curitiba but this meant that Agi was getting closer to getting into 400/900 parity in our attempt to climax together on 500/1000. Florianopolis was a fairly pleasant city. Well, actually it enjoyed a fine location, some nice old buildings and the money was straightforward. Only problem was; that that meant expensive beer and food. We came across, and resisted a 2 litre bottle of red wine for £1 in Iguazu Falls, which once again showed the inconsistency in pricing. No wonder we saw many more homeless people in 4 days in Brazil than we had in 3 1/2 weeks in Argentina.

We had a first for dinner that night. A very enthusiastic, young, English speaking - the latter being a rare treat - waiter enticed us to sample his fare in the local market. I clocked that the prices were really quite high. £6-7 for some of the beers. We decided to share a very tasty litre of local, and most welcome after finally achieving 2 days of abstinence, Belgian white beer. We pondered the menu and took the waiter up on his suggestion to share a local fish dish. He showed us a picture of it, so I hadn't clocked it on the menu. I panicked when I did. £70! I checked that I hadn't mixed up the price. I hadn't. I apologised and said I would have to cancel the order. "I can make you a special offer. How about R$210 including tax?" Basically 50% off. Still pricey - Argentina had truly spoiled us - but it sounded tasty and wasn't it just! I guess I didn't haggle as such but it was a first for either of us to strike a deal on a restaurant meal. "If you don't ask for the special offer, you don't get the special offer", he informed us with a cheeky grin. Noted, should we return to Brazil. Or maybe we should try it everywhere.

We finished off our latest South American venture with a very tidy MasterCard Priceless rooftop restaurant in São Paulo. A new one on me, MasterCard Priceless restaurants? We won't be rushing back to Brazil unless we have a change in finances or they do, but it was a pleasant end to another fantastic month or so on the road. I was quite sad to leave Argentina, not quite so, Brazil. São Paulo is just a bit too big, busy and, sorry to say, rough, for my tastes. It made me keener to return to Europe than I would have been from Argentina.

945 (me)/430 (Agi) airports. I've already done more in 2022 than in 2021 and Agi is closing the gap. I can't say the finishing line is anywhere near in sight. We need Stinky Penguin fit to push us along the way. Hopefully the summer will be kind to us and our other goals will become much closer, or even achieved in one case. And hopefully the mask police, who have been at their worst behaviour on our LATAM flights will have taken a sabbatical.

Let's see....

# CHAPTER 4

Yessssss!!!! We did it (so did Leeds - even more of a miracle)! Did what? I hear you ask, dear reader. Well, I could keep you in suspense for a couple of pages but we were so proud of our achievement I just have to share. We finished National Trail number 14: for us, the biggy. None other than the South West Coast Path, all 630 miles of it.

Yes, I know. It's not Everest (although it is pointed out in the guide books that the ups and downs equate to 3 ascents and descents of said mountain). Yes, I know, tons of folk accomplish it, many in one go with tent and god knows what else on their backs. Nevertheless we have done it, in our own way. We did walk the remaining 270 miles in 18 consecutive days which I think we should be, and are, rightly proud of. Actually, I was so proud that on our last day I couldn't help but tell everybody we stopped to talk to that we were finishing the whole thing. Whilst everyone was most complimentary on our achievement, it's fair to say that they all sounded very surprised. We didn't blame them. We openly admit that we do not look like long distance walkers. We simply do not wear or carry the gear that seems mandatory for most walkers. To be honest, I'd started telling people when we only had 6,5,4,3,2 days left. OK, to be completely honest, only when asked you understand, I'd been saying we only had 270 miles left and downwards each day.

It seems it's what you do on the walk. Not everybody, of course, not in towns and villages but most people we met in the middle of nowhere seemed keen to stop for a break and to swap stories. Convention seems that the vast majority, doing it in one go, start in Minehead and finish in Poole. This means that they have a very, very high chance of walking the first 300 odd miles into anything from a stiff breeze to a very strong wind.

Not for us thanks. I didn't think I was a wind dodger until Agnes mentioned it on our first stint on the SWCP. Well, it's not a dodger but a utiliser I would say. We started in Minehead heading west but pretty soon changed direction as we were encountering a moderate to stiff breeze. It's fair to say that we enjoyed many a wind assisted mile out of the 630. These hardy folk who walk come rain or shine are clearly not bothered. Or they are but just put up with it.

We also managed to notch up a further 17 Wetherspoons along the way, including our 700th in Camborne, where we booked into the hotel to celebrate. We ended up staying 4 nights as it was so convenient for the walk, and conveniently priced compared to coastal options. The bathroom in our fabulous room was bigger than some bedrooms we'd stayed in. Aggers had read somewhere that the walk-in shower in room 4 (that's a guess) was particularly impressive and, we were in luck and it didn't disappoint. The pub internally was pretty decent too.

We celebrated in Bideford and Barnstaple (x2) on completion of the walk. All 3 are virtually on the route but had torturously closed just a couple of days before we passed through back in March 2020. Of the other 13 pubs on this tour, in our opinion, 2 fell straight into the excellent category: Exeter - The Imperial - and Bodmin (sadly since closed). 5 we considered very good: Okehampton, Perranporth, St Austell, Crediton (for its garden) and Helston (upgraded for the 4 free breakfasts we received on a return visit after a minor error in the order). The remaining 6 in Falmouth, St Ives, Penzance, Newquay, Truro and Exeter - Sawyers Arms - were good solid Spoon offerings; is there such a thing as a bad Wetherspoon (apart from Thornton Heath)!?

Before I forget, I know that those of you who haven't worked it out, will be gagging to know what Leeds achieved. Well, with the odds stacked against them and, with my not insignificant sacrifice, they managed to avoid relegation on the last day of the season. Not that I'm superstitious but, as we were walking the Pembrokeshire Coast Path when England won the cricket World Cup in 2019, the Hadrian's Wall Path when Ben Stokes did what he does from time to time, later the same year and were walking the Pennine Way on six occasions when Leeds won matches to seal promotion in 2020 it was obvious that Leeds' only hope was for us to be walking a National Trail whilst they battled away at Brentford.

We had planned on a 15 mile walk on the day in question. We had even booked a B&B that morning for our destination. When we stopped a couple of hours short of our overnight for some refreshments it was only 3pm. I said to Aggers that this wasn't going to work: we would be finished at 5pm and the match wouldn't finish until 6. Like the kind lady she is, she agreed to plod on another 7 miles to Padstow. This would mean a 23 mile walk from Newquay. It was fairly flat, the sun was out and what breeze there was behind us. Ideal walking conditions for us.....and Leeds United.

We were rewarded with our decision to continue by finding the most delightful little B&B in Padstow. The owners were both in their 80s, as was their dog, I think, and as quintessentially British eccentrics as you could wish to meet. Our lovely little room even had a balcony, although the sun had retired before we did. The kind lady who we had prebooked was not upset at our cancellation and wished us well on our way to Padstow.

To be completely honest the real reason we kept going was because of the weather forecast the following day but we were able to do Leeds a huge favour in the process. Not that I'm superstitious you understand. I realise our walking had no bearing on the outcome of the match, but it's not a bad little run I've got going there, is it?

Before I tell those of you not that familiar with Cornwall how bloody great it is, particularly from a walking perspective, I must just share the addition of one more airport before we went for a 270 mile stroll. Aggers and I rightly feel that almost every day is a special one for us. Many may be on the point of projectile vomiting at the cheesy nature of that statement but it's true. So.... what to do on those special days, i.e., birthdays? A few years back I took Aggers on a surprise birthday trip to The Canaries. You may also scoff at that but there's a bit more to them than the average holiday maker experiences. I had 2 airports left, La Gomera and El Hierro. In addition Agnes would add Tenerife North and Las Palmas.

Not that she knew it and didn't want to, to the point that she suggested I pack a bag for her to keep the element of surprise until we were in the departure lounge. I met her at East Croydon train station, platform 3, from her work, with a glass of champagne. You didn't know I could be such a romantic, did you? Once in the departure lounge at Gatwick South, Spoons of course, romance again, there weren't too many options showing on the board. Agi excluded Tenerife South from her guesses as we had been there on our way to La Palma a couple of years ago. I'm sure she would've kept her disappointment to herself if it did transpire that I was treating her to 5 days in Playa de las Americas. On second thoughts, maybe not.

I suggested that our final destination may not feature on the board. She started to think of onwards from Barcelona, Alicante.... Glasgow! Therefore, it was only when we reached the gate that she was aware of our first destination and I could finally spill the beans on our itinerary. We flew to Tenerife South and took a ferry over early the next morning from Los Cristianos to La Gomera. Apart from the wind, what an extremely pretty and pleasant island.

Via a rather chilly Tenerife North onwards we went to El Hierro. Quite a strange island made even stranger by the accommodation I had chosen for Agi's actual birthday. Normally, as the saying goes, if something seems too good to be true it is. I had found this private room, attached to a larger house by the sea. No beach but it seemed incredibly cheap compared to what it claimed to offer. Apart from the fact that it was located in a volcanic rock field and looked like something from Thunderbirds it wasn't too good to be true. We had a lovely room and the icing on the cake (I'm trying to think of something funny to say to link in with on top of the volcanic rock but can't) was a guided tour of the underground tunnel from the main house to the ocean. Someone, not the current owner who was a self-confessed alcohol and drug abuser in his previous life, had been smoking something quite strong.

The owner, I forget his name, was a Brit from London who had moved out to El Hierro in an attempt to dry out and marry his El Hierro lover. They had only recently bought this place, hence why our room was so cheap, and were keen to share the tunnel with us. On entry there was a bath filled with blood coloured water - apparently natural, caused by the colour of the rock it was made from rather than some gory goings on - and a bar which new owner obviously needed to keep dry. We had to wear helmets to negotiate the tunnel in order to avoid suffering severe head injuries - hat hard ons to fellow Partridge enthusiasts - but made it to the exit some 50 metres away. It really was quite bizarre.

As was our accommodation in Gran Canaria. Another destination I thought I would never return to but, not only was it the cheapest and quickest way home from El Hierro but it was Agnes's birthday and Las Palmas would be new for her. We also had a chance to visit the city of Las Palmas which was most pleasant. I had prebooked an apartment in a small town in the hills not far from Las Palmas airport. When we arrived in the evening a very friendly young Romanian guy showed us to our room. A couple of reviews on Booking.com had warned of not receiving the room they had paid for. Neither did we!! Ile, probably the most famous Romanian to those my age so I'll use that name, felt we were not happy with the room. We were but he insisted to show us a better one for the same price. Well, why not? It was still a birthday trip wasn't it? Our 5 bedroom bastard house (Thanks again Mr Partridge)!! I kid you not. This was ridiculous. It really was 5 bedrooms, 3 bathrooms, 2 living rooms and a kitchen on 3 floors. All for the £20 I'd lavished on the last night of the trip. It seemed rude not to have a game of hide and seek. Ile seemed surprised that we were surprised with our upgrade. We may have blagged a few in our time but this was the ultimate: double room with en-suite to 5 bedroom house.

It was a lovely trip. Canaries complete for me, airport wise, and would be for Agi a couple of years later. These islands really do still have plenty to offer to the more discerning tourist as well as those who just want the 3 S's, which we want as well! So impressed was Agnieszka with my packing skills that when I suggested a surprise trip for her birthday just gone, she immediately said that I would be packing for her! Non-negotiable.

We only had a five day window of opportunity due to other commitments. Fortunately I came to a decision quite quickly and, whilst I was pretty confident that Agnes would be pleased with my choice of destination, there was, as usual, an angle for me: I had long wanted to go to Plovdiv. Agnes had mentioned on a few occasions that she had never been to Bulgaria and wanted to. My previous visit to Sofia, as I may have mentioned in BID, had been extremely brief so I was also keen to visit this city properly. We both really liked Plovdiv a lot. It didn't disappoint. We took a delightful narrow gauge railway journey to the ski resort of Bansko, 4 1/2 hours to cover less than 100 kms and, overall, had a ruddy nice time. Most importantly, apart from the airports obviously, Agnes was, again, delighted with her backpack contents.

I had managed to keep the destination secret until we got to the gate. This time there were a few options but Agnes was very pleased when she saw where we were heading. It was only when she opened her bag at our apartment in Sofia that I realised she still had no idea how I had chosen to dress her. She really is very trusting.

Right, back in Cornwall and we were very pleased to be.....back in Cornwall. We had chosen not to even look into the campervan/motorhome option. The roads were just getting narrower and the overnight parking options more limited the further south west we ventured last time. We didn't want to book any beds in advance as we were determined to continue enjoy walking, and that meant avoiding the rain. We pretty much managed that. We walked from Falmouth to Fowey in the first 3 days, stopping at a B&B and Airbnb along the way. On our return to Falmouth we reintroduced ourselves to Couchsurfing.

Our host, I'll change his name, just in case, was a very kind chap indeed. In fact, I won't change his name, I'll just refer to him as he. Within about 2 minutes of our arrival he informed us that he was bipolar but not to worry as he hadn't had a psychotic episode since his last voluntary hospital stay a few weeks ago. This could be an interesting evening, and it was. Sorry, this isn't going to work. He needs a name. Tim was very, very open about his illness, condition, whatever is politically more correct. He'd smoked strong dope from the age of about 10 and was fairly convinced, understandably so, that this had brought about his mental health issues.

Tim was off the booze as it had been playing havoc with his mood stability so we abstained too. Well, we'd actually notched Truro Spoon on our way so we weren't exactly completely dry that day. Tim shared a very pleasant curry he had cooked up with us and it really was an example of when Couchsurfing works, it can be an extremely enjoyable experience. We even slept on his couch!

I was going to continue to list our route but I'm not sure that is fair on you, dear reader. What I will say is that, unlike the 3 authors' long distance walk books we have read we met a lot of interesting people along the way. Thanks again to Vivobarefoot, unlike the authors', our feet didn't ache at the end of the days, even if our legs normally did. Perhaps it was something to do with the time of year that we had more chats along the way? Or maybe we are just more open? This I'm not so sure as I felt the authors were all keen to have stories on other walkers.

We met the Kennedys from Vancouver who were walking a section of the coast for a week. I thought they were about my age but Mrs K was 70 and Mr 68! What a fine effort. On one stopover we ended up in the same B&B and another we bumped into them in the pub, as we did Johannes, the Austrian-Swiss who was coming over a week a year to walk a section. It makes me feel very proud that folk from such beautiful parts of the world come over to little old Blighty for a stomp.

We met many folk of all ages, shapes and sizes, doing the whole thing in one go. Fair play to them but I wish to carry no more than a toothbrush, toothpaste, spare socks, underwear, a bottle of water and maybe some wet gear on my back. That means we will generally walk no more than 3 or 4 days before repositioning the car and restocking the bag, changing clothes. It works for us.

There's no disputing that this walk can be tough at times for average walkers like us but I cannot overstate how stunningly beautiful it is for probably 600 of the 630 miles. And I managed not to injure myself again! I thought I knew Cornwall but I certainly didn't. There are so many simply stunning beaches in places I had never heard of, and too many to mention here. The well-known beauty spots of Mevagissey, St Ives, Fowey, Boscastle and Padstow did not disappoint. The unknowns, to us, of Porthleven, Portloe, Charlestown, Port Issac, Perranporth and St Agnes, to name but a few were further delights.

Interspersed with our Spoon stay in Camborne and another prolonged stay in the Darlington Hotel in Camelford we enjoyed a couple of superb B&Bs. The buses and, to a lesser extent, trains were very accommodating for reaching the path and our car. Our friend the sun shone at least part of every day and on several days, pretty much all day causing the sea to shimmer in that gorgeous turquoise colour normally associated with parts of the Mediterranean, Caribbean Sea, Indian and Pacific Oceans and even the Polish Baltic coastline. We managed to finish the walk with a kind of symmetry for us. I'm not sure too many who have walked the whole thing will have finished in Hartland Quay (15 miles north of Bude) but we did. That's where we had to abandon in March 2020 and that's where we joined the last remaining line over 2 years later. As you know, I think, it didn't actually take us 2 years, 2 months, 12 days to walk 630 miles. It actually took us 47 days which is a daily average of 13.4042553191 miles. Let's call it 13.5. Not bad eh? Considering that some rain affected days meant we only walked 5-8 miles you can see that we packed in a few 20+ milers.

We hope to finish the last of the remaining National Trails, for us, before the nights start drawing in too much. May is a fantastic time to walk in UK, particularly Cornwall. The crowds have yet to materialise and the days are long enough for rain dodgers like us to have the best window of opportunity to get a good stretch in. Even UK weather can normally fit in a good few dry hours out of 16. The last of the remaining National Trails being the Pennine Bridleway which actually is not finished. It currently ends, and has done for many years, in a fairly nondescript point in the Yorkshire Dales. I believe the plan is/was for it also to reach the Scottish Border but there appears to be no progress.

So, like the England Coast Path, we will do what exists. However, we hope to finish the Pennine Bridleway in one hit. With regard to the England Coast Path, unlike Peter who would think nothing of travelling 400 miles round trip to "do" 100 yards of new train track, we will wait until reasonably lengthy sections are open.

We did not have much time at home to rest our weary legs before we were off on a little European airport collecting exercise. Not the numbers we achieved in Colombia, or even Argentina but we can't always airport binge can we? I had planned a cheeky little 8 flight routing for 2 weeks for the ridiculous sum of £92 each in total. The absurdity of the cost of flying in Europe appears to know no bounds. I'm sure prices will increase with the ever astronomical rises in fuel for our cars but, in the meantime, we will make hay while the sun doth shine.

Wanna know how it went?

# CHAPTER 5

Well, potentially, how it's going as we're still on it at the moment. We are currently in Trebinje. Where? I wouldn't blame you for asking. In fact, I would be suitably impressed if you said, "Alan, don't be so condescending. Of course, it's in the south west of Bosnia & Herzegovina, actually Republika Srpska". We had certainly never heard of it.

Now we have completed all but one of the eight flights planned I feel it is safe to share the proposed itinerary:
Luton - Satu Mare
Oradea - Bergamo
Bergamo - Suceava
Bacău - Rome Ciampino
Rome Fiumicino - Pristina
Pristina - Vienna
Vienna - Tuzla
Sarajevo - Luton

All for change out of £100 each courtesy 7/8 of Wizzair and 1/8 Ryanair. 7 newbies for me and 9 for Aggers. The press had been, and still is, full of stories of how people's travel plans have been royally screwed up, mainly by easyJet and BA but some mention of Wizzair too. We have been remarkably fortunate on our recent trips to Colombia and Argentina - not one delay of any note. I had mentioned on more than one occasion that our luck must surely run out and Europe was more likely to be the venue for that.

After a rather early start to Luton, 0230, and a minor drama that our previous free parking spot 20 minutes' walk from the airport had been converted into residents only (we hadn't used it in over 3 years!), we got away from lousy Luton on time. No longer than usual queues, just the normal horrible experience that this airport, and Stansted, specialise in. Well, you don't have to do it do you, I hear you opine. Well, I pretty much do actually if I'm to get to 1000 any time soon.

Take the rough with the smooth is yet another of my favourite proverbs. Luton and Stansted are very rough, in my opinion, but very smooth for adding new European airports with a UK departure. My main gripe with both is the bloody shops. If we wanted to go shopping, which we don't, we would go to Westfield or similar. If we did want to go shopping we would go to Oxted charity shops or a nice market somewhere. We wouldn't buy a plane ticket and go shopping in Luton or Stansted airport. This horrible plan of forcing you to walk through endless shops to get to your departure gate is not their curse exclusively. It's spreading, as we have seen on this trip.

Let me repeat again, this is one of our few gripes in life, we know it's inconsequential and what a darn lucky existence we live. As I recall being told what my dear grandmother said, after being told by one of her daughters that there were people worse off than her, after she had had a stroke which left her slightly paralysed and needing to learn to talk again: "but I don't have their problems to deal with, I have mine". It may sound selfish but it is true. It's stuck with me for 50 years now. Most people in the world may well be charmed by aforesaid airport shopping opportunities. We'd rather have a bit more room to sit down.

We were happy to be back in Romania. It was our 5th visit. Another short one as I stupidly only realised when I looked at the itinerary again after we left for the second time. I really am such an idiot at times. Maybe because there were 4 new airports planned there and only 2 in Bosnia & Herzegovina my brain thought Romania was the main focus of the trip. No matter that I had scheduled 4 nights there and 6 in B&H.

Our first trip to Romania resulted in a missed flight but an alternative new airport. If I have told this story before I apologise and maybe my editor (dream on!) will delete this but I'm pretty sure I haven't, well; maybe 60/40. Agnieszka had wangled a not totally necessary work trip and invited me to join her. She would make her appointments on Friday and Monday so we could stretch the trip to 6 days in total. I think it fair to say that I had only heard of Bucharest, Constanta and Craiova before I started looking into that trip.

Craiova? Well, my European adventures with Leeds started in 1979. I missed out on the glory years where they competed in Europe for 10 consecutive years, I think, but once I had free/cheap flights there was nothing to stop me. Well, actually there was: the Iron Curtain. My excitement at our opponents in the first round was unbridled. Valletta. The match was on a Wednesday night and it just so happened that Dan Air had night flights Tuesday and Thursday. My old mate 92 had booked a 3 night organised trip. I could sleep on his floor for the night of the match.

It was September, still very warm in Malta. I am fascinated by snippets that are stored in our brains. I can remember the names of the Dan Air captains on each flight. I had to travel on the flight deck each way as the flights were full. It was up to the captain if they were happy for you to occupy the jump seat. 92 had to share a room. His companion was a strange chap. Didn't say much at all. 92 complained about his smelly feet, in fact, his general odour. He said the guy didn't have any change of clothes. Now, I reckon I've seen this guy at virtually every Leeds away match I've been to in the last 20-30 years. I don't remember seeing him in the 10 years after Malta. If you're a footy fan I'm sure you know the score: out of a few thousand faces (much less if you're a Millwall fan!) you always see a few that you don't know personally but they are just always there.

I'd often thought of saying something about Malta to Mr Smelly Feet. He always had this somewhat gormless look on his face so I reckoned that he wouldn't remember me after 10+ years. When I went to the Spurs v Leeds Under 23 game in February to add the new ground I met a couple of mates in the Spoon in Highbury & Islington beforehand. Who should be in there but Mr SF himself! Why was he attending an Under 23 game on a Monday night in London? I knew he was from Yorkshire, originally at least. I cracked. I approached him. Of course he didn't remember me, but he claimed that he did remember someone kipping on his floor, 43 years later! Not only did he go to every Leeds game but he attended most, if not all, of the U23 games too. Dedication? Addiction? Madness? You can decide.

Having thrashed Valetta 4-0 in Malta, bizarrely on a sand pitch (yeah UEFA, football was fun before you helped screw it up), I took the home win for granted and eagerly awaited the draw for the next round: Universitatea Craiova!! Where the hell was that? I'm sure a few diehards made it on an organised trip but back then, it was a bit beyond me. I figured I'd wait for round 3. There was to be no round 3 (we lost 0-2 both home and away). In fact, there was to be no European adventures with Leeds for over 10 years and it would be more than 35 before I made my Romanian debut!

It actually proved quite challenging to include new airports whilst following Leeds in Europe. I did mange Genoa en route to AS Monaco in our second season back (where we belong - as the t-shirt said), Vigo on the way back from Deportivo La Coruna and Florence, having bizarrely played Hapoel Tel Aviv there. Sixteen other European games failed to bring any new airports. Spartak Moscow did result in a new airport but, if you ploughed through BID, you'll know there was no match.

Whilst I'm not much of a one for friendly football matches they did provide the excuse for a new airport on a couple of occasions: Galway would have added 2 had the firemen not been on strike in Derry but at least Knock was a kind of pilgrimage for me, if not for the normal reason - I'm not religious, let alone Catholic. Further afield another pre-season fixture should have also added 2 new airports. We were playing Green Town of Hangzhou, as you do. I planned to fly via Hong Kong to an airport in Shanghai, I think. I say, I think, because I was sure that this airport began with M but Wiki tells me that the only other civil airport in Shanghai, other than Pudong which I ended up flying to and from is Hongqiao. This rings no bells. I've searched through China airports and not found one beginning with M that does ring a bell. It's time to move on.

Bizarre that Leeds would play this fixture (money obviously). More bizarre that there were a few hundred Leeds fans there doing all 3 meaningless games on the tour, the others being in Thailand and Oz. Did any of them have ulterior motives too? It was ridiculously hot to sit and watch football in the evening let alone play it.

Leading me back nicely to Romania is the fact that I missed the flight to Hong Kong and, therefore, the onward connection to the mystery new airport. I had to settle for a flight the next day to Pudong, which was delayed over 4 hours. My error the previous evening becoming more costly. Why did I miss the flight? Well, without going into too much detail, I had an illicit meeting at Heathrow, completely lost track of time, until it was too late to check in. Silly boy!

So back to that first Romania trip. Actually it's coming back to me..... so we can move on, swiftly (IYRBID you may recall my recall of the first Romania trip; it's near the end!) to this one. Not much to write home about Satu Mare. Pleasant enough town centre. Nice small airport. Walking distance to town, just. The train ride to Oradea was a blast from the past. The scenery was modest, well, flat and uninteresting really, but what made the journey enjoyable was the antiquated nature of the train. As I've said before, we love a good train ride, to get us between airports especially. This old fella/girl, whichever you prefer, but I know means of transport are generally referred to as female for some reason, was of the compartment with a sliding door and corridor variety. Long, long since disappeared in UK and most other countries, they are nearly always comfortable and spacious and if you don't have one to yourselves tend to make striking up conversation more likely.

Oradea was a most pleasant surprise. Plenty of nice, historical structures, a fine large pedestrianised square, and a fast flowing river by which we enjoyed a very welcome pint and dinner. Considering our early start to Luton we were on good form and had found ourselves a very agreeable apartment to rest for the evening. There was only one problem: I received an email from Wizzair informing of a potential Italian air traffic strike the following day from 1000 to 1800 and to be aware that our flight may be delayed or cancelled. Our run of good fortune seemed likely to be coming to an end. I also received notification of a schedule change from Ryanair.

I had received no fewer than 18 schedule change notifications from Wizzair in the month after I had booked the flights, 2 of which informed us that our flight had been moved by a day. One of which is for a future trip a week after our return from this one. Ryanair's schedule change was different: our flight had been moved forward by 40 minutes. This was in order for us to arrive in Bergamo before the strike began. Not a bad idea. What were a couple of indecisives like us to do?

Why, you may ask were we flying via Bergamo just to go back to Romania? Simple really: it was 14 hours by train from Oradea to Suceava or £100+ on flights via Bucharest versus £12.50 on flights via Bergamo and 9 hours including a pleasant layover of 5 hours in Bergamo. I say pleasant because I remembered flying to Bergamo on a there and back towards the end of my Dan Air days and the airport being rather pleasantly located close to the mountains.

So, thanks to Ryanair it seemed certain we could get to Italy but it didn't seem that Wizzair intended to delay our flight by a couple of hours so that we could depart, once the strike finished. The next available flight to Suceava was in 4 days' time. No use to us as we were flying from Bacău in 3. For the sake of one new airport was it worth the risk of getting stuck in Italy? We both figured it would be at our own expense, even though Wizzair mentioned in their correspondence that they may cover any hotel expense. We didn't trust them. Booking.com wasn't showing any availability in Bergamo for less than £200! What was occurring there!?

We considered the option of going straight to Bacău to pick up our journey from there. This would mean missing out on 2 new airports. Aggers fell asleep. I continued in my attempts to come to terms with this tragic scenario. Seeing as you may not know me, that last sentence is in jest. I was gutted at the prospect but, at the risk of repeating myself, I know how lucky I am that my worries are so utterly trivial in the bigger scheme.

It was an hour walk to Oradea airport. Before Aggers nodded off we had agreed that we would start walking to the airport and make a plan/decision en route. I received confirmation overnight that the flight from Bergamo to Suceava was cancelled but I had found a flight to Bucharest the following morning which was available. Aggers will accept a very basic bed for the night. She will even sleep on the beach if it's warm enough. What she will not do is kip at the airport overnight, something I hadn't done for a very, very long time but had in the past.

We set off for the airport with the threat hanging over me that if I wanted to add Oradea was I prepared to pay £200+ for the privilege? There was conflicting information on Google that not only were Italian air traffic controllers striking but airline staff in Italy as well. Airlines will obviously try to minimise their expenditure on passengers on delays and cancellations, so no doubt Wizzair would hide behind the ATC strike as being beyond their control, even if their crew were also taking action as reported, between 1000 and 1400 along with their friends from Ryanair and easyJet.

Of course I was terrified at the prospect of a £200+ hotel bill but addicts go to extreme lengths don't they? We stopped twice on our walk to the airport to try and make a decision, to the point that we were in danger of missing the flight and the decision being made for us. What had been added to the equation was that the weather forecast for Bergamo was really quite unpleasant. Were we to get stuck there we wouldn't be doing much sightseeing. It was down to me to make a decision, Aggers decided. She was happy to proceed so long as I knew her terms to do so: splash the cash if need be.

I couldn't help myself. I booked the flight to Bucharest, said a quick prayer to the travel friendly gods and suggested we quickened our step if we didn't want to miss our rescheduled flight. In Google we trust, or more accurately forget not to. It transpired that the remainder of the walking route they insisted we took to Oradea airport was inside the perimeter fencing of the airport. We really didn't fancy that. We realised why it refused to reroute us soon enough as the actual route available was along a busy dual carriageway with no path. Clearly Google takes health and safety more seriously than us.

We reached the brand new terminal building safely, only to be told by security that Ryanair departed from the other terminal. What on earth was an airport this size doing with two terminals? Ryanair were in the old terminal. Of course they were. Probably refusing to pay increased costs for the new one. I can't knock them or the others for their attitude to costs. If they weren't so tight then the fares would be higher, wouldn't they? In spite of (or is it despite? I've just checked Google and apparently either will suffice) security's best efforts to stop it, the flight left at the new departure time. We arrived in a sunny Bergamo after a very scenic approach, as I remembered some 30+ years previously. Chaos, unsurprisingly, reigned in the terminal building. Ryanair has a lot of flights from Bergamo. This day it had a lot of cancellations.

Fortunately, by virtue of the fact that Wizzair only had 4 in the whole day I could take a ticket for the other airline help desk not Ryanair. After a quick phone call the agent informed me that Wizzair would provide hotel accommodation and to come back to desks 12-14 (why I have included that detail, even I struggle to understand) at 1300. It was 1000. Whilst I had been getting the airline info Aggers had popped off to tourist information and learnt we could get an all-day bus pass for 5 euros each. It was less than 10 minutes to the city centre. Not a bad place to get stuck, particularly compared to any of the London airports, with the exception possibly of London City.

We nipped into the city for a very pleasant al fresco brunch. It looked a fine place with the walled old city perched on one of the surrounding hills. I was happy to right a wrong of a there and back and seeing nothing other than from the air which had loomed for 30+ years. Bergamo was packed with university aged youngsters. It must've been end of term party time. Seriously, they were everywhere.

We headed back to the airport on a packed bus which proceeded to breakdown. Whilst our replacement bus waited patiently at the red traffic lights at a busy dual carriageway an Uber Eats, or similar, moped rider decided not to. He shot through the lights and proceeded to get mowed down by a pretty fast car. Food everywhere. Miraculously he got up and staggered to the pavement. I do not make light of this incident. I thought, momentarily, the rider may have died before our eyes. It is actually unclear whether our lights were just changing and the car went through a red or if the moped really was on a suicide mission.

What popped into my head resulted from recently watching an episode of The Other One on I-Player. They had gone into some detail about the targets Deliveroo and Uber Eats riders must meet. It's a comedy show so may not even be true but my immediate reaction to this event was that the rider was trying to make a target delivery time, hence him skipping the light. Now the food wasn't going to arrive at all!

To our surprise when we got back to the airport the ground staff informed us that Wizzair would indeed put us up for the night. They would even give us an evening meal and breakfast. The only issue was that they were having a bit of difficulty finding any rooms. We had actually found a room for 70 euros in the city centre. We were informed that we could book this and reclaim the money from Wizzair. We were sceptical about how long it would take Wizzair to return our out of pocket expenses, and more importantly, if they actually would. With thunderstorms still forecast we decided we would leave the accommodation in the hands of Wizzair and set off back to the city to return at 1700 as instructed, food and other crash debris all cleaned up nicely, by the way.

Bergamo really is a nice city and I was £200 in credit! We could even afford a beer stop, with small snacks which, as it transpired was quite fortuitous. Wizzair did deliver on the hotel room but the whole organisation was a shambles. We didn't leave until 1930. Out of 4 flights Wizzair miraculously only had 10 passengers to accommodate, including us. One woman with 2 small kids was looking forward to 4 nights at Wizzair's expense before the next flight to Suceava! We hoped her hotel offered more than ours which was a Fawlty Towers experience, of sorts. The owner/manager wasn't mad and we didn't have a Spanish chef. In fact, we didn't have a chef at all. We couldn't dine at Wizzair's expense because the hotel didn't have a kitchen, let alone a chef. It was lashing down with rain and the hotel was in the middle of an industrial estate.

We decided on an early night, grateful we'd had a few crisps and olives with our beer. We felt sorry for our 2 fellow passengers going to Sofia who had 2 nights in this establishment, even more so when we found out that breakfast was limited to a packaged croissant and an admittedly, very decent cup of coffee. Agnes was extremely sceptical that our transfer back to the airport would materialise in the morning. We spoke to the handling agent via the hotel manager and he promised us that there would be a transfer for us at 0645.

I told Aggers it would be fine, not that I had anything to base it on, and it was. A deluxe Mercedes limo pitched up at exactly 0645 and the extremely courteous driver even apologised for being on time and not early! Back to a significantly less chaotic airport and we were off to Bucharest a few hours later. Considering we had paid £4 each for our tickets we really felt quite lucky that Wizzair looked after us. However, we learnt that they had no choice. It is apparently Italian law that, no matter what the cause, they have to provide accommodation if required.

We were off to Bacău one airport light, Bacău being a similar distance from Bucharest as it is from Suceava. We're not too disappointed that we'll need another trip to Romania one day if we are to tick off Suceava and we do still have Constanta to visit if we're to complete Romania options (for any anoraks, Arad doesn't seem to have any flights at the time of writing).

We met a Romanian chap who lived in New Addington on our train to Bucharest station - small world (as it's only a few miles from where we live). We treated ourselves to a first class ticket for the 4 hour ride to Bacău and a litre bottle of the local lager each. Bacău doesn't have much to offer but we did enjoy a lakeside dinner, and a very nice wholesome breakfast in our very reasonable hotel after the first night. We found an apartment just 5 minutes' walk from the airport for our rescheduled early morning flight to Rome so, all in all, considered that luck was still, very much with us.

# CHAPTER 6

Wizzair had decided that we needed more time in Rome. They moved our flight from Bacău forward by 5 hours and our next flight to Pristina backwards by 4 hours. We didn't really need any longer in Bacău but would rather have arrived in Pristina at 7pm as planned, than 11pm. Particularly as they had also then decided to move our flight out of Pristina forward by a day, cutting our stay down to less than 24 hours.

"Flying in and out of Pristina, Alan? That's not your usual form, is it?" I imagine you pondering. Well, just like I'm not going to devote a full chapter to the tourist hotspots of Rome, I'll try to be brief on my musings on Yugoslavian/Balkan politics. I'm actually getting ahead of myself but it is relevant. Whilst being cautious and checking the uk.gov website to see if there were still any Covid related entry restrictions which could affect our mini tour, I stumbled across the fact that you cannot enter Serbia from Kosovo without having already been in Serbia!

What a nonsense. Serbia doesn't recognise Kosovo as an independent nation - of course it doesn't - therefore, if you enter Serbia from Kosovo, it deems it an illegal entry. Just to clarify, you can enter Kosovo from Serbia but not vice versa unless you've done the former first. My plan had been to travel by bus/train from Kosovo to Nis and fly from there onwards. What about if we went via Macedonia, into Serbia? Nope, not if you don't already have a Serbian stamp of entry.

My initial reaction was that if we just turned up at the border it would probably be fine. A little more research, however, indicated that this would definitely not be the case with attempting to go direct from Kosovo to Serbia. It also looked very unlikely if we went via Macedonia. So, I had decided not to risk it and had begrudgingly, booked a return flight from

Pristina back to Vienna, where we would now have to spend 2 nights rather than 1.

Aggers and I had both been to Rome before; her once, and I on several occasions. Obviously, I had notched both Ciampino and Fiumicino airports. Aggers couldn't remember which one she had been to, but, as there was only one on her list it wasn't a deal breaker, as we were using both. We were both quite looking forward to reacquainting ourselves with Rome but it didn't take long to be reminded of one of the downsides of this city and country.

For those not in the know, Ciampino although the original Rome airport, is a pretty small affair only used by the low-cost boys and even they use Fiumicino as well. We made our way to the small Airport Information booth. Don't you find that these, when manned, can be pretty hopeless at times? In many places they don't need to know much but we have found on several occasions that they can't even tell you about public transport options or taxi fares. Some like Bergamo, can be really helpful. Others.... the proverbial chocolate teapots.

This little baby in Ciampino, however? If you want abuse, they dish it out for free. Looking back, I am absolutely astonished at how they both spoke to us. Condescending doesn't do it justice. Agnes politely enquired of the female staff what our options were for getting to the coast, as we were struggling to find accommodation in the city centre under £200! "Well, Italy is surrounded by coast, almost to the point it is an island. What coast do you want?" Err, probably don't need a geography lesson on Italy, thanks, we were both thinking, but Agnes politely responded that we were planning to go to the coast near Fiumicino airport and could we take a train? "No, you can't!" The lady then proceeded to produce a map which showed the train line to the coast. She also decided she would give us a lecture on the whole transport system surrounding Rome.

At this point I intervened as it was developing into a full-blown argument. On reflection, I really wished I'd let them fight it out, but my non-confrontational attitude kicked in and I tried to keep the peace. The guy, who hadn't said too much decided to join in and tell me that I clearly hadn't travelled much and that Rome was a dangerous city in parts and that we should be careful. Nice introduction, pal! I told him that we lived in London (not strictly true as Woldingham is anything but London, but he wasn't to know) and contrary to the opinion he and his charming colleague had decided to form, we hadn't just stepped off a plane into a foreign country for the first time in our lives!

It went on for a few minutes longer in the same vein before we decided to walk away, but not before the final put down. "Where are you staying in Rome?". "Well, we don't have anything booked yet," said Agnes. "What!? You've come to Rome on a Saturday night without a hotel booking? You won't find anywhere to stay for a start". OK bye, thanks for your help and we'll see about that!

It was, to be fair, looking like we wouldn't find anywhere to stay in the city on our budget. We were looking more and more at the coast but every now and then an option would pop up on Booking.com for the city centre at a half decent price. Unfortunately, they seemed to be snapped up before we could book them. We decided to head to the city for some breakfast and look afresh at where we would hopefully lay our heads for the night. We had worked our own way out how to get there as I really didn't fancy another lecture from the information dudes.

Whilst we waited for the train, I kept plugging away on Booking.com and to our immense satisfaction managed to book Hotel Babyface (yes seriously, that was its name and on arrival, we learnt that it had a sister; Richbaby!), close to the main station for £60. Up yours Ciampino know alls! I did think that Babyface may be too good to be true, but no. Not only did we have a very nice room, we had our very own courtyard. Our welcome was so in contrast to the information desk's that I asked the receptionist where he was from. Albania. We had a nice chat and when I asked him where we could get a bottle of wine, he told us not to bother, he would give us wine! We weren't sure if something was lost in translation.

We did have a very pleasant day wandering around Rome's main tourist areas but I was shocked at how little I remembered, even by my standards. What also surprised us was just how unkept these parts of the city were now. Lonely Planet shared our opinion and went on to say that the city has suffered from neglect for a number of years. Public grassed areas all terribly overgrown, untidy, full of rubbish, pavements in a right old mess. One of the world's most famous and visited cities and not a hint that it fancied looking good. Nonetheless, it is undoubtedly a fabulous city.

We returned to our little sanctuary (the hotel was very small, just a few rooms between Richbaby and Babyface) armed with a bottle of wine and a pizza to enjoy in our courtyard. Our Albanian friend, on clocking our bottle of wine, almost seemed offended that we had not taken him up on his offer. We invited him to join us in our courtyard for a glass of our wine. He accepted and proceeded to bring his own bottle too, fortunately he didn't want any pizza. We spent a very pleasant evening hearing about his country and his travels and family. We told him we would be going to Albania soon and that his town was on our radar. He hadn't been home for 3 years so we said we would look in on his parents. Maybe we would?

He left us after a while but not before he insisted on giving us another bottle of red. We decided we would leave it with our bags so not as to appear greedy. When we returned the next afternoon to collect them before heading to Fiumicino, he insisted that we took the wine with us. Obviously, we had to drink it before passing through security, no great hardship.

Whilst Rome would never have been on our radar, we were pleased we had had the opportunity to spend some time there but were eager to head off to lesser known, to us, places. We knew nothing about Pristina or Kosovo. Thanks to Wizzair we would only learn about Pristina as we now had no time to head out of the city.

# CHAPTER 7

Never judge a book by its cover: one of, if not my favourite proverbs. They were a motley bunch on the flight to Pristina. Loud, aggressive, scary looking mothers. For me, there's always a different feeling arriving somewhere new and unfamiliar at night. Not only was it very dark when we arrived in Pristina, it was also peeing down. Reluctantly we had no option but to fork out 25 euros for a taxi to our hotel. Quite strange that the euro is the Kosovo currency. Apparently, they had been using the old German Mark well before they gained independence. Even stranger was the fact that our flight from Rome cost exactly the same, for the two of us, as the taxi ride.

We had had a small taste of the politics of the former Yugoslavia on previous visits to Croatia and Bosnia & Herzegovina (Agnes rightly insists on using its full name since it was pointed out to us by our very, very nice host in Trebinje that we were in Herzegovina not Bosnia, and that they, Herzegovinans, found it disrespectful when people referred to their country as just Bosnia. It's a bit of a mouthful, Bosnia & Herzegovina, isn't it, so yep, B&H from now on). We also had a little insight to the sheer tragedy and brutality of the 1990s wars.

As you know I'm neither politically or religiously motivated so these wars to me were a terrible example of man's insanity and inhumanity towards his fellow man. Just like I keep saying I'm not writing a travel book (yet I'm writing a lot about travel lately), I'm also not writing a history book. Those of you interested in modern history/warfare will know a lot more about the Yugoslav conflicts than I still do. Those of you not, may not care to learn more.

I first visited Yugoslavia in 1979 with Jackie; first wife, and her parents on a 2-week package holiday. Apart from skiing it was probably my second and last holiday of that genre, the first being 10 years earlier when my father had a win on the horses and packed us off to Majorca for 2 weeks, Gatwick fittingly being my first ever airport and Palma my first overseas. I only flew twice before my 16th birthday. Maybe this had some bearing on my excesses since?

I have very fond memories of that first Yugoslavia trip, even though Jackie and I were forced to share a room each with her mum and dad rather than each other. Me with Ted and her with Rita just in case you were picturing some even weirder set up with the 4 of us in one room. I don't have such fond memories of my second visit 9 years later. My father had recently died and Jackie and I separated. Apparently, according to the medically trained, this was why I was having a breakdown. I was convinced it was because I had been partaking in too many class A's for my brain's liking, culminating in an extremely excessive dose of magic mushrooms.

I won't dwell on this as I still don't understand what was happening to me. Acute anxiety resulting in panic attacks? Probably. A breakdown? Partially as apart from one night shift I never missed work. Depression? Well, that takes many forms so maybe another yes. Almost intolerable mental anguish/pain? Most definitely. There was a point that I felt I really could tolerate no more and I think it was mainly because my dad had only died 6 months previously that, for my mum's sake, I sought medical help rather than figuring out which way to take my own life.

This situation lasted well over a year, not all day, every day but there were days when it was a case of getting through each hour at a time, not a day at a time. One upside of this episode in my life is that I believe it made me a far more compassionate chap than before it. Back in the late 80s any mental health issue was pretty much a taboo. Now it's pretty popular, almost fashionable. Apologies, I am certainly not being dismissive but it's all getting a bit serious so let's get back to the main subject.

In the midst of a complete brain fog I set off on a Saga holidays' Dan Air flight to Ohrid. Where? Apparently old folk liked the big lake there. I stood out like the proverbial, being 28 years old, whereas every other passenger was at least over 60. It was one of those trips I look back on and think how did it happen with only the flights being preplanned. I didn't visit the lake, although I saw it from above. I made my way to Skopje, by bus I think, for a flight to Belgrade. As I arrived in the evening and had a very early morning flight to Ljubljana I chose to kip at the airport: not a great experience.

I do remember a stroll around Ljubljana before heading off to Pula for a flight home a day, or maybe two later. I was 5 airports to the good but it wasn't much use to me in my current state. I tried another trip to Corsica to clear my head. I'd already notched Calvi and Ajaccio in happier days so headed down to Figari. This little gem of an airport was in the middle of nowhere in the far south of the island and naturally, I had no plan how to reach Bastia in the far north. I decided to hitch. Not only did I get a ride all the way pretty quickly, but the kind Corsican chap put me up for the night. He must have thought I was a right miserable sod. I really was.

My return journey from Bastia involved flying via Berlin to Saarbrucken, by land to Luxembourg from whence I flew home via Paris. 4 more airports but I was still very, very unhappy indeed. Maybe a trip to the Shetland Isles would help. Another 4 to the total but still I couldn't get my old mojo back.

Gradually the normal times began to outweigh the abnormal. I feel I'm one of the lucky ones. I've heard stories of less fortunate people than I taking one way acid trips, for example. Our couch surfer in Falmouth has clearly not been so lucky. My magic mushrooms trip did have a return segment but at times, it felt like an open return, valid for a year, which I kept trying to use but failed repeatedly to complete the journey.

But I digress! My first visit to the former Yugoslavia was a much happier occasion. Although at the time it was tinged with sadness because Agnes and I were going through the friends only stage. Now we've just celebrated our first wedding anniversary I have only fond memories of it. I may well have already mentioned that we flew to Split, as this was long on my to do list of Dan Air destinations I'd failed to visit during that wonderful airline's life.

In order to get back on track I'll be as brief as I can about the previous trips. This first one resulted in another Dan Air tick, Trieste, on our return. In a strange quirk Agnes did not fly back with me as I had to return the day before her. I had hoped that the trip may result in us becoming boy/girlfriend again but she was having none of it, not that I actually tried.

Next on the list was Zadar. This was a Ryanair tick I'd been after for a while. I'm not sure why this one interested me so much but it did. When Agnes suggested I accompany her on a work trip to Paris it was down to me to work out a roundabout route. We took a ferry towards our ultimate destination the next day with 2 options: either we proceed to Mali Losinj, a sizeable island with numerous accommodation options or we get off at Ist, a tiny island with no accommodation showing on Booking.com or Airbnb. Obviously, but after not inconsiderable indecision, we chose the latter.

As we were nearing Ist, Aggers decided it might be prudent to ask one of the crew if they knew anywhere we could stay. I was directed to a fellow passenger who, in broken English, immediately pointed to a lady and said, "you stay with lady there, pay her 25 Euros". So that's what we did. Said lady spoke very little English but there's some similarities between Polish and Croatian languages, or whatever you want to call Yugoslavian these days. We quite literally, took her luggage for her in a wheelbarrow to the other side of the island. She had a lovely house overlooking the other harbour from where we would take a boat onwards the next morning.

Sadly, this lovely house had a very sad story, we learned. Her husband had died just before he finished building it and she had been living alone since, for the last 5 years or so. Her children and grandchildren did visit but she, understandably, seemed a bit like me on my previous visit to Croatia, when it was Yugoslavia. At least she had a good reason.

Via further overnights on the islands of Mali Losinj and Cresc we made our way to Rijeka where we repeated the bus journey to Trieste together this time. A train to Venice gave us enough time to take a gondola ride and have an ice cream in this one-off city before catching an evening flight to Paris. I had taken a jump seat ride to Venice one night shift in my early Dan Air days and it had taken me almost 20 years to actually visit the city, courtesy of Ryanair using Treviso (another unfulfilled Dan Air number) as their idea of Venice.

I had 3 more airports I wanted to visit in Croatia but the schedules never worked in our favour to make it whilst still working. Ryanair used to fly to Osijek occasionally from Stansted but had stopped altogether so I feared that might remain unfulfilled. No, it wouldn't. There was, unknown to me, a domestic airline that flew twice a day, Monday to Friday from Osijek to Zagreb for a very agreeable price. Now we had the time, all I had to do was find somewhere to fly into near Osijek.

One benefit of our frequent visits to Poland, apart from Agnes's mum's chocolate vodka (it's so thick you eat it, rather than drink it), is some of the destinations Wizzair now fly to from Katowice. We had enjoyed a short break in the beautiful city of Lviv and I now had this ingenious route planned back to Blighty: Lviv - Berlin (Schonefeld, in case you're wondering - the Germans being already 7 years behind schedule on opening Brandenburg) - Banja Luka, bus, Osijek - Zagreb, train, Rijeka - Stansted. Not just 3 remaining airports in Croatia but 2 more to get there. I was rightly very proud of myself. There is a flight from Zagreb to a couple of the Croatian islands but they are clearly only for the rich.

It seems inappropriate to mention a visit to Ukraine without mentioning how that country is now enduring what B&H, in particular, did. Having seen 3 fine cities there before Russia chose to ruin them is in stark contrast, for us, to seeing those in Croatia and B&H being largely rebuilt whilst still bearing scars of the wars almost 30 years ago.

After the trip I'm in the middle of telling you about we travelled to Kiev Zhulzany, I'd done Kiev Boryspil about 10 years earlier, on a work trip, the flight being notable as the last time I smoked a cigarette on board: nothing to be proud of, I know. I think the reason I chose to smoke on board an aircraft was kind of payback - I don't know who to - for all those smoke-filled flights I had had to endure as a non-smoker before the ban. Looking back isn't it ludicrous that smoking was ever allowed on aircraft? As a standby passenger, beggars can't be choosers (another nice proverb), I'd frequently endured 10 hours or more breathing in as much smoke as the smoker themselves. The Air Ukraine flight was pretty empty so I wasn't harming too many more than myself. I liked Kiev a lot on that first visit and even more so when we went back. We had arrived via Turku and Tallinn and took a train to Kharkiv, from whence we continued to Katowice.

I fear not only these regions are being destroyed but at some point, in the not-too-distant future, the idiots who run this world will press the self-destruct button, to the point that Covid restrictions will have felt like a mild interruption to our idyllic lifestyle. Sorry, that's a bit morbid, hopefully I'm being over pessimistic.

Back on track, sort of. I'd never heard of Banja Luka. Not much to write home about as LP says because the Serbs destroyed all the buildings of any note. Who lives there now? You've got it, 90% Serbs!! Utter, utter lunacy!

We took a couple of buses to Brod, I think, to walk across the border into Croatian Brod and another bus on to Osijek. Our kind host met us at the bus station. Well, that was a kind act but his reasoning as to why Osijek had very little crime - no blacks (not his word but a less offensive version), no gypsies - a little less friendly. His apartment wasn't too great either but we were in situ for the long-awaited, for me, flight from Osijek to Zagreb. Osijek is a pleasant enough riverside big town/small city. Part of the city is modern and pedestrianised with bars and restaurants. Most of the buildings in the old city are still riddled with sniper fire and many derelict.

After an enjoyable couple of days we took a 0430 taxi ride out to the airport. On arrival, it reminded me of an experience on my last visit to New Zealand. Obviously I'm going to tell you about that trip before I tell you why I was reminded of it. It was one of my better blags. The Cook Islands Tourist Board was not only prepared to give us some money to produce a brochure for them. They were also prepared to fund a visit there for me.

I took this as an opportunity to fly around the world eastwards having finally done so westwards a mere 10 years or so earlier. Now, you're going to think I will digress to that trip. Ha! Wrong! Why? Because there's a very topical story on that which I'll come to later. The Tourist Board rather unfairly placed a limit on how much they would spend to get me there and back. This necessitated the first part of the journey to contain an element of risk which would bust the whole trip if it materialised. I had a 3 hour connection in Los Angeles for the onward journey to Papeete, French Polynesia. What's the big deal?

Well, the big deal was that I was in the infancy of my newly discovered travel anxiety. Perhaps this was prompted by an incident a few months previously. I was treating myself to a quick little Greek Islands trip. I had only allowed an hour or so for a connection in Athens, which if missed, would mess things up. However, I was still in the prepared to risk it phase, having moved on recently from 3 decades of carefree travel planning. I took off from Heathrow on time so all was well. I, this doesn't sound right, we, even though I was travelling alone sounds better, approached the runway at Athens in clear blue skies. Hold on. What's occurring? Still quite a height from landing but we were definitely climbing again.

The captain came on the mic pretty swiftly to allay, I'm sure, most passengers' fears, but not mine. There was an aircraft which needed to return to Athens with a medical emergency on board. Obviously, I was very sorry that someone was in a far more precarious situation than me, but I couldn't suppress my main thought that I may very well miss my connecting flight to Ikaria. How selfish! Me or the medical emergency? You decide. We circled for what obviously seemed like an eternity to me but, in reality, was probably no more than 30 minutes. Fortunately, we were ahead of schedule so ended up landing about 10 minutes late. Panic over. I know you're dying to know what the rest of that trip entailed: ferry from Ikaria to Leros via Samos, flight to Astypalea, ferry to Kalymnos and flight back to Athens. 4 new airports, in case you didn't bother to count them and 4 fabulous islands - I'd already been to Samos.

So... back to Los Angeles. We/I left Heathrow on time. First hurdle, hurdled. Surely 2 hours would be long enough to crawl through the notoriously painful US immigration and customs. It was a breeze. Why the sweat? Well, if I didn't catch the flight to Papeete, I would miss the once-a-week flight from there to Rarotonga. I had no desire to get stuck in French Polynesia. Jackie and I had had a rather less than satisfactory holiday there in 1985. That's putting it quite mildly. We planned to stay 2 weeks and left after 1. Yes, Bora Bora was rather idyllic, but not in constant rain and wind. Yes, Rangiroa looked like the perfect island hideaway from the air but, once on land, where we could afford to stay, the golden sand beach we saw from the air was actually all broken shells. No running water, a return to Tahiti, more rain and running out of money prompted a rather early departure to California.

There was one flight a week so it really was decision time. It was just too expensive and wet for us. At least the rain in San Francisco was cheaper! And yes, when I landed back in Papeete this time, it was pissing down. It was pissing down the next morning after an overnight in probably the worst value for money establishment I've ever come across. £5 dorm at best, £50 dump in reality.

Cook Islands really were delightful. No French for a start. I only had 2 options to fly to outlying islands, which I naturally took or would have done. The local airline had the audacity to cancel a flight to Aiki, as I was the only passenger booked and wasn't paying anything for the ticket. Even though Atutaki was as good as it gets for dreamy islands and the main island most pleasant, I had seen everything they had to offer. So rather than sit around for another day I chose to leave early for New Zealand.

New Zealand, apart from Zimbabwe, was the only test playing nation I had yet to see England play cricket in, hence my stop there on the way home. I was due to fly to Wellington for the cricket, but, on my way to Auckland from Rarotonga, on a rather unfriendly 0320 departure, arriving 25 hours later on a 3-hour flight (I'm fascinated by time change so crossing the international date line is the peak of excitement for me), I learnt that Air New Zealand offered the opportunity to travel standby, anywhere on their domestic network, for around £25. I won't bore you with the details but I hopped on a quick flight to Roturua, a bus to Taupo and a flight from there, very early the next morning, to Wanganui and another bus to Wellington. Taupo is where the similarity with Osijek arises.

The flight was very early and when I got to the airport the small terminal building was locked up. I didn't need to panic for too long as the co-pilot appeared with a set of keys and sprung everything into action. This wasn't a private flight from Shoreham. This was a scheduled service with a renowned airline and here was one of the pilots opening the place up as if it were the keys to his home. 3 unexpected new airports, minus one expected, a fine game of T20 cricket, not my favourite version but it'll do and a chance to briefly visit more of New Zealand than I expected.

Back to Osijek. The terminal was a similar size to Taupo, the lights were off. However, the door was open. We nipped in for a scout around. Just one old lady with an awful lot of luggage. We had an hour until departure, not an employee in sight. It was quite a weird situation. The old lady seemed relieved to see us and in broken English, enquired as to whether we planned to fly to Zagreb. As it transpired, once the workers arrived, it was just the 3 of us on a little Trade Air LET410 operated by Van Air Europe. From memory about 20 seats but spotters can correct me.

We liked Zagreb, took a train to Rijeka and headed off to the island of Krk. Rijeka was the last remaining Dan Air destination in the former Yugoslavia for me to visit. Bizarrely the airport is located nowhere near Rijeka, but on Krk Island. The island is linked by a bridge to the mainland but it was almost as if the good folk of Rijeka had seen Ryanair coming many moons before they did. To save Ryanair the inconvenience of looking for an airport 50 miles from Rijeka, in the middle of nowhere, which they could call Rijeka, they did it for them.

Nearly there. Where? Back in modern day Pristina, Kosovo. Just before that though, Aggers had treated me to a most pleasant birthday treat to Montenegro in 2016. Of course, I booked the flights but the rest was down to her. Actually, I'm sure Dan Air would have flown to Tivat once upon a time. For us, easyJet did, finally, several hours late - one of the toilet doors was broken, unfortunately the one with a crew seat attached to the outside of it. A beautifully located airport, a splendid evening in delightful Kotor, memorable also for the location where we heard the result of the uncalled for Brexit referendum the next morning.

We toured round Montenegro for a few days, spending my actual birthday overlooking the island of Sveti Stefan. Why do I mention this? Well, the local government kicked the locals off the tiny island and handed it over to a hotel chain. No backhanders involved for sure!! The locals quite rightly were not impressed. Some rather rich Arab dude had hired the whole place for a celebration, flown in Simply Red and Fat Boy Slim, amongst others. I've no idea whether we shared birthdays, or if it was even a birthday celebration. Whilst I appreciated the not inconsiderable free firework display the music was a tad irritating. As part of their protest the locals had set up a temporary sound system to drown out Mick and Norman. It only partly worked so we had an unsavoury mix of the worst of euro trash hip hop along with "Money's Too Tight To Mention", which it certainly appeared not to be.

Another curiosity about Sveti Stefan was that on the beach directly next to the causeway to it, the charge for sun loungers varied between 5-20 euros depending on which row you were in. We stayed on our ample balcony. We flew back from Podgorica, although we didn't see the city. Whilst on a roll of fairly uninteresting observations - yes I know, the contents of both books you would be correct to opine - we noticed that a pretty damn large lake that was on the Lonely Planet map did not feature on Google at all. It was most definitely there. We stopped for a photo. It is on Google now, but back in 2016 it most definitely was not.

OK, back to Pristina.....

# CHAPTER 8

As it turned out it wasn't too much of a disappointment that Wizzair curtailed our stay in Pristina. We may have had enough time to rent a car for 24 hours and venture further afield if they hadn't but they had, so we didn't. It's a pleasant enough city, but small, so we really did only need a few hours to see it.

So we were off to Vienna which, funnily enough we are again now, as I write. Aggers had been many times courtesy of having an Austrian boyfriend for a while. Not now you would hopefully not be surprised to learn. I had been once when Dan Air flew a scheduled service there. It was January, so I don't think I ventured out much. Why did I go in the first place, then? We had one free ticket to use each year on scheduled services and I needed to use mine before it ran out. You should be able to work out the rest. Aggers reckoned it was a fine city. She wasn't wrong and I was very happy to have a much better understanding and impression of the recently voted, World's most liveable city. Yeah, wait until Croydon gets city status, Vienna!

Due to the fact we now had 2 nights in the most liveable city, which is certainly not the most affordable city, I was in Couchsurfing mode. Having failed miserably in Rome, I thought I'd have another go. I found a couple of candidates and this time got a positive response. What an interesting experience. Our host was an Uighur refugee and his family. We didn't know too much about the plight of the Uighur people, other than that the good China democracy really wasn't being very nice to them at all.

Sutuk as a host couldn't do enough for us. We had dinner upon our late arrival, a room to ourselves and a hearty breakfast before we left. We were certainly far more well-informed on this shameful and tragic situation after a good few hours of listening to Sutuk. He had fled to Turkey 6 years ago. When he returned to visit his family in China, he was chucked in jail for 5 weeks. The authorities would only release him if he agreed to spy on them once back in Turkey. He agreed, in order to get out of China. Once back in Turkey he fled to Austria and sought political asylum, which he achieved.

He and his wife have no chance to return to their homeland and visit their families. They haven't even been able to contact them in any shape or form for 5 years. He fears his brothers will be in prison/correctional institutions, if not dead. The situation in that region of China he described to us is truly horrific.

He invited us to stay a second evening. We declined on a number of accounts: although his English was very good, he spoke so quickly it was extremely difficult to understand him. This was the main reason. Also, he was veering more and more onto the subject of religion, and Allah in particular. We wanted to see some of Vienna while we were there and it just so happened it was our 1st wedding anniversary that second day. Call us selfish but we had listened, with great interest and concentration to Sutuk's stories but it probably wasn't how we would choose to celebrate our first anniversary.

We bade our farewell and suggested we may stay on our return to Vienna (he seemed quite put out* that we didn't want to cancel our hotel for the night and lose the 50 quid we had splashed out, oh well). I have to share this: I actually finished this chapter just before we landed in Vienna again. Hopefully you would expect me to achieve more than the above output in 2 hours. Well, I did. In fact, I finished the chapter but, inexplicably, my ancient iPad decided to delete everything from the * above. This isn't the first time it's chosen to misbehave but it was certainly the most damaging. Ever since the advent of email I've struggled to replicate what I have written if it vanishes. Why am I bothering you with this? Well, not only do I want to encourage you to travel and collect, if you aren't already, I also want to, if you feel there's the inkling of an urge, get you closer to putting pen to paper, well fingers to keyboard and tell your story. I really was quite angry. Why, when I erred on the side of caution and copied the latest diatribe I'd written, did my iPad decide to copy about 20% of it and delete the rest?

I tried to console myself by recounting the unfortunate incident I had read about in the Metro a couple of years back: this fella had cycled around the world, written a book about it, was on his way to a publisher, I think, when as reported, he popped into a cafe for a takeaway coffee. He left his bike outside, as you would, left it unlocked, as you probably wouldn't, although this was in Barnes from memory and, almost unbelievably, left his computer in a bag on his bike. I like to believe what I read in the Metro. When he completed his purchase and came back to his bike it was no longer there. More importantly and if true, far more devastatingly, neither was his laptop! It contained the only copy of his manuscript. I'm not sure why you would bother to contact a newspaper if the story wasn't true. He must've been truly, absolutely gutted if it was true.

So, I'm only 3/4 of a not particularly long chapter down but it instils in me a bit of writer's block. It's taken me 6 days to face rewriting. So here goes.....

I've actually resorted to 1 finger typing on my phone, which doesn't seem much slower than 2 fingers on my iPad, which I'm still sulking with. I actually have what I've written so far saved in 4 different email accounts so hopefully the still to be published "But I Digress" is safe enough.

We are currently enduring an air traffic delay on Wizzair. In my Dan Air days, they were ridiculously common and unpleasantly lengthy at times, as were technical delays. These days both are extremely uncommon. On a positive note, this gives me longer to hopefully finish this chapter, depending on how much I digress!

What I didn't write previously was that the experience of

that poor chap who, supposedly, lost all his work, (yeah, I know it was a bit daft and naive of him, but you've still got to sympathise) reminded me of a couple of my own bicycle mishaps: I went to watch Leeds play at Watford one evening in the League Cup in 1992. We'd just won the league, so were pretty decent and even pessimistic me expected us to win. Cantona was useless and we lost 2-1, I think. To cap off a miserable evening, when I returned to Victoria Station to collect my bike, only the front wheel remained. Bastard/s!

On another occasion when I used to leave my bike at East Croydon Station on my way to Gatwick, I returned after one night shift to find it no longer where I left it. This resulted in me deciding to take my replacement bike to Gatwick with me. The consequence of this was one evening I forgot that I had the bike with me, back in the day when trains had a guard's van where bikes travelled. I only realised after the night shift when I went to go home that the bike was not padlocked up in its usual place. Initially, I thought this one had completed my own hattrick of stolen bikes. Then it dawned on me that it was my own stupidity that caused me to be 3 bikes down. What a twat!

I did actually complete my hattrick of bike thefts some 22 years later when some bastard (I know it wasn't bastards because the police reviewed the CCTV footage, to no avail unfortunately) stole my pretty nice new bike from Whyteleafe South Station in broad daylight. I could digress from here onto bike crashes, girlfriend thefts (I don't think I had any of those luckily) etc but let's crack on now I'm over the loss; of the chapter, not the bikes.

Seeing as I don't know how long it's going to take us to finish our collections and how much excitement we'll have along the way, it's quite tricky to know how much to write on each addition to the total and even how much to digress. I guess if it's getting too long, I'll just speed up to the end.

We did enjoy a very pleasant wedding anniversary in Vienna. The next day we met up with Uli, Aggers's ex. I only mention this because it seemed quite odd that, having not seen each other in 10+ years, he suggested we go for a swim in the Danube. Maybe he wanted to see Aggers in a bikini? He did and we did...go for a swim. After a pleasant lunch Uli dropped us at the airport for our flight to airport number 951 (or so I thought!), Tuzla. A small, nicely located airport from where we treated ourselves to a hire car which we would drop at airport number 952 (or so I thought!). I say treated because car hire and fuel prices have risen so massively recently that it is no longer an option we would automatically consider.

Obviously, you're dying to know why the numbers above are in question. I'm dying to tell you too, so I'm going to be as brief as possible about our stay in B&H. That'll also help me to move on from trying to remember what I wrote about it first time. It's a beautiful country, the people are very friendly, it's cheap to eat, drink and sleep and the weather was lovely. Nothing to dislike although our fellow drivers were amongst the worst, if not the worst, I'd encountered in Europe. Still, like India, amongst others, no road rage.

We visited Srebrenica Memorial Museum, a truly harrowing reminder of man's inhumanity to his fellow man. A beautiful 6-hour drive through wonderfully varied scenery took us to a delightful overnight stop in Trebinje, in the strangely named, but extremely friendly Porto Bello Hotel. Onwards to Neum, B&H's only seaside access. It seems a bit harsh that Croatia nabbed so much of the coast line and Montenegro the rest, but it was very agreeable to hit the coast, albeit briefly.

On our route up to airport 952 (or so I thought) we made several stops including an overnight in Mostar - a truly stunning small city, even if there were rather too many tourists and the inevitable tat for sale for our liking. As it was almost on our way, we had stopped at Medugorje. As you know, neither of us are much into religion in the slightest, but our good friend Colin had mentioned that he hoped to make a pilgrimage there. Neither of us had heard of it but, apparently, it was the new Lourdes.

If we are both sceptics when it comes to religion this took it to another level: in 1981, 6 teenagers had climbed a nearby hill and seen an apparition of the Virgin Mary. So now we have Apparition Hill that Catholics flock to in their thousands, even though the Vatican, 40 years on, is yet to officially accept the veracity of the teenagers' claims. Maybe the Pope came to the same conclusion as us. Nonetheless China, most likely, as well as the locals, has benefitted from the inevitable junk souvenirs that accompany such a place.

Our biggest issue, though, was that initially we climbed the wrong bloody hill! Cross Mountain! It was damned hot, extremely rocky and uneven and about 12 times further than Apparition Hill, and we were both in flip flops. Dare I say it, but Agnes was pretty cross when I broke it to her just over half way up that, the reason we weren't meeting many pilgrims was that this climb was too much for most of them, particularly in this heat.

As it transpired it didn't seem that too many made it up Apparition Hill, preferring the shops and the church. At least we felt, having decided after Agnes had quaffed a well-deserved beer, we were here so we may as will shoot up Apparition Hill (maybe the teenagers had been shooting up, up there!) too, that our efforts for Colin's sake had caused us some minor temporary suffering along the way.

We really liked Sarajevo too. We visited The Tunnel Museum and The Childhood Museum to further educate ourselves. I'm old enough to remember the war there but trying to envisage this city besieged for 4 years was beyond my imagination. It's just baffling how it could start in the first place, let alone continue for so long.

We enjoyed a pleasant flight back to Luton on an unusual half empty Wizzair flight. The time on-board flew past as I wrote, as it did when a week later, we flew back to Vienna. The last 2 hours have also sped along as we still sit waiting to depart for Katowice now, the reason for our delay becoming slightly unclear.

Now, I've recovered this chapter I can tell you about 951 and

ALAN FORBES

952, or so I thought!

# CHAPTER 9

While we were in Colombia my friend Nail (sic), he of Venezuelan rucksack repacking infamy, had contacted me for some advice on flying over the Grand Canyon. I immediately had a feeling, call it a sixth sense, that Grand Canyon was not on my list. It wasn't, but I had to wait until we got home to erase that 0.01% of doubt that time had caused me to question whether I had actually taken a flight there or not. The 1999 diary entry said I had. Quite why I hadn't stuck it on the list, I know not. I can only think that I was not as desperate back then to add to the numbers.

I pondered on whether I should add it at this late stage, thus rendering celebrations for airports 700, 800 and 900 invalid. I decided I would ponder some more. Whilst researching the itinerary for that last trip, I stumbled across a Wizzair Norwegian destination; Harstad/Narvik with an IATA code EVE. Alarm bells added to my normal volume of tinnitus. Aggers and I had done a quick there and back to Evenes on our Norwegian odyssey. A quick check on Wikipedia revealed that Evenes airport was now, more commonly, known as Harstad/Narvik. I was pretty sure Narvik was on my list from my 1988 Norway trip. It was. Dilemma solved. I could just slot Grand Canyon in where Evenes was.

I'll try to be brief. Since finally putting my flights on an excel spreadsheet 2 years ago I planned to list the airports on a separate sheet but had, so far, failed to make time for this. With Agi's help, at last, a grey day in Blighty prompted me to get my shit together. What if the numbers didn't tally up with my oh so messed up written list? I was actually quite surprised that they didn't. It took me the best part of a day to check the 952, or so I thought, hand written total against the computerised total.

Bugger!! On the same page I'd listed Labuan twice. I was one down on the total. On my numerous business trips to Malaysia, more specifically Sabah, Borneo it had always troubled me that time had prevented me from taking any of the several flights that Malaysia Airlines flew to remote spots inaccessible by land. Perhaps this frustration resulted in me sticking Labuan down twice? I had managed to fly to Kota Kinabalu via Macau, Clark (near Manila), Kuching and the delightfully named Bandar Seri Bagwan so that these long trips weren't all lacking in any additions to my total, but adding Labuan twice was just blatant cheating.

Obviously, it was a genuine mistake but I was crestfallen. Not for long. Unbelievably, I had numbered Manston as 582, between 652 and 653. Did I really take this collection lark seriously? Clearly not, but the numbers were back on an even keel. But, hang on, they weren't. The computer said I had 954 airports. My scraps of paper said 952! This was nothing short of sensational. I was about to add 2 airports to my collection without leaving our apartment!

The computer told me that Luang Prabang and Mana, whilst on the flights lists, were not accounted for on the airport list in date order. The computer was bloody well right, don't you know? In 2001 I treated myself to finally flying round the world. I had been as far west as French Polynesia and as far east as Christchurch but had always gone back the same way. Commitments necessitated a quick trip, with Fiji being my main stopover. There are plenty of flights to small islands there but I only managed to fly to 3. Why, then, had I left Mana off the list? Don't ask me.

I told you I was fascinated by time change. I also told you I'd tell you about my other circumnavigation of our planet (I know it's not that much of an achievement doing it on commercial flights). This was the ultimate. I left Nadi at 2215 on Saturday only to arrive in Los Angeles at 1000 the same morning. My enjoyment was only tempered by sitting across from the man with the smelliest feet I'd ever encountered. As I was travelling on a staff ticket, I didn't feel I could ask him to put his shoes back on, not that he'd have known I was a freeloader. They really did pong though.

A few years later, I didn't have a bucket list but I fulfilled a long-held desire to visit Angkor Wat. I coupled it with a quick side trip to Laos. Why the hell was Luang Prabang not on my list of airports? Well 954 it was, so who cares?

There's still one question over the exact total which I don't think I can ever answer. There was actually an airport at Narvik as well as Evenes. I'm sure you remember that Evenes is commercially known as Harstad/Narvik. Well, when I visited in 1988 both Narvik and Harstad/Narvik (Evenes) were both operational. My records show I went to Narvik in 1988 but I think I've just demonstrated that they leave a little to be desired. I can't categorically state that I went to Narvik in 1988 and, therefore count Harstad/Narvik (Evenes) as another airport. From what I read I think it probably was Narvik I went to first and not Harstad/Narvik but, I would rather be one over the total than one light.

Sorry about all that but the collectors and addicts amongst you will, may, understand. On the subject of numbers would you count countries on your list, if you have one, such as Yugoslavia, Czechoslovakia, USSR, East Germany that no longer exist, as well as their respective replacements? Fortunately, I'm not counting. It's too complicated as I've alluded to before.

Just before I move onto 955 (which I thought was going to be 953) let's talk Wetherspoons. I'm actually glad I didn't make too much fuss about milestones along the way, airport wise. Potosi had a nice story to it as number 800, but it's now 802. What matters is getting number 1000 right, or 1001. Maybe I'll celebrate both. So why talk Wetherspoons when we're on 709 - hardly a landmark? Well, since our appearance in the Summer 2019 edition of Wetherspoon News magazine, I have to admit to pretty much reading each quarterly publication from cover to cover. Although I admit this is partly down to my

OCD tendencies, it does also present an opportunity to refresh my mind on pubs we've visited, which are featured within. Additionally, it whets my appetite to read about pubs we've yet to visit.

Whilst many features are about the staff and fundraising, there are numerous short articles on customers. Again, and rightly so, many of these concern fundraising for charity, but some are about people like us. Yes, they do exist. Apart from one chap who's featured a couple of times (he is the leader of an alternative political party), most of the customers featured have significantly less pubs in their collection than us. I noticed one article where the couple had been featured previously but were still well behind us.

We are neither attention-seekers nor braggers but I quite fancied another appearance. I contacted the girl/lady who had facilitated our debut appearance in the mag. Yes, she did still work there and she would be delighted to feature us again. The photographer was dispatched to meet us in Hailsham Spoon. The real reason for telling you this though is that we received breakfast "on the house" - an achievement I would rank alongside a couple of complimentary beers from Ryanair. Needless to say we, but I in particular, as Aggers isn't so sad as me, eagerly await the publication.

So, we were quite chuffed with our productive week back in Blighty which also included a very enjoyable birthday celebration with the family in a caravan. Now there's a collection - caravan sites? Not for us thanks. After another pretty pleasant 24 hours in Vienna, 955 awaited. It should have only been 3 hours but Wizzair decided to change the day of our onward flight. I had been to watch England play in Tirana around 20 years ago. It seemed quite bizarre that a country the size of Albania only offered one commercial airport opportunity but until just a few weeks ago, it did. Rather than chastise Wizzair for depriving us of a day in Albania I would rather thank them for providing us with another route to Poland.

Aggers was very keen to visit Albania once she learnt that Wizzair flew to Tirana from her nearest home town airport, Katowice. Obviously, I needed a further incentive. The commencement of a twice weekly service from Vienna to Kukes, coupled with Wizzair also starting to fly to Vienna from Gatwick provided it. I was also pleased we could reach Poland without another Stansted or Luton visit. That particular positive soon became quite negative. Bugger me, if I thought they were bad, my dear old friend Gatwick was giving them both a right old run for their money. The security experience Gatwick was currently offering made both Stansted and Luton seem pretty user-friendly.

No matter, we were off to Kukes and what a delightful little airport it was. Situated in the mountainous north of the country, its location, coupled with the warmth and early evening colours made it one of those invigorating arrival experiences. Even the immigration staff were friendly. Mind you, the novelty probably hadn't worn off and only having 3 flights per day could hardly be too strenuous. We were more than happy to walk the 5 kilometres to the town centre. The scenery was gorgeous and so was the weather. We were both glad we collect airports.

We had barely walked 10 minutes when a couple stopped to offer us a lift into town. We weren't too sure at first, as it was such a fine evening for a stroll, but it seemed a bit rude to turn down their kindness. Now it turned out that this couple weren't going to Kukes. They were off to Tirana. So were we......tomorrow. Lonely Planet (LP from now on) didn't even mention Kukes. Our driver, Bledar, and his wife, Clementine, both said that the town had little going for it, other than its location. They would be more than happy for us to accompany them to Tirana. Only problem was that, as Booking.com only offered one property in Kukes, we had booked it in advance. Our new "friends" insisted on taking us to the hotel to see if we could cancel without charge. We could, so off we went to Tirana, nicely ahead of schedule.

It was a most enjoyable drive through beautiful mountain scenery. We learned that Kukes, bizarrely, provided the majority of Albanian immigration to UK. Although only young children when he died, our friends related many stories from the time of their country's 50-year oppression at the hands of Enver Hoxha, a dictator that made Ceausescu and some of the others sound like pussies. We enjoyed their company immensely and it was great to learn more about a country that had remained a mystery to us up until now. If it's true that men with small willies like big, flash cars (which I'm sure it isn't) then the Albanian boys don't measure up too well. Top of the range German models were in abundance, and a significant number wore UK number plates. Initially I wondered why Brits would drive all the way to Albania. Drrrr! These weren't Brits at the wheel. These were Albanians returning to their homeland for a well-deserved holiday. Call me a sceptical, narrow minded racist but I was prepared to stereotype how these drivers had obtained the funds required to purchase such a model. Actually, we were informed later that the cars were most likely stolen, so I was being kind, in my observation!

Bledar said that Albanians valued a flash car above anything else and would gladly live in a squat or similar, if it meant they could drive around in a large Merc or BMW. He also said that during Hoxha's time if you had a village of 50 people, 15 would be working for the secret police! If you tried to escape the country, the government would kill any family you left behind. Perhaps that explained why people didn't chance a swim over to Corfu, it's that close (or maybe they did). What a charmer this man really was (not)! The most unbelievable statistic about him and his cronies, for us, was the 170,000 bunkers they had built in the country due to his paranoia about a nuclear attack. These were constructed between around 1967-1986. Wikipedia gives quite good but brief details on this bizarre obsession. And yes, that's 170,000, although 230,000 were planned. Maybe they'd have got to 230,000 if he hadn't popped his clogs!

We did visit the main bunker in Tirana which was constructed for Hoxha and his generals to use. It even contained a theatre and was a vast place. Many of the bunkers were more like pillboxes with room for two or three people. The modern history of Albania is yet another example of how one complete and utter bastard can ruin the lives of so many. That said, Bledar said he cried when Hoxha died. He also told us that although Albania is nominally considered to be 70% Muslim, 80% of those Muslims don't care about religion. You really wouldn't know you were in a Muslim country any more than you would if you were in Luton.

Bledar and Clementine were picking up their children on the outskirts of Tirana, so offered to drop us at the bus stop so we could continue into the city. We had yet to visit an ATM so were without any local currency for the bus. No bother. They gave us the bus fare. Admittedly it was only about 15p each but it's the gesture that counts. What very, very kind people. Bledar had lived for 3 years in Northampton. He liked England, particularly the pub culture but he just couldn't handle the weather. We had a lot in common. We would be genuinely pleased if they ever made it to UK and we could return their hospitality.

We picked up a car the next morning and headed off to Berat and after an overnight, onwards to Gjirokastra, both deservedly UNESCO World Heritage Sites. Well worth visiting both, for sure. Charming old towns, wonderfully situated but both quite different from each other. Highly recommended. We then headed down to the coast for our final two days. Quite what LP found "delightful" about Ksamil was completely beyond both of us. The book was only 3 years old and the place was a mess. Sarande, the self-appointed capital of the Albanian Riviera was no better. Both overdeveloped, crowded hell holes as far as we were concerned. We headed north and the coastal scenery was beautiful and in places, quite dramatic.

We found a lower key and far less ruined beach spot after a good few hours, to spend the evening and improve our impressions of the Albanian Med. I would normally greet the news of a new airport construction with a degree of joy, if it was one I would be likely to visit. However, when we learnt that an airport should open in Vlore in 2024 our fears for the region deepened. Obviously, I've had to have a quick google on this: it's being built totally within a protected area which provides shelter to 62 species of birds! If it wasn't so sad, it would be comical. What protection are they providing to these birds if not from low flying aeroplanes!?

Vlore will be Albania's largest airport. Not much of a claim when there's only two others, one of which - Kukes - only has parking for three aircraft. Jumping the gun slightly, but whilst on the Albanian airports, Tirana may have parking for many more than three planes but airside in the impressive looking, from the outside, terminal barely provided enough seating for that number, let alone any more. Bodies everywhere. I don't remember much about my previous visit to Tirana but that terminal looked pretty new. It didn't look like much consideration had been given to any increase in passenger numbers. Maybe you knew that Mother Teresa was half Albanian? We didn't. See how airport collecting educates us? Tirana airport is named in her honour.

Before we headed to Tirana airport, we spent our final afternoon and evening in Durres on the coast rather than visit the capital again. We knew it would be busy, given its proximity to the capital, but bloody hell (on earth) - it was truly horrible. Row upon row of sunbeds for miles on end. Big overflowing wheelie bins, positioned almost in the sea. We decided to head off to the amphitheatre in the original area of the city. Bloody good job we did. The contrast between the actual city one side of the port and the beach resort the other, couldn't have been starker. The seafront was tastefully developed and devoid of any of the "amenities" the resort area offered. Consequently, people were in short supply, even though the few restaurants were so, so, so much nicer looking than the multitude on offer t'other side. We enjoyed an idyllic last dinner on the ocean, had a quick butchers at the amphitheatre, wandered through the pedestrian area where the locals had emerged once the temperature dropped and finally waded through the sea of sunbeds back to our, actually not too bad, pad for the night.

Overall, we loved Albania. We expected the coast to be a let-down and it didn't let us down. The rest exceeded our expectations. The climate was superb, slightly too hot if anything but that would only ever be an observation, never a complaint (unless in the Middle East).

Aggers got one airport closer, having gone two behind after my unexpected additions, with Tirana. Could we achieve our aim of climaxing on 500/1000 airports simultaneously, with foreplay at the last Spoon on departure? Sounds quite sexy? Best we go and do a few Spoons....

# CHAPTER 10

Well seeing as it's been nearly 5 months since I last put pen to paper (obviously I'm not putting pen to paper quite literally. In fact, I'm trying a new method which I discovered while writing an email to my cousin. I'm recording - amazing when it works, speeds things up considerably, so if you notice a change in the writing style.... new paragraph new paragraph - clearly not working as well as the other day!) I'm sure you would be disappointed if we hadn't added any new Wetherspoons to our collection in this time but we have, and some, but first let me share with you my current anxiety. Yes, of course it is airport collecting related and I actually feel it has been under control until yesterday full stop (told you it's not working as well as I hoped). In fact, it was still under control yesterday but if the weather hadn't been kind to us I don't know how I would have felt.

We are on a break from Wetherspoon as we are spending the first part of the winter away from northern Europe. Now, plenty of planning had to go into this, firstly because of the massive increase in long haul airfares and secondly, to ensure that we went to a destination which would enable us to reach our targets sooner rather than later full stop new paragraph new paragraph!!

I won't bore you with the details, suffice to say that we decided to return to the Far East. We are currently in Bario, deep in the heart of Sarawak, Malaysian Borneo. It is a delightful place, however, we would not like to get stuck here for too long. Yesterday we woke up in Miri - the gateway to small airport collecting paradise - to heavy rain and thick low cloud. Not ideal weather conditions for flying into very short runways in the jungle, surrounded by mountains. But I surprised myself with just how relaxed I was that the flight may be cancelled. It wasn't and we enjoyed a delightful flight via Marudi to Bario with 2 other passengers.

Once we had settled on Malaysia as our main destination, I set to work on trying to maximize the number of airports we could add. Through work I had been to Sabah many times but never had the time to visit some intriguing sounding airports nearby in Sarawak; namely Long Akah, Long Banga, Long Lallang, Long Seridan and Bakelalan (long acre long bangor long lalanne long sarah dan back call alan, so much for the recording!).

The frequencies of these flights were far less than I hoped. All told I would estimate that I spent the best part of 20 hours trying to work out a route that would enable us to visit all the airports in Sarawak and I failed miserably. I could not understand why we could fly to an airport but not fly onwards from the same airport on the same plane. Unfortunately, with the jungle terrain, it would not be possible to fly to, for example, Long Banga and fly back from Long Lallang, even though they are only about 60 kilometres apart. There is no road or river to connect them. Therefore, our normal method of into one airport and out of another, would not work. The flights were nice and cheap but this did not help when I couldn't book them.

Once we got to Sarawak it became clear why: although the aircraft operating are Twin Otters with 20 seats, because of runway length restrictions, they only sell between 7 to 9 seats per flight and some destinations are only served once or twice per week. Today we had planned a there and back to Long Seridan from Bario. We had been lucky enough to secure seats on these flights a few days ago. We awoke to very low cloud again and lots of barking dogs and cockerels. I surprised myself again at how relaxed I was. Maybe it is because we are getting very close to 1000 and 500 each? Maybe, at last, I really am completely putting things into perspective? Whatever, I was relaxed. Again, the cloud cleared and the sun broke through. When Agnieszka suggested that we took our bags with us in case the flight took us to Long Seridan but couldn't return us to

Bario, instead continuing to Miri, in which case our bags would be stranded a mere 11 hours away by dirt road, I was relaxed enough to decline this suggestion. Yet again the Twin Otter took off early with one other passenger and this really was the best of sightseeing flying you can imagine. It seemed like we flew through the mountains rather than above them and the tiny village of Long Seridan was beautifully located. We would like to have stayed there but could not imagine using 10 days of our time before the next flight!

We have met the same pilots on several occasions and they now understand why we are flying there and back with them. While I am recording, the black clouds are gathering again. It is after all, the middle of the rainy season so I can now start to worry about our flight from Bario back to Miri tomorrow. Will we get stuck in Bario? Whether we do or don't we will not regret coming here. It is a simply charming place. The locals are so friendly, the paddy fields are incredibly green, surrounded by delightful hills and mountains. It really is a treat amongst our many treats.

Just to keep you up to date with the rest of the potential anxiety inducing plans facing me: should we get back to Miri tomorrow we will attempt to hitchhike to Bandar Seri Bagwan, Brunei. If you're not familiar with the geography in this area it is really strange. Brunei is separated into 2 parts which entails 4 border crossings. Unless you take the new bridge to stay in Brunei without passing through Sarawak again, if that makes sense. There are no longer any buses running from Miri to BSB, as the locals call it, or Bandar. Bandar Seri Bagwan really is a bit of a mouthful, isn't it? You now have to fill out and pay for a request, on line, each time you want to enter or leave Brunei. Who knows why? We need to get to Lawas in Sarawak from BSB; apparently also no bus service.

We want to visit Bandar but not the airport. Aggers is getting precariously close to being less than 500 behind me. She is in favour of the dual celebration so we are bizarrely, trying to avoid any new airports solely adding to her total. In my desperation to add new airports en route to and from Kota

Kinabalu on numerous previous work trips I had transited Bandar on one occasion - a strange 20-minute flight with Royal Brunei where Allah said a prayer for us over the entertainment system before take-off.

We have succeeded in booking a flight from Bakelalan to Lawas. However, we could not find a flight to Bakelalan so we are trying to find a ride on the logging track! You see, these are the lengths we must go to - choose to go to, to reach our goals. I'm sure there is an easier way but this is the fun way, isn't it? I'll hopefully be back to let you know before too long if the weather and logistics have been in our favour.

What hasn't succeeded or been in my favour is recording this chapter. It's actually proved a miserable failure and taken me longer to correct, amend and add to it than it would've done to write it in the first place!

# CHAPTER 11

So....... how many new Spoons do you think we did since our celebrations after completing the SWCP? Come on, have a guess. Well, obviously I'm not going to tell you now, but I will tell you how we discovered even more of our lovely homeland along the way. When we set off on our first Spoons trip, this time round, we didn't even know how much of a Spoons trip it would be. We had thoughts to start the rest of the Pennine Bridleway which would mean visiting a vastly reduced number of new pubs. We had 5 days due to a family commitment.

Depending on when I finish, let alone attempt to publish this book, the UK summer of 2022 may be a very distant memory. We may even have had hotter ones since. The media really did go totally over the top. Yes, it was hot; very hot. Very, very hot by UK standards but, for 2 days! It was nice and warm before the 2-day mega heatwave and where we were, pissed it down, with resultant drop in temperatures straight after. That said, we decided it really was a tad unfavourable for long distance walking. Our time would be better suited to exploring the coastline of Lancashire.

Actually, when we headed north, with a breakfast stop - 710 for those of you counting - and canal side walk in Stourbridge, we were still indecisive. After further stops in Stafford (2 pubs), Uttoxeter and Cheadle - all 3 being very pleasant towns we had never been to - we were still indecisive. What had been a unique experience was welcoming the normally chilling Wetherspoon's air-conditioning! We are neither fans of air-conditioning nor sitting inside when it's warm out. However, in a first for us, seriously ever in UK, we chose to sit in the pubs rather than outside in the shade. The 39 degrees really was quite warm even out of the sun.

After a very pleasant evening in the garden and company of Nail (sic) the rucksack repacker we made a decision the next morning: no long-distance walking, just pubs for the next 4 days. We didn't regret it. 26 pubs at a nice relaxed pace. We discovered that Warrington is a very pleasant town, not a northern dump. As for Crosby, Formby and Southport; what a remarkably nice coastline. We walked a fair bit of it. In true UK fashion the weather changed, at least in the north west. It was still warm enough for the locals to be out in numbers on the beach but it clouded over considerably.

As usual, away from the main access points the beach was deserted. Not only does the tide at Southport shock with just how far it goes out but the town itself is extremely pleasant, boasting 2 Spoons. I allowed myself a quick visit to Southport FC. They were a league club back in the 70's but never since. They are still at the same ground. Peter has finally completed his 92 football league grounds and he got me thinking. Fitting in with his increasingly frequent bus and train travel since he retired, he has also been visiting some non-league grounds of clubs that were formerly league clubs. Maybe I should visit Kidderminster and Boston, both of which fall into that category, along with Southport and Workington? I'm not sure how that would sit with the 92 club aficionados. Well I am actually. They would 100% not approve. Boston may have moved grounds since they were a football league club (no internet in Bario to check) as have Bradford Park Avenue. I could not count them.

As I've said before, my/our collections, my/our rules. As we've yet to do the Spoon in the latter I could be tempted. Talking of football grounds, I managed to add the new AFC Wimbledon and Brentford to my list - even getting to see Leeds at The Bees. Lost 5-2 sadly but both nice enough grounds for newbies. Just the dreaded Barrow and far more appealing Harrogate to go. Apologies non footy folks.

Meanwhile, back to the Spoons. After a night in Southport (potential, only potential, for a new collection) we hopped over to Preston; another town only seen previously from a footy perspective and offering some fine old buildings and 2 more pubs, The Twelve Tellers being a fine example of the aforementioned architecture, we headed over to Lytham, had a pint and hopped on a train to Blackpool South. Interesting situation with train track for those of that persuasion. Not us particularly, but I believe Mr Beeching may have been responsible for the lack of track between Blackpool South and Blackpool Central.

I had warned Agnes about Blackpool. To be fair it's only really that southern end that's tacky; the Spoon down there, The Velvet Coaster, fitting in quite nicely although it has a rather nice rooftop. We had a lovely stroll along the beach all the way back to Lytham St Anne's to tick off The Trawl Boat Inn before heading up the Fylde coast to Fleetwood and Cleveleys, pubs and towns both mid to lower table. We stayed up the north end of town. The beach was really quite lovely in places and enjoyed views over to the Isle of Man at sunset, quite rare apparently, seeing IOM that is. One more added to the new potential collection in the process. You're dying to know aren't you, but I would be getting ahead of myself. I'll tell you when we've added a few more.

The next morning we completed the Blackpool hat trick of Spoons before heading south via Leyland (why had it never occurred to me that this was the origin of Leyland lorries - favourites of my childhood?) and Ormskirk to the suburbs of Liverpool. The Frank Hornby in Maghull deserves a mention out of 5 pubs in the Liverpool suburbs which completed our days "work"; plenty more nostalgia from my youngest days to enjoy. The next morning was truly miserable. All those bemoaning the heatwave were most likely cursing the steady and heavy rain. This sadly meant we saw little of St Helens, Widnes and Runcorn apart from the Spoons, none of which would live particularly long in the memory.

We had promised ourselves another car-less Spoons jolly. After a quick weekend home, we headed north again - to Sheffield. We hoped to go by train but this involved silly money, so Megabus it was. I even treated Aggers to prebooked front row seats, top deck. Some rather splendid pubs, the converted swimming pool, which is now The Rawson Spring in Hillsborough, being the pick of the 11 we ticked off in and around Sheffield, passing 750 in the process. What was notable about this 2-day Spoon fest was the phone call Aggers received whilst we broke our fast in The Sheaf Island. A news agency in Birmingham had spotted her Instagram updates and wanted to do an article on us. Once they learned we didn't just collect Wetherspoons their interest grew. Less than 2 weeks later Agnes was a page 3 girl in the Sun!

Actually I was also a page 3 geezer and neither of us had to take any clothes off! What amused us was how we learned which of our friends were Sun readers. Knowledge that the article existed came from a quite unlikely source (the agency had neglected to tell us): I thought Nicola was posher than that. She said her husband read it. We were and are not courting any publicity in the media for our collecting but I thought it may just help me get a publisher. It hasn't.

Further articles appeared on line with the expected trolling - hoping we died of food poisoning in Spoons seemed a bit harsh! As did the response to one reader's question: "what's she doing with that old geezer?" was followed with "have you seen the state of her, who else would have her!" Fortunately Aggers saw the funny side. What amused me was, "that guy used to be my landlord, he's alright" from a rather charming girl I had neither seen nor heard of for over 35 years. The People, yes, only the classiest rags for us, covered our airport collecting in print whilst The Mail Online managed to attract more abusive responses, the pick of the bunch being "thank you Alan and Agnes for destroying the planet. How utterly selfish you are". Yep, we're managing to do that all by ourselves. Remarkably clever of us, eh?

I'm still after an appearance in the Metro though and negotiations have started! Unfortunately the Spoon winter magazine had been delayed by a month so we had to wait patiently for our follow up appearance there.

After taking a well-earned break from collecting to attend my son's rather delightful wedding and my first Polish wedding too it was time to head off for that heady combination of Spooning and walking. The logistics of walking the southern end of the Pennine Bridleway with a combination of Mazda and public transport looked nothing short of a pain in the backside. The weather forecast was pretty inconvenient for fair weather walkers such as ourselves, too. The reality of both was far less problematic.

We notched off the 5 remaining Spoons in the Nottingham area on our way north. The second of these was notable for the conversation we enjoyed outside The Last Post in Beeston (also noteworthy for the manager's special - fish and chips £3.99 - not to be sniffed at in these inflationary times). When the bartender brought our drinks but failed to take away the pile of empties a kind chap on the next table proffered, "welcome to Wetherspoons" accompanied with a friendly smile and chuckle. I felt it worth mentioning that we were familiar with Spoon's service and why. Also that we weren't phased by it. He, and his 2 mates, were quite astounded not only by our number but the fact that we collected Spoons. This wasn't a one-way conversation. One of them had sparked Agi's interest as he was sporting a polo shirt with PKO logo, a Polish bank. Turns out he was "collecting" Park Runs. I wasn't familiar with this concept. Aggers was, but we were both suitably impressed that amongst his 250+ strong collection were several Polish ones. If, like me, you were unaware of Park Run, they are 5km organised runs every Sunday. Aga hinted that this could be the start of something but that she would be walking them.

One of the guys, in his 50s, and with a few Spoons under his belt, was gobsmacked when Aggers produced a copy of the latest Best magazine containing a double page spread interview with her and accompanying photos. He did no less than sprint across the road to get himself a copy. He returned, gutted that it had sold out. He was not perturbed that this was the best-selling women's/ladies'/girls' magazine. He determined to get himself a copy - for his wife! We could have chatted for a while longer but we had the other 3 Spoons to visit before overnighting for a second time at The Portman Hotel in Chesterfield; a fine Spoon hotel.

The forecast for the next day was grim. In fact it was already raining as we left Chesterfield. Rather than leave the car at our finishing point we decided to start walking as soon as possible as the worst of the weather was due in the afternoon. As I write it is hammering down outside in Bario, after a beautiful day. Plenty of cause for a sleepless night! As the Pennine Bridleway, you may recall, is primarily intended for horse riders and cyclists it is understandably much more even than its nearby friend The Pennine Way. We saw hardly any of either over the next 9 days and certainly none that looked like they may be attempting the whole thing. However, we never look like we're out for more than a day so "never judge a book by its cover" sprung to mind once more.

The walk starts at Middleton Top, not far from Matlock. We planned to have a breakfast at the previously visited Spoon there. Just as well we didn't. It was no more. As the start of the trail follows an old rail track (thanks again to Mr Beeching) we made good progress and the weather was massively better than predicted. We covered the 18 miles to Blackwell Turn in good time. This was handily placed on the Buxton to Matlock road and whilst the bus we rushed for was rather inconveniently nearly an hour late we made our connection to from whence we started and jumped in the Mazda just as it started to rain.

It would be no exaggeration to say it absolutely hammered it down for the next hour and a half as we sloshed our way to Buxton. We were, once again, grateful that we were flexible with our plans, having started walking a good 3 hours before we intended.

We stayed in a grand old hotel in Buxton. I recalled that I had previously stayed there with my mum, son and youngest daughter about 15 years ago whilst ticking off Macclesfield (v Leeds). When I asked if either remembered it, my son enlightened me that we had stayed there again, about 5 years on, en route from ticking off Fleetwood (not v Leeds!) to Alton Towers! Buxton is a charming town with an excellent Wetherspoon. I enticed Agnes, with a curry along the way, into a wander out to the non-league footy ground. Of far more interest to me was the cricket ground where snow had famously stopped play in June (!!!) in a county championship match between Derbyshire and Lancashire in the mid-1970s. First class cricket had not been played there for some time but I was delighted to see that the pavilion walls were adorned with press cuttings from that day.

Now, back to this fine old hotel - Palace Hotel, I think. By now we knew that this was a Britannia Hotel. We had not known this when we booked into Southport and Blackpool. Our only previous experience of this chain was in Nottingham, way back, on our first Spoon inspired jolly (it also included a failed microlight flight and Leeds 0 Wolves 1). The hotel was a modern, soulless place which we felt was overpriced even though it was city centre on a Saturday night. We were not interested in staying in another Britannia.

I'd like to say how things have changed with Britannia. Not so. Their hotels only generate between 5-6/10 on booking.com. I just read that they have been voted worst hotel chain in UK for the last 10 years. Result! It's not easy to achieve that level of consistency. However, having now stayed in Southport, Blackpool, Buxton, Manchester, Bolton and Liverpool I've given them 10/10 each time. Apart from Bolton which was like Crossroads Motel - if you're old enough to remember that soap classic - the other 5 were very centrally located, charming old buildings with sensational foyers. Other than Blackpool and Bolton, where we were warned that the rooms were quite small, the rooms were huge with very, very high ceilings; almost like mini suites. How could you possibly complain!? Well, I suppose if you paid £300+ you wouldn't quite feel that you'd nabbed yourself a bargain. We did - only paying between £39-49.

After we had stayed in The Adelphi in Liverpool I did stumble across a very unfortunate story in the Metro: a young girl had returned to her room to reapply her makeup and the wardrobe had fallen on her and killed her. That is tragic and leaves no room for any sick British humour for me but I wonder how much Britannia was to blame. Several Liverpudlians warned us against staying in The Adelphi but we were not to be deterred and personally, had no complaints at all.

Having said all that Aggers is less than lukewarm to try and stay in all 66. I think we need to branch out more but you never know.

We walked, we Spooned, the weather behaved. Once again we felt blessed with our chosen lifestyle. After another dry 18 miler on day 2 after breakfast in the very fine Buxton Spoon, we returned to rest our weary legs in the comfort of The Palace. Day 3 was curtailed to 10 miles due to weather forecast and logistics but that enabled us to add 5 more pubs. Of particular note in the southern suburbs of Manchester was The Sedge Lynn in Chorlton-Cum-Hardy. Even if the pub had been bang average the town name would live long in the memory. But it wasn't, it was a delightful old billiard hall conversion if my memory serves me correctly. We were also pleased to take our post walk refreshments in The Smithy Fold in Glossop. We had been caught out some 18 months ago by it being closed for refurbishment when we tried to grab a pint there in the latter stages of The Pennine Way. That was before I called ahead to make sure a pub was open - when I remembered. Stockport, East Didsbury and Urmston preceded the Sedge Lynn; unwittingly we had saved the best 'til last this day, just like Great Malvern.

We bashed out a commendable 21 miles after 3 Spoons for breakfasts (the standard 1/2 breakfast wrap, 1/2 breakfast wrap, coffees routine in Fallowfield, Rusholme and Ashton-under-Lyne) before returning to the Manchester Britannia via Manchester Wetherspoon - a crowded, quite unmemorable pub with an equally boring name. The walking was not strenuous compared to some coastal walking and it was never as remote as the Pennine Way. Manchester, in particular, was often in view most of the day and Burnley made several appearances.

Talking of Burnley, we often receive acts of human kindness on our travels. Not so much in UK, although we did hitchhike with remarkable and swift success in Norfolk. When walking The Peddars Way (and Norfolk Coast Path, to give it its full title) the bus journeys involved to recover the car were laborious in the extreme - 3 buses, 3 hours to cover 15 miles, for example. We resorted to putting our thumbs out. On almost every occasion the first vehicle stopped - a coal lorry driver, with coal imported from Australia! An old lady out picking cow parsley who asked us to sit in the back in case we weren't trustworthy.

We also hitched a ride in Pembrokeshire. The lady in question picked us up because her young daughter had asked her why we were walking with our thumbs out? "Then you must pick them up after you drop me off."

We were not the recipients in Burnley but as we walked into town 2 young lads of around 14 stopped to ask a homeless chap if he was hungry. He answered in the affirmative. They proceeded to hand over their McDonald's to him. Nice, eh?

No idea why, but I thought Stalybridge would be a nice town. Perhaps because we are generally pleasantly surprised by around 90% of the towns we visit that are previously unknown to us. Sadly it wasn't. Stalybridge felt like its heyday had long been and gone. Pretty nice pub for a breakfast wrap but we were also soon gone. The Harbord Harbord in Middleton for coffees will not stay prominent in the memory for too long either.

We were pretty knackered after our 22-mile day to be honest. The Vivobarefoots continued to feel as comfortable as slippers. I don't think I've mentioned these beautiful shoes before but try them. I'm not on commission. I'd just like fellow walkers to be as blister and sore toes free as we are. We've only ever seen one other walker in them on our National Trails and he was as sold as us. Peter is a proud owner of a pair on our recommendation. Only problem is that they are not waterproof. Unless you shell out on the boots, but the shoes are super light and compact so perfect for our hand luggage only style.

Talking of which, we used to curse Wizzair and Ryanair for reducing even further our free allowance (easyJet just finally, followed suit). Now we thank them. No unnecessarily heavy bags for us. As most of our trips are no longer than 6/7 weeks we are pleased with ourselves that we take less than most folk would for a weekend - and I don't believe we smell too bad!

Back to our overnight after the 22-mile day. We stayed in a very traditional style, small, old English pub directly on the route. No fancy food, just bloody tasty old pub grub. A Friday night live band, with a healthy audience and a friendly landlady. The basic rooms upstairs were fine too and we were told that the band would be done by 9pm, which they were. What could go wrong? Well, this pub, pretty much in the middle of nowhere, turned into a banging night club from about midnight until 3 am.

I don't want to sound too ancient but it really was pretty annoying and totally unexpected. Unfortunately, the landlady, who had left the premises before we retired, as had the band, didn't ask us in the morning how we'd slept. I was a bit grumpy so decided I'd let her know anyway. She didn't seem to believe me at first - didn't apologise but did get on the phone to one of her bar staff. Apparently, said bar staff had been under strict orders to clear the pub by midnight and turn the music off. She told her boss that the punters were having none of it, she couldn't control them and they insisted on pumping the music hard.

It was the bastard waiting for his taxi who really pissed me off. From 2 until 3 he must've changed songs 40 times. It was like being back in Colombia. We learned in the morning that a little jukebox with an incredibly powerful speaker was the culprit, right under our room. The landlady said that if she had known they would carry on she'd have stuck us in the back room. I politely suggested that this really wouldn't have made much difference.

Seeing as she really hadn't mastered the art of an apology, let alone a sincere one we were quite surprised when she took 50% off our room charge. I said that she didn't need to do that and that I didn't want her to be out of pocket. She told me not to worry, it would be coming out of her bar manager's wages! Harsh! Clearly, she couldn't give us our sleep back but at least it meant we'd had a very fine free dinner. It didn't affect our walking capabilities anyway and we covered another 18+ miles in good time, catching a bus to Burnley for a couple of pints in the surprisingly nice Boot Inn, an expected fabulous curry in a rather large curry house and an overnight in a rather charming B&B, in Burnley of all places and close enough to Turf Moor to attract visiting footy fans.

If you're wondering why I'm going into a fair bit of detail on how we tackled this walk, if not the walk itself, well, I'm not sure either. I think it's probably because it's the last of the 15, and I'm feeling a bit nostalgic about them. There's a lot of planning goes into these walking days - how far to go, where to overnight, public transport options, when to get reunited with Mazda. It's not only the walking that is quite satisfying but also when the plans work out, which they always do in the end.

The Pennine Bridleway planning is further complicated by having a 47-mile loop section and the section past the loop having no guide book to help with logistics. It is though, another really rather lovely walk in the main. We had learnt about a week before we set off that it had been agreed to turn the coast-to-coast Wainwright's Way into a National Trail. So, whilst we would be 15/15 if we finished The Pennine Bridleway we were quite happy that there would be more to do.

They're a funny old lot these National Trails makers. Apart from their signposting, which I've ranted about before and which, apart from being non-existent on a pedestrian only section of this walk has been the best. Actually, that really was bloody ridiculous. Clearly, they don't want horses to get lost but don't care about us poor old walkers. I believe I've also mentioned the creation of the England Coast Path. They have a section on their website, advising which sections of it are open, which have been approved but not opened and which are awaiting approval. How can the section currently open as the SWCP not even be approved as England Coast Path too!? It's already there and open for goodness sakes!! We are confused.

The Pennine Bridleway was due to be completed in 2005. It still isn't. Wainwright's Way's conversion to a National Trail is due to be completed sometime in 2025. Apparently, it's going to cost £5.6 million to convert it! Quote: "The new National Trail is expected to follow closely the existing route." Our dilemma for next summer: do we knock off the 190 miles before it's a National Trail? What if we later discover significant diversions? Tricky one, eh? Bit like doing a former football league ground and counting it as a league ground.

Day 7 felt like a very tiring 18.5 miles and we had to call on all our Spoon's desire to head off to Leigh and Walkden: 2 fairly unremarkable towns and pubs, before resting our weary legs (but not feet, thank you Vivo) at Crossroads Motel - sorry Bolton Britannia. But that was Greater Manchester Wetherspoons done and dusted. We could head off to Yorkshire the next morning to crack on with getting that side of the Pennine's J D Wetherspoon in better order. 4 pubs before a 20-mile walk (Cleckheaton, Bradford, Shipley and Bingley) did have me wondering whether we'd arrive at The Maypole Inn in Long Preston before dark, but we did. What a fabulous room they provided - top-drawer. Unfortunately, the welcome was distinctly bottom-drawer. You know how sometimes you walk into a local village pub and not being local, you get the eyeballs? Well, this was worse. "That'll be £86; cash or card?" That was literally the first words the barmaid said to us when she finally managed to get Mr Halfwit Local to work out how a credit card machine worked! No greeting, no here's your key. Just where's our money. Very, very poor.

This could have been a charming place but it was truly spoiled by the human element. Our departure mimicked our arrival: no "how was your breakfast?" or "did you sleep well?" or "enjoy your stay?". "Have you paid?" Welcome to God's own county, indeed! We asked for an omelette at breakfast. "Sorry we don't have any omelettes", yet you produced 2 fried eggs for each of us. Maybe you need a new chef or a lesson in customer service. What you did offer though, apart from the room which really does warrant a second mention, was the possibility for us to finish the walk before heading over to Leeds for my first visit to Elland Road since BC (before Covid). Rather than having to return the next day to finish the last section, we could crack on with another good day collecting Spoons.

As we had walked the sections north of Settle last year, we could conveniently finish this and our 15 walks with the 10-mile Settle Loop. I think we were both as proud to get to the finish of all 15 as we were of the SWCP. It was actually a right old slog uphill out of Settle to get to where we had turned off on the loop but at least that meant a stroll back on ourselves to get back to Settle for the train to Keighley and onwards bus to reunite ourselves with Mazda. Settle and its station are both lovely places. As we knew we wouldn't have any time to celebrate in a Leeds Spoon before kick-off we enjoyed a mandatory beer on Settle station.

Unfortunately, Leeds didn't manage to crown the day with a win, why would they? We met Peter for a celebratory breakfast, for us, the next morning in the simply outstanding Headingley Wetherspoon - the relatively newly opened Golden Beam. What a fabulous pub. After 4 more not bad pubs (Leeds (newly reopened Stick or Twist), Chapel Allerton, Bramley and Pudsey) and a good bit of walking in between, the Otley Spoon and town provided a fitting culmination to a fine day of Spooning before the customary joviality of an overnight with Mrs Hamilton of Yeadon.

2 more days of sightseeing and Spoonseeing included another 9 pubs; Cross Gates, Garforth and both (underwhelming) York pubs on day 1 and Selby, 2 x Mansfield, Sutton-in-Ashfield and Kirkby-in-Ashfield on day 2. Mansfield yet again was a town with a pleasant centre, missed on my footy visit almost 40 years earlier. I couldn't resist a quick trip back to Field Mill (Mansfield F.C.'s home). I had no memory of it. The Stag

and Pheasant looked nondescript from the outside but was anything but inside. Whilst it's always a shame when a Spoon closes hopefully the Mansfield locals will be happy that The Widow Frost bit the dust out of their 2. I doubt we'll be heading into Mansfield again so it doesn't really affect us. Could we have done more? Yes, but we were trying to pick a special for number 800. Having royally cocked up our number 600 plan, we were determined to get this right. York is undoubtedly a splendid city with a stack of history, so we wondered why its 2 Wetherspoons both had, literally, no history on their walls whatsoever. Very poor show.

We're not done on Spoons yet for the year, although we are done on National Trails, for now - congratulations to us! Thank you very much - but I've got some serious airport worrying to do. I think I would've been OK if a "friend" hadn't sent me a serious weather warning for the next 6 days - in Malay! All I could get from him is that it's due to be very wet and very windy. I'm going to tell you why I am, or was, so desperate, even more than usual, maybe, to add Bakelalan and Lawas to our totals.

# CHAPTER 12

I had no reason to panic in Bario in the end, but I just can't help feeling that our luck will run out. The weather behaved very kindly for our departure. Even though I was slightly alarmed when the staff at the airport explained that the previous flight took off late because of the cloud base. It looked distinctly good to us. Our plane arrived on time and left on time. We had a final dramatic view of Long Seridan and Mulu airports from the air before landing back in Miri for our transit to Brunei. We took another ridiculously cheap Grab to the border: think Uber, which they don't have here. We walked through the length of the respective immigration border controls with no hassle, just the heat to contend with.

We managed to hitch a ride, almost immediately, to the nearest town; Kuala Belait, around 15 miles away. In yet another act of kindness our lift giver, not sure if there's an actual word for someone who gives hitchhikers a lift, informed us that there would be no bus from KB to BSB. We needed to go to the next town Seria, where we could hopefully still get a bus. He then told us that he would happily take us there as he wasn't in a hurry. It may have only been another 7 or 8 miles but it's the principle, isn't it?

He enquired at the rather grubby and almost deserted bus station if there would be another bus and was told by a rather clueless looking young girl that there would be, at 5. Great, we were in business, so off our lift giver went, good deed accomplished. No sooner had he left than the girl, when I tried to confirm what she had told our man was true, said, "no, no, no more bus". Great. Seria really looked a fairly unattractive proposition to spend any time, let alone the night, from where we were standing. Our guide book described it as a nondescript oil town, with a British army barracks. Lovely stuff.

Luckily the girl had been right first time. A bus did turn up. Rather less fortunately the bus driver was in keeping with the surroundings. You know how some people can just have a really unsavoury demeanour? Well, this guy did. He was slovenly in the extreme, loud, no manners, bolshy, but worst of all, opened his door every 2 minutes to clear out the contents of his throat and mouth. It was utterly disgusting. We were sat directly behind him. I had to move in the end.

For a country flooded in oil money, Brunei's public transport system sucks. Probably for 2 reasons: most people, apart from immigrant workers, have a car and the chief clearly keeps most of it for himself. Apparently, he owns 2 x A340s, 1 x B747 and a private jet. That's probably more than the national flag carrier. No comment.

Our shitty old bus got us into BSB in the end where public transport, including most taxis finishes at 1800. I had arranged some Couchsurfing for our 2 nights there. We had found a reasonably priced basic hotel but thought it might be more interesting to stay with someone with some local knowledge. Our hostess lived a 20-minute cab ride out of town. Getting a cab proved quite a challenge. We borrowed some Wi-Fi off a swanky hotel but as warned, Dart (Brunei's version of Uber) proved to be useless. We were directed to the city's taxi stand - nothing. We approached a young dude in a limo. Not for a lift, although that would've been handy. He flagged down a passing old banger. The old boy agreed to take us for B$15. Dart had offered us B$8 but had no drivers. I got him down to B$10 and just before we drove off limo boy told us we could pay B$8. He even gave us his number in case we needed any help in the next couple of days.

We found our hostess's home despite the best efforts of numerous barking dogs to scare us away. Fortunately, they were all behind wire fences. She was hungover and immediately offered us a beer, which was quite ironic in a country as supposedly Islamic as Brunei. It's a funny old place, Bandar - a small, spacious city, with some fine mosques, a nice riverfront but just a bit lacking. After a very pleasant curry lunch the next day with a couple of other couchsurfers; both immigrant workers, one from India and the other Indonesia, the former of whom absolutely insisted to pay for all 5 of us before dropping us at the city wharf - very kind gestures indeed - we hired a boat for a lovely river ride. The main purpose was to see proboscis monkeys. We did see about half a dozen of them but unfortunately, at a distance where you couldn't make out their rather substantial hooters, which for Aggers, was the main attraction. Still, they were very entertaining.

Before leaving the city we not only found a taxi but this guy agreed to take us to the border the next morning for B$20. This seemed unbelievably cheap to us as it was about 25 miles and we'd paid B$10 to go 5 minutes down the road to the curry house. We caught the last bus (at 1700!) out to our lodgings and enjoyed the doggy bag remains of our curry. The next morning, we had a quick butchers around the bizarre Regalia Museum, proudly displaying some of the sultanate's opulence. Not sure who's worse, him or our royal family.

Our preplanned taxi driver was there at 1000, as agreed and happily took us across South East Asia's longest bridge to the Malay border for our bargain price. He even WhatsApped me a thank you message for the business later. Quite why this bridge has been built is beyond us. The weird geography of Brunei means it's almost like a sandwich with a Sarawak filling. The top piece of bread, depending on which way you look at it, is so sparsely populated that the bridge was nearly devoid of traffic. The land is virtually all Forest Reserve or National Park. What the bridge does do is negate the need for 2 border crossings to reach the top deck from BSB on the lower slice - of bread. Well, I suppose the Sultanate needs to spend his money on something. At least he didn't have the gall to charge a toll.

Another swift immigration passage ensued to get us back into Sarawak. The only problem we had was that the first dozen or so vehicles didn't stop for us. Admittedly half of them didn't have any room. For a girl who once hitchhiked from Poland to Southern Spain and back, Agi is surprisingly disgusted when the first passing vehicle doesn't stop to welcome us aboard. It was very hot and 15 miles to Lawas so we really did need a lift. And we got one after about 20 minutes and just a few more vehicles.

So, we had reached Lawas: an unremarkable town but with a lovely riverside setting with mountains in the distance. Whilst in Miri we had fortuitously met a delightful young lady from Bakelalan. We told her of our desire to visit her village and the driving force behind it. Whilst in Long Akah, for all of 20 minutes, we had met an equally delightful young lady from Brunei but originally from Long Akah. She had returned to her home village to vote. We could tell by the brown dye on her index finger, which we had been informed was how they vote here: with their finger! Sylvia from Brunei, had most helpfully supplied us with the names of some drivers she knew who may be able to take us from Lawas to Bakelalan. Esther from Miri/Bakelalan, just happened to know a couple of these guys too. She also had an uncle who was due to make the trip. She also had an uncle who had a Homestay in Bakelalan. She also had another uncle who had a Homestay in Lawas.

Esther was so into our planned journey. She was determined to get us to Bakelalan. Just to explain: I had managed to book us a flight from Bakelalan to Lawas on the Wednesday. We just had to get there. The flight on Monday was full. Esther's auntie worked for MASwings, the subsidiary of Malaysia Airlines which operates the rural Twin Otter services. She thought she might be able to magic us a couple of seats, but she couldn't. What she did manage to help us with was confirming our ride with Balang, probably another relative, to Bakelalan. Sadly, he couldn't take us on Monday, only Tuesday, which would mean just one night in Bakelalan rather than 2 and a full day.

Now, my friend Howard, who we are due to stay with in Sabah, decided to send me a weather warning, as I mentioned. I truly believe, without this, that I may have been a little less stressed but no, it's been full on thanks to him. Although it rained during the night in Lawas we awoke to the best morning yet of the whole trip - not a cloud in the sky, not even over the distant mountains. Balang turned up in his pick up over an hour before the agreed meeting time. We were still breaking our fast over by the river. Although we didn't set off until the agreed hour of 1000, by the time he'd loaded up with cargo and 4 other passengers, the dirt road to Bakelalan was nowhere near as bad as Esther, amongst others, had led us to believe. We've certainly been on a lot worse, and some. Once past the first 10-15 miles the environs of which were massively mashed up by all kinds of different mechanical vehicles, doing who knows what to the landscape, the jungle/rainforest was in the main, remarkably untouched, apart from a few small village settlements along the way.

The scenery was spectacular and the 5 1/2-hour ride was most enjoyable, if mildly uncomfortable. We were happy to be travelling in the covered, but open sided, back of the vehicle rather than in the air-conditioned cab. The weather was great until, as it does, it all changed and lashed it down. It then cleared just as quickly and we arrived in Bakelalan in glorious afternoon sunshine. What a gem of a place, for us. The runway takes up half the village, literally. Bakelalan is tiny compared to Bario. The valley in which it is situated is tiny again, compared to Bario. Landing a Twin Otter here looks far and above the challenge of landing in Long Seridan, let alone Bario.

If only our plane was due to come in the afternoon, not the next morning. Well, if it had been, I would have been panicking the whole journey up, whether we would make it in time, wouldn't I? Anyway, as Aggers keeps reminding me: what will be, will be. Our Homestay here, arranged by Esther wasn't quite, in fact it's far from, on a par with Jane's hospitality in Bario but, it is quite literally about 15 metres from the runway. A plane spotter's paradise if there were more than 3 flights per week! But, undoubtedly, an airport collector's paradise. There is a little gate to take you across the runway to the tiny terminal building the other side. I wonder if they lock it when a plane is due. We walked the length of the runway yesterday, because we could. I remarked that I thought that to be a first. We had driven a moped along a defunct runway in Vietnam, wandered onto a closed runway in Cape Verde and, on this trip, watched kids play football on the closed runway in downtown Bintulu, but walking up and down an active commercial runway? An airport collector's high.

Sarawak has moved and upgraded several of its airports. We just missed the old strip in Mukah, which only closed last year. Bario moved its runway a while back. Bintulu and Sibu moved out of town to new locations, the former this century. Plans are afoot to move Lawas' tiny airport to a new location, out of town. There's nowhere to move Bakelalan's runway, so it'll be here for a while, if we need to come back!

We mused that, even if we did have to make the return journey by road, we were glad we came. Yes, we will be disappointed, very, not to fly out of Bakelalan but, as I mentioned, I'm not so desperate on the numbers. Neither is Aggers. To her credit she bypassed BSB airport (one bus even stopped at the terminal) several times and was steadfast in her decision not to request or insist that I built it into our itinerary. Apart from the very noisy generators from 6 until midnight it is idyllic and if the airport tick is achieved, I think it'll go straight into the top 5. I'd never really given that any thought until our news agency "friend" requested it for both pub and airport articles.

As I write dawn has broken to reveal heavily overcast skies. Gone is the beautiful sunshine of yesterday evening. We can but hope that the cloud burns off to facilitate a landing for our 1030 flight, and, if not, there is still transport available to return us to Lawas...... (if that tension doesn't have you turning the page straight to the next chapter nothing will).

# CHAPTER 13

Unlucky for some? I considered to continue as chapter 12 but, really? As if this cloud is going to lift just because I don't write about it in chapter 13. The mist over the runway is currently so low, you feel you could jump up and touch it. Better still, blow it away. The tension is unbearable. Really? No it isn't. It's all in perspective. Where there's hope. These MASwings boys seem to be quite sensible about their schedules: there are no early morning flights to the rural airfields and none past 3pm. They clearly recognise their window of opportunity. The mist through the valleys really is quite magical, so long as it doesn't out stay our welcome to it.

While we're waiting, let me just bring you up to speed with some other trivia from this trip. Plotting our route to South East Asia at an agreeable price, unsurprisingly led us to Bangkok. The start of that route was quite surprising even to me. I knew Wizzair were getting into Abu Dhabi big time but just not quite as big.

(I've just been out for a cloud base inspection from the runway. I'm nowhere near enough of a wordsmith to describe to you how magical it really is. The mist and cloud swirling around through the jungle clad hills is just nature at its best, though. The airport fireman has arrived on his motorbike, to supplement the existing fire brigade motorbike! I've never noticed a fire service at an airport before with 2 fire extinguishers! Even in the Orkney Islands they have a proper fire truck and the aeroplanes are half the size! Somebody is sweeping the terminal floor. It did look a bit grubby yesterday and it wasn't locked up, obviously. All this being observed from our Homestay balcony and still 3 hours before departure. I feel genuinely excited by the spectacle rather than anxious).

In my less cautious approach of yonder year, we could have flown from Gatwick via Catania to Abu Dhabi for £40!! That is just utterly ridiculous. That would have involved a 1-hour connection; with the same airline. Unfortunately Wizzair don't offer the option to book connecting flights. I'm sure that's solely because they don't want the financial pain if you miss the connection through their fault. It clearly wasn't worth the risk as we could go a day earlier with easyJet for an extra £20 and have a look around Catania. We had both been before on our way back from Lampedusa on my birthday trip, but didn't see the city. It's not a bad place at all and the weather for early November was a treat. Wizzair took us to Abu Dhabi for £21! 5 1/2-hour flight. That is a bargain in anyone's book. Our friends, Indigo, took us via Mumbai/Bombay (one more for Agnes) to Bangkok.

Now this routing would be considered a pain by most but one benefit we noticed, with the 4 hour stops in Abu Dhabi and Mumbai was the complete lack of jetlag over the following days. It seemed wrong to pass through Thailand without popping up to Chiang Mai to visit our friends, Budgie, Poppy and Arthur. Admittedly, it's not a stroll up the road but, if we could incorporate some new airports along the way we had the time. In addition, 2 other friends just happened to be passing through Chiang Mai at the same time.

On our previous visit, 3 years almost to the day, we had flown to Phitsanoluk, followed by a scenic 6-hour train ride to Chiang Mai. It is a very fine city and, although not determined by a previous football visit, my impressions then were far and above those of my first visit in 1984. We hired a car for a week and toured the Northern Highlands before catching a flight from Chiang Mai to Khon Kaen for an onward airport extravaganza in Vietnam. This time we flew to Limbang the next day, followed by a mere 1-hour bus ride to Chiang Mai. After a delightful 3 days we took a 6-hour bus ride through the mountains to Nan: a most pleasant city with a charming riverside setting.

It was time to start our journey south, with a couple of new airports in the bag. Via Bangkok we reached Hat Yai. For those of you who have never been to the old Bangkok Airport, since reopened for low-cost carriers, it never ceases to amaze me that a full on 18-hole golf course exists between the 2 runways! Arriving on a jumbo or similar, early morning from Europe it always made me chuckle to look out of the window and see so many golfers. The noise must've been intense. Less so now with smaller, quieter and fewer planes but still, why would you? Even stranger is there appears to be no security fencing between the fairways and the runways. I, for one, would surely have shanked or hooked a ball onto the runway.

(Bakelalan update: we are checked in, the cloud has lifted to what I would perceive is acceptable to any pilot other than the biggest pussy. If only it lasts for the next hour. I was amused when we left our Homestay when the girl asked who was taking us to the airport! They really don't like walking in Sarawak. Seriously, it's less than 70 metres from Homestay to the terminal. Further update: we've been ushered into the departure lounge. There are 20 seats for when they carried a full payload. I've been too busy chatting to the very friendly check in lad to write. His other job is birdwatching. There are 3 check in staff for a maximum of 9 passengers. Today we are 6. I've just been asked to sign the airport visitors' book! Another first. And another: Aggers is the first Pole in the book, going back to 2012! I'm the first Brit since 2018. IT'S COMING....IT'S LANDED! The joy is unbridled. We had been considering if we could get Malaysia Airlines and/or Tourism Malaysia to sponsor us for a return to Bakelalan for our 500/1000th. Now we can turn our attention to Long Banga and Long Lellang, if they're interested. We didn't particularly fancy another 5-6 hours on the dirt road for one thing, let alone the fact that by road is 25% more expensive than flying. Check this out. The plane arrived 20 minutes early and we are now 10 minutes past departure time. Why? Because the pilots have gone off for some noodles).

Safely back in Lawas, you may be thinking that I'm a bit

of a drama queen re the airport weather. "Assumption is the mother of all f*ck ups" as the saying goes and I've certainly learnt that a few times. "Never assume", yet we still do. So, just because the low cloud normally clears by 1000 and the rains normally don't start until after 1500 in this neck of the woods, I'm not going to assume it will be the case. In Bario, for example, just after we landed, it started to drizzle around midday and then stopped around 1600, the skies cleared and we had beautiful weather at our favourite time of day. Actually, Agnes just forwarded me a blog by a dude on Bakelalan Airport (there are folk more anal than I then) in which he writes at length about the weather issues and numerous cancellations. Justification of sorts for me.

Anyway, enough said. Our remaining 5 (7 for Aggers) new airports planned for this trip should be weather angst free. No short runways, no mountainous terrain, as such. When we arrived in Hat Yai it was peeing down. When we left 24 hours later it was still raining. This was a complete shock to the system after the lovely weather oop north. Aggers was full of foreboding. We were heading into the monsoon season in Borneo for sure, but it should've been dry in Southern Thailand, I think. There is a marked distinction between the monsoon season on the east and west coasts, even though the distance can be as little as 50 miles as the crow flies. I recall one July leaving Koh Samui in beautiful sunshine and arriving 20 minutes later in a downpour in Phuket. Actually that trip is worth a quick mention, particularly as I'm conscious that I've digressed very little lately. Come to think of it, as the title of this book is not "But I Digress", but, obviously "Let Me Finish", I'll have a better chance if I stick to this title. In the quote made famous by Bamber Gascoigne (I think and RIP, I know): "I've started, so I'll finish". This trip was way back in the early 90s and EVA Air were very kindly flying me to Taipei. Whilst in Taiwan I managed to notch 5 domestic airports but, more interesting for me, U-Tapao and Hua Hin on my way back through Thailand, in addition to Surat Thani and Koh Samui. 10 new airports on a work trip. Probably my best effort in that category. There have been more memorable, 5 in Madagascar for example, but for sheer numbers I'm pretty sure that was a winner. I feel very fortunate to have had an all-expenses paid business class trip courtesy of Air Madagascar amongst much good fortune in life.

Admittedly, back on track, Hat Yai is nearer the east coast but as we flew in this particular day it was very thick cloud as far as the eye could see. I'd passed through Hat Yai by bus almost 40 years ago and spent a rather uninspiring evening in a cockroach infested, drab hotel. What I had seen of the city meant that there was only one reason to go there. That purpose achieved we set off by minibus to Songkhla on the east coast. It was raining so heavily that the driver took pity on his passengers, ourselves included, by making several diversions from his main road route in order to minimise their and our drenchings.

It continued to tip it down all evening but fortunately a local eatery could be reached without emerging from the awnings covering the 20 metres from our apartment. Excellent food but a rather sad story from the proprietor who, when we enquired where she had learned her English, informed us that her British husband of some 35 years had passed away some 2 years ago and that she still missed him every single day. I think our runny eyes were caused by a combination of spices and emotion. It had virtually stopped raining in the morning, the strength of the rain having woken both of us several times during the night. The guide book spoke quite glowingly about the historical area of Songkhla, which had tempted us there in the first place. It would seem a shame to leave without seeing anything.

We promptly headed out to make the most of what would most likely, and proved to be a small window of opportunity to get to know Songkhla a tad without getting drenched. A short walk over a hill, extremely heavily populated by monkeys brought us to a pretty pleasant beach. We enjoyed a decent coffee overlooking the sea and watched the sky gradually turn more threatening. We headed off to the historical quarter via a quick butchers at the quite substantial lake. By Thai, and far east in general, standards it was really quite charming. It started raining again and before long was hammering it down once more, but not before we had purchased a couple of Disney-themed looking, gaudy, but practical and no doubt Chinese, umbrellas. We asked a kind gentleman if we could shelter by his shop. Well, we didn't actually know whether he was kind or not, but he offered to bring us out a couple of chairs, which was a nice touch.

The rain eased and we headed off and found a small establishment where we enjoyed a simply divine brunch. What Thailand lacks in cuteness, or architecture in many, if not most of its towns and cities, apart from temples, obviously, it sure makes up for in its culinary delights. We were glad we had seen most of what Songkhla had to offer. It does have some charming old buildings, some great murals and a bunch of cute eateries. One would assume it attracts a certain level of tourists but it was pretty deserted during our brief visit.

Now, don't you just love it when a plan comes together? Or more precisely, when no plan comes together, perfectly. We were to make our way across the Thai/Malay border to our next airport; sorry destination: Alor Setar, or strangely, also Alor Star. Rome2Rio is normally a useful starting place for public transport options but can certainly be a bit hit and miss. Guidebooks, however recent, can be out of date. Locals can try to help and do the opposite. Having explored all those options we had come to the conclusion that we would most likely have to catch a bus from Hat Yai as it was unclear if the train still ran and if it did, it was once a day. As you may recall, we so prefer the railway to the road. Therefore, we asked the minibus driver if he would drop us at the station, considering that the buses supposedly departed from there too. Our minibus driver completed the journey from Songkhla which, by the way, does have a not insignificant runway of its own - the rain broke our enthusiasm to go take a peep - but no scheduled services, in about half the time we took to get there. Within 10 minutes of arriving at Hat Yai Station we were leaving on the only train, in the foreseeable future, heading south with change from a £1.

Splendid and tremendous.

We cleared immigration and customs pretty swiftly and 20 minutes later were pulling out of the Malay station on our way to Alor Setar, with change from £2. Back of the net(work)! I was pretty chuffed that my Malaysian currency (£100+ worth) from 13 years ago was still legal tender. The contrast between the Thai and Malaysian railway and equipment (not the right word, I know, but word blindness has got me here. Stock! Rolling stock, actually. Thanks, Google) could not be starker: think London Overground v Flying Scotsman in fading glory. You'll likely know which we preferred. The Thai old banger, obviously not a steam engine but I'm trying to create an image, chugged out of Hat Yai passing numerous derelict engines, carriages, other rolling stock, overgrown sidings and disused tracks. The station had seen better days too but the carriages were fitted with ceiling fans and the massive windows were wide open - India style, but without the bars. It was delightful and also weird to think that the opulent Orient Express most likely utilised the same track. We stopped at a couple of quaint old stations and the border station itself was a very small affair.

Contrast this with what we found the other side. A large modern station with glistening track. A modern train with that lack of separation between carriages that London Overground and Underground amongst others, favour. Bizarrely though, the glass was completely shattered on about 80% of the windows. It was fridge like inside. With more stops we covered roughly 30% more distance in 25% less time. Speed isn't always king, however.

When we left the very modern station at Alor Setar we passed the old station which had been converted into a bar and English style, named The Railway Tavern. We could spy a selection of craft beers inside but sadly for Aggers at least, it was closed both times we passed. I think it's fair to say that I'm missing alcohol less than her. Not that we've been completely dry but we haven't been searching it out. In most places we've been so far in Malaysia, it's certainly not been that visible and in those stores that do stock beer, the choice and price has been unappealing.

Alor Setar wasn't a bad place for an overnight. We visited the birthplace of the former Prime Minister, Mahathir Mohamad. Interesting chap. After having been in power for 22 years from 1981, he returned in 2018 in his 90s and just ran again, unsuccessfully, aged 97! We took a slight chance the next day by taking a train 1 stop to Anak Bukit for 20p. Google is generally pretty good with walking directions, apart from when it wanted us to walk within the security fencing to Oradea Airport. So, when it showed a convoluted 3-hour walk from the station to Alor Setar Airport we were slightly concerned. We could've taken a 15-minute cab ride but where's the fun in that? We fiddled around a bit with the start point of the walk and managed to turn it into a 45-minute walk through beautifully lush paddy fields. As you know we like to walk to and from airports wherever possible and walking through Asia's magic green carpets, on this occasion, was a real, if sweaty, treat. On our last European adventure (of which more later) we had to transit and overnight in Rome again. After the debacle on arrival in Ciampino last time we were a little bit more clued up. We found a place to stay 3 stops from the nearest train station to the airport from where it would be a 45-minute walk to the airport. As it transpired we ended up only going back one stop as the walk would be a similar distance. What we didn't know was that Google had us walking along part of the Via Appia Antica: built in 312 BC it connected Rome with Brindisi. Just shows you what you can learn on an airport walk.

We flew to Subang; the old Kuala Lumpur airport. Like the old Bangkok it had been closed down when they built the new one and reopened, albeit on a much smaller scale to Don Mueang. There are a handful of domestic flights and more importantly for us, one international. We had booked a small hotel just over a mile from the airport. To be honest, the airport was more like a small shopping mall than an airport. For the number of flights - none able to carry more than 70 odd passengers - the number of shops was mental. Google told us we could walk to the hotel in 30 minutes. Only if you were prepared to walk on the motorway. They don't mention that. We tried to find an alternative but to no avail. There wasn't exactly a line of waiting taxis, in fact there were none and Grab drivers were none too interested either. I didn't blame them. Not exactly a moneymaking trip we were offering them.

In another act of special human kindness early the next morning, the young night receptionist who called us a Grab for the airport simply refused to take the money for it. It was only £2.20 but that would've bought him a nice dinner. I tried to insist he take it but he literally started to run away. I thought I was meant to tip him if anything. Now, the reason we flew to Subang was because it had led me to discover, to my immense surprise and satisfaction, that Singapore has more than one commercial airport. Primarily, well almost exclusively for private jets, Seletar provides one scheduled service, 4-5 daily from KL (Subang). It's a bit pricier than I would normally shell out for a 1-hour flight but too good an opportunity to pass up. Aggers had never been to Singapore and my 2 previous visits had been fleeting, one of which it rained constantly. On my second, dry, but very brief (1 night) visit, my opinion of the place had improved, compared to the longer drenched version. This time I could somewhat, appreciate the attraction.

We arrived at 0745 so had the whole day before crossing the border back into Malaysia for our next flight - and massively cheaper accommodation. Seletar is primarily set up for those who can afford a private jet, but a local bus does pass by. It reminded me of Biggin Hill on steroids. Funnily enough I worked at Biggin Hill for 2 weeks a few years back, but it's not on our list. It is in our thoughts as a potential for the 500/1000th if we don't come up with anywhere more exotic. We can actually walk there from our flat. It's not ours but we're lucky enough to keep all our worldlies there and call it home for now. We took the bus, which we were told by the driver, would go to the city centre. After almost an hour we had made little progress, seemingly going round in circles and stopping almost every 100 metres. Another nation of non-walkers.

The driver pulled into a large bus station. Unnoticed by us, everybody had alighted. The driver came up and told us it was the last stop. I queried this as we were barely any closer to the city centre than when we landed. He apologised and in perfect English, told me that he hadn't understood me when I asked if he was going to the city centre. Right!

After catching a city centre bus which proceeded to stop even more frequently and make even less progress, Aggers was getting rather impatient. Fair enough, we wanted a day seeing Singapore's sights, not its endless blocks of apartments. We tried our luck with the metro and finally, arrived where we wanted to be. A 10-mile journey had taken us 135 minutes! We broke our fast with a delightful curry in Little India and had a good old stomp round the city. It really does have a lot more to offer than I had given it credit for previously. We had been advised that it could take 2-3 hours to cross the border back to Malaysia at busy times, so being a Sunday evening, we waited til 9pm to take a local bus out there. Singapore may be pretty expensive on the whole but their public transport system is both very cheap and very plentiful. Our border crossing was painless if vast. We had a pleasant wander round the compact, old area of Johor Bharu the next morning before catching the bus out to JB Airport. Our Borneo adventure was about to begin. Our approach into Kuching was very turbulent and it was very wet on the ground. We made use of our new umbrellas as we searched for a suitable eatery. It seemed that Agnes' warning to me that she wasn't prepared to spend a month in the rains of Borneo may very likely come to fruition.

# CHAPTER 14

I'm sure the weather didn't improve because it knew I wouldn't be writing about it in chapter 13, nevertheless it did. I had only passed through Kuching very briefly on one of my visits to Sabah and had no memory of the city itself. Seen in the dark and rain it didn't look too inspiring. Fortunately for us, the next morning the clouds gradually broke and we enjoyed a damn fine coffee at a charming riverside setting. We went over the stylish pedestrian bridge to an orchid farm. Not many orchids in bloom and when we asked the dude on information when the flowering season was he said he didn't know. Incompetence on a par with the average airport/tourist information centre. Seriously, if you work in an orchid farm surely you know when they bloom. You couldn't put it down to a language barrier as his English was fine.

We had waited in the morning for the free electric bus to the Semenggoh Nature Reserve to get a chance to see some Orangutans. It turned up an hour late which meant we would miss morning feeding time. So, we decided we would take the 1200 bus and catch the afternoon feed. It left 15 minutes early! So, we decided to take a taxi, with our new friend, 76-year old Margaret from Ottawa, of Polish descent, who we'd met in the farm. Our excellent taxi driver took us for something to eat and drink as we were a bit early. The guys in the ticket office kindly told us that the chances of seeing any orangutans was very slim, due to it being fruit season. When I pressed them on how slim, they offered us less than 1%! Undeterred, we decided we'd go for that greater than 99% disappointment, seeing as we were there and the flora was pretty nice too.

We were delighted when one huge male and a youngster made an unexpected appearance and kept us entertained for the best part of an hour, at very close quarters. OK, so they're not

100% in the wild but they're free to roam what remains of their habitat, hence why sightings were far from guaranteed. We met Margaret for a Laksa dinner. She's a plucky old bird, travelling round Asia, solo in her mid-70s. Mind you she's lived in Thailand and is extremely well travelled in Asia. Our paths were to cross again in Miri. She'd been to Kuching 5 years ago so introduced us to her favourite den for Laksa. The place had changed hands but the food was of the same high quality at a very low price. It tipped it down again on our way back to the hotel but Aggers' threat of bailing out early from Borneo was receding after a fine day.

It took another step backwards after the 1 ringgit bus fare to Bako National Park. Apparently, a promotional fare of roughly 18p has been in place since they opened up after Covid lockdown, to encourage folk onto buses. That's all very well but the services are unreliable and infrequent. There were very few passengers at all taking advantage on the journeys we made. Bako National Park is about an hour from Kuching but a different world altogether. Very, very peaceful. We didn't see any wildlife, apart from some quite charming bearded pigs, even though there were many signs warning us to keep out of the sea due to the presence of crocodiles, but the scenery in general and beaches in particular were awesome. Back in Kuching, we took a final picture of the cat roundabout and enjoyed a lovely sunset, accompanied by a rare beer, over the river. I had no idea that Kuching means cat in Malay. They've really gone to town on it and even have a cat museum.

The next morning the free electric bus turned up on time to take us to the airport, void of any other passengers. It's an hour ride and the bus is very modern, so someone has put a lot of cash into this venture. Our airport madness was about to begin (I think the route from Nan, south to Kuching was fairly sane but you may disagree). Tanjung Manis has one flight per day from Kuching, nothing else. It looked in the middle of nowhere on Google. There's a lot of rivers in Sarawak. However, Google did show a road route to our next destination, Sibu. It was only 100 km. We had over 24 hours to get there. Surely, we could hitchhike if we needed to. We didn't need to.

We were met with another act of remarkable kindness on arrival. Tanjung Manis airport was indeed in the middle of nowhere. It had a cute little terminal and there was a lot of staff floating around for one 20-seater flight per day. Remarkably it also had a small shop. I approached a very smiley lady and asked her if she knew how we could reach town and from there, how we could travel to Sibu. "Please give me 5 minutes and I will take you". What, to Sibu? I didn't say that, funnily enough and assumed she meant to town. When she saw Aggers reappear from the toilet her smile grew even more. Yet again, keeping off the tourist trail brings its rewards. Not only did this lovely lady take us to the jetty, some 20 kms away, she took us via a tour of the local market and the beaches. She wished we'd been able to stay for dinner with her family - so did we. She helped us try a few different fruits at the market and bought herself, what I thought was a pretty pricey bag of dried prawns (£4ish). She gave us an option of catching the bus all the way to Sibu - promotional fare 1 ringgit - or a boat to Sarikei and a 1 ringgit bus from there.

We fancied a bit of river action so splashed out on the boat journey. We were rewarded by seeing dolphins and a crocodile before we left the jetty - the latter clearly being quite rare as a few locals snapped away on their phones (see what I've done there? Not only splashed out on a river journey but snapped a picture of a crocodile too, quite the comedian!). Ex wife Jackie asked if I recalled her and I calling these rivers in Malaysia, peanut butter rivers when I sent her another random cat picture with peanut butter river background. I didn't, but I could see what we'd meant, nigh on 40 years ago. Our lovely Tanjung Manis lady presented us with the dried prawns as a parting gift. We didn't particularly want them, but she insisted and of course, refused any offer of money. We have saved them as a Christmas gift for Agi's dad. Talking of which, it had been quite odd to see the Xmas decs up all over the country, particularly when a snowman is involved. At least they allow them. With fruit and dried prawns added to our minimal luggage we bade farewell to our latest kind person.

The boat journey was nice, the bus OK, once we had finally established when it would leave, and Sibu not that great. We decided to spoil ourselves and booked into a very plush hotel with a pool magnificently situated overlooking the massive splurge of peanut butter and the promise of a tempting buffet breakfast, all for £30. The room was 5-star, again overlooking the peanut butter, the pool very refreshing and like the heathens we occasionally are, we only left the establishment for dinner. It was raining again after all. The buffet breakfast didn't disappoint and after a swift wander round the huge market we were finally off to the airport by bus, over an hour later than we had been told we would be.

The journey was rather slow due to the traffic at first and then the driver never getting out of third gear. We jumped off at the airport turn off, sweated some on the walk to the terminal and caught our flight to Bintulu. Both Sibu and Bintulu airports are pretty new and just like new football grounds in general, have been built some distance from town and lack the character and charm of their old counterparts, if more efficient. Bintulu's old runway, bang in the centre of the city is still there. Apart from that, nothing to say about Bintulu other than the curry was splendid.

The next day the bus to Mukah left an hour late but lost no further time on the rather unremarkable journey. Just as I was thinking that Bintulu was a bit of an airport tick only, Mukah revived the feeling of reward that the airport collecting so often brings. Our guidebook only mentioned the nearby Kampung (village) as an attraction, nothing about Mukah itself. We thought it was a very pleasant place - lots of wide open, grassy spaces, some fine mosques and other buildings and a pretty decent beach. It was warm but the walk to the Kampung on the river was well worth it. We headed to the beach. Such a rarity we seemed to be in this town that folk were lowering their car windows as they passed to ask where we were from and where we were going (when I had enquired with Tanjung Manis lady if they received many foreign visitors, she said she recalled 4 in the last 6 years!). Being a Saturday evening, the beach was lively which was nice to see. It was a fair hike from town so we didn't turn down a lift from another kind stranger. When she dropped us, she insisted we meet for lunch the next day. When we said we couldn't she almost begged us to meet for breakfast at 8.

I'm absolutely certain we were at the right place. We waited until 8.30 but she never showed up. She was so keen it will remain a mystery long past our 500/1000th airport. We went back to the now deserted beach for a lovely Sunday morning stroll and pondered once more, over how lovely our lives were. Mukah's old airport, which had only closed just over a year ago, was located less than 50 metres from us but remained invisible behind the thick foliage. We would have to content ourselves with an aerial view once we had reacquainted ourselves with the MASwings Twin Otter at the obviously, out of town new airport, which we did on the short (well, long, for a MASwings Twin Otter) hop to Miri.

MASwings deserve a mention. On their ATR flights which we used from Sibu to Bintulu and to Mulu and back from Miri, they offer you peanuts, cake and a drink. On Twin Otter flights to or from Miri, they offer you peanuts and water before you embark or after you disembark. A bit of unnecessary TLC, a blast from the airline service of the past, considering the flights are no more than 30 minutes. Every flight we took, 16 in total, was on time or early. If only they weren't so difficult to book we would have visited almost all their destinations. As it was, I settled on 14 new airports with them, 16 for Aggers.

We liked Miri. The new area on reclaimed land, contained a small seafront cafe which provided us with 3 utterly superb sunsets accompanied by excellent coffee. We had our first, up close encounter with a fabulously nosed hornbill after normally eagle-eyed Agnes had originally mistaken it for a wooden one. Perhaps because it was perched on a man-made feeding station within a designated nesting area, she was sceptical of the sighting. I gave it no more than a cursory glance, trusting her far superior eyesight and specifically, bird spotting capabilities. She decided we would do a circuit and return later in the hope of seeing a real hornbill, seeing as we'd caught a Grab out to the nature reserve for this specific purpose. Imagine her surprise when the wooden hornbill was no longer on its man-made perch but had magically, relocated itself to the top of a coconut tree. Admittedly they do stay remarkably still but it was an error infinitely more likely to be made by yours truly. I'm no birder by any stretch, but they are magnificent creatures, well the long-beaked ones in particular.

Miri was our base for our trips to Mulu and Bario, both of which were superb. I'd long wanted to visit Mulu Caves on many of my numerous work visits to Kota Kinabalu (KK) but had just never had the spare time. Our guidebook had warned us that "if it were ever possible to Disneyfy the jungle, and with Singapore-style efficiency, Mulu had succeeded". What a load of drivel, in our opinion. Granted, if the 250 maximum visitor limit is reached during a visit I'm sure it would feel a little different but, as barely 5% of that figure was in attendance during our visit, we couldn't agree less. We walked 10 minutes from the small airfield to our delightfully understated Homestay. A&A Homestay! Yes, we liked that name, for sure. Our host didn't look a day shy of 80 and electricity was only available from 6pm to midnight. Far from a Disney experience. The staff at the National Park were efficient, not always the case in Borneo admittedly, but the guides left you to make your own way back - you couldn't get lost, unless you're incredibly stupid, but I wouldn't imagine Disney taking any chances with some of their clientele. Yes, raised boardwalks are provided but seriously, who wants to get covered in leeches, trudging through mud and water, if you don't have to. Anyway, the caves were and are a truly magnificent quirk of nature, the dusk noises of the frogs in particular, hilarious and the canopy walk tested my vertigo levels, if not very surprisingly, Agnes'. We only did Mulu-lite, partly based on weather forecast, but if I'm totally honest, more on airline schedules providing other opportunities. We didn't fancy a 4-day trek to The Pinnacles (we were rewarded for being heathens with a stunning view on our flight from Bario to Long Seridan) and whilst certainly not of the seen one cave (lake, mountain, beach, mosque etc etc) seen them all brigade, we were happy with our decision. I don't think you would be disappointed if you stayed longer. There's even a Marriott Resort, thankfully out of our sight, if that's your bag. It was extremely hot in Mulu, for us, but at least the rain stayed away.

After 2 more Miri sunsets we were off, via Marudi to Bario. As I've talked about Bario already, I would just like to add how wonderful our Longhouse experience with our host Jane, was. It really was remarkably long. It felt a bit deserted even though 15 out of a possible 23 families still inhabited it. Jane, apart from overfeeding us and displaying repeated astonishment that we would walk the 3 kms to and from the airport, was just charming. She spent so much time with us during our 2-night stay, joining us for meals, but eating very little, enlightening us on the way of life of the Kelabit people. Ever seen those ladies with the incredibly huge holes in their stretched earlobes? Well, there's 6 of them left in Bario. We felt their balls/earrings; not without their permission, you understand. They're ludicrously heavy. A girl/woman was considered unattractive and unmarriable if her ears didn't stretch almost to her shoulders. Hence, their ears were pierced almost immediately after birth and weights attached. I only hope they started with grams and not kilograms! The charming ladies we spoke to said that it was a painful experience at times and didn't blame the more recent generations for taking their chances on nabbing a local lad with their ears as standard. These ladies were not a tourist gimmick, please be assured. We were the only travellers in town.

Once we had made it back to Miri, through Brunei and up to Bakelalan and back it was time after a leisurely stopover in Lawas (we treated ourselves to another bargain pool/buffet breakfast combo to celebrate our Bakelalan success) time to head to Sabah. Just one more act of kindness to mention before we do. We wanted to find a proper coffee to enjoy riverside, on our first day in Lawas. As I may've already mentioned, they don't half drink some shite in Malaysia. No wonder they have one of the highest diabetes rates in the world. Forget to say no sugar at your peril. Sometimes, even if you do, it's still present. Consider sachets of coffee that contain sugar, margarine, wheat, oh, and a bit of coffee and you get the gist. We've found some pretty decent stuff in supermarkets to use in our rooms but, unless you happen upon a Starbucks or similar, vendors are prone to satisfying the local craving for Nescafe with added "benefits". The setting of several box type cafés and eateries riverside was ideal, the availability of sugar and shite free coffee less so. Step up an English-speaking local to the rescue. Having understood and translated our wishes to the vendor we received a coffee of required standard. After a pleasant conversation he bade us farewell and told us the coffees were on him. I'm sure it didn't make a massive dent in his wallet but yet again, it's the thought that counts. Our ride to Bakelalan was also enhanced by our facilitator; he didn't drive, preferring to sit in the back with us, and sharing his limited beer stock. Another very nice gesture.

Our last Twin Otter flight strangely went in completely the opposite direction to Limpang before heading to KK. For us this was perfect as we could notch Limpang, without having to return to Miri. When we quizzed our jovial, to the point of hysterical, pilots why this was, they merely shrugged, said they didn't have a clue about their schedules and proceeded to laugh some more. There are no runway restrictions at Limpang - most flights are by ATR72 to KK - although Lawas, before they build the new airport, can only accommodate Twin Otters. This still didn't explain the routing but we were happy as pigs in poop. It was my first visit to Sabah in almost 13 years. Suffice to say, if you want an example of how destructive addiction can be, I need look no further than my ex-business partner. Throw selfishness, greed, denial, recklessness, (Christ, I sound like a football pundit: particularly Hansen, Shearer or Murphy, so I'll stop there) into the mix and disaster was due at some point. There's another whole story in that, which I won't be writing, but let's just say after passing through immigration untroubled, I wasn't the only one who thought there may have been a remote chance of me being apprehended - as in the past my signature had been forged, making me a director of no less than 5 companies which all went bust owing a good number of locals an even better some of money.

That hurdle not materialising, it was time to visit some old and new haunts and put Aggers out of her misery, as she had listened to me bore on about Sabah on far too numerous occasions.

# CHAPTER 15

KK had changed so much between my first visit in 1992 and my last in 2010. It had certainly expanded further in the last 12-13 years too. After the comparative sleepiness of Sarawak and even Brunei, KK was a bit of a shock. What a big airport, even though one of the terminals is no longer in use. We were met at the airport by a kind lady who had been quite badly wronged by my ex-business partner. Clearly, she hadn't tarred me with the same brush, rightly so. We'd never met but she proceeded to give us a guided tour of KK that I doubt the tourist office could have matched.

The next day we hired a car and drove up to Kudat. Fortunately, I had ticked off the small airport there, as there were currently no MASwings flights. Aggers was not disappointed as she is getting very close to parity for our big numbers. The beaches at Kelambu Cove and Tip of Borneo were as delightful and unspoilt as I remembered bar one significant difference: the amount of plastic rubbish, most horrendous at the former, was just utterly soul destroying. Our "friend" (I find it difficult to be straight out there with friend if I haven't seen or spoken to someone for 15 years, no matter how well we reconnect) who we stayed with at his inland jungle lodge, told us that a group of them had totally cleared the beach 6 weeks previously! What we saw was only 6 weeks' worth of human-generated garbage. He also told us that they had approached the local government minister, volunteering to keep the beach clean for free. All they needed was something, somewhere to dispose of the rubbish. This git told them he was retiring in 2 years and was not interested. Goodbye!

After 2 pleasant days and noisy nights from nature's most welcome orchestra we headed to the Crocker Range and the village of Kundasang, for a view of 4,000 metre Mt Kinabalu. It was unsurprisingly, covered in cloud. Would it be clear in the morning? You bet, and actually during the night too. I wasn't interested in England's progress in the World Cup, so it must've been pure coincidence that I was awake from 0330. Actually, it was too chilly to sleep well. The thin blanket provided and my thermal top were inadequate for the temperature change at 2,000 metres asl. Aggers coped slightly better. We enjoyed a nice cup of our own coffee on the chilly balcony and marvelled at the view in front of us before the clouds started to roll in.

One other "friend" owned a delightful home 500 metres above KK. The views of the city, coastline and islands below were stunning. Despite the weather turning rather wet, we enjoyed a splendid 6-hour lunch with him and his wife. We don't really miss or crave other unavailable foods on our travels but pesto sauce, chips, a selection of cheeses and some superb fish were most welcome, especially the cheese. Back down in KK we met with more "friends". One of Agnieszka's old college friends had emigrated to USA, some 20 years ago. She, her husband and 2 daughters had set off for a year of travels in July. They happened to need to leave Bali for a visa run. Initially planning to go to Oz, they diverted to KK, specifically to meet us. A lot of planning had gone on between them and Aggers to arrange a meet. They were due to join us on the trip to Kudat but she, the friend, got sick. I didn't realise people were still taking Covid tests, but she did and the result wasn't in her favour. We agreed to meet them outdoors but she took a turn for the worse. Before leaving for Kudat we ended up having a couple of beers with the husband and daughter; neither of whom Aggers had met before. The daughter was 11 so had a piece of cake instead, while the other daughter had bailed out of their world trip in Poland.

It wasn't a disaster, but it would've been a shame for Aggers not to meet up when they were literally a few 100 metres apart, having spent the last 20 years on different continents. Luckily, for us, she felt worse before she felt better, thus delaying their planned departure to Kuching. Albeit, much more briefly than planned, Agi and Karolina were finally able to reacquaint.

Obviously, it was difficult to cram a 20-year catch up into 2 hours but they had a go.

I was starting to question my own logic when I was booking flights to Tawau and Lahad Datu, the 2 remaining airports for me to visit in Sabah. Neither city/town received any positive comments in our guidebook. It would have been rather pointless to fly to Tawau, just to return from Lahad Datu as the journey between didn't appear to offer anything of particular interest. Amongst Sabah's Nature Reserves I had failed miserably to visit any, other than Kinabalu Park and Turtle Island. It would be a push but we could fit in a visit to Sukau, in the Kinabatangan Nature Reserve. The natural route is to fly in and out of Sandakan. Not a chance for us; already visited several times by me and to be avoided by Agi. Our research indicated there was one bus from Tawau, leaving 30 minutes after our flight was due to arrive. Tawau's new airport was obviously way out of town, by some 20 kms, but at least it was on the way from Tawau to Lahad Datu, although 3.5 kms from the main road. Maybe we could flag it down, if it had any spare seats and we arrived in time?

We arrived 15 minutes early and set off to the main road. Barely 200 metres into our stride a very kind chap stopped to offer us a lift to the main road. This looked promising. We were getting a ride without even stretching our thumbs out. Pretty soon 2 pick-up trucks stopped on the main road to try and help us on our way, but they were going to Semporna. In the right direction, but a turn off about 150 kms short of Lahad Datu. Drrrrr! What were we thinking? Like we were going to get there in one ride! We didn't have long to rue our novice mistake. Pretty soon another pick-up stopped, again heading for Semporna. He very kindly dropped us off just past the turn off. He told us a bus should be along soon and, we think, asked a couple of locals to help us get a bus. They were quite perplexed when we started putting our thumbs out: "No, no, no. Bus come la". Well, the bus wasn't quick enough. Having learnt from our schoolboy error we gratefully grabbed our next lift to the Kunak turn off.

We were just over half way to Lahad Datu. Things looked a little trickier here though. Numerous minivans passed by, all of which were full, only one actually with a Lahad Datu sign and many on the school run. Finally, well after about 20 minutes (we've all waited much longer for a London bus, have we not?), but it was very warm, Martin stopped and yes, he was off to Lahad Datu. His English was very limited but his kindness wasn't. Almost immediately he stopped to get himself a drink. Of course, he gave us a lovely can of ice-cold coffee too. This was too kind to bother about the sugar content even for Aga. He then proceeded to drop us at the bus station which I'm sure wasn't his destination. We had arrived over an hour before the bus would have, if it was on time. We had time to break our fast before meeting with our preplanned car hire to get to Sukau.

So far, we had been pleasantly surprised by the lack of intrusion of palm oil plantations. This changed dramatically. They were virtually constant from Tawau to Sukau, and I'm sure onwards to Sandakan. Consequently, the potholed road on which we drove was inundated with lorries transporting the stuff. Neither of us feel the Western world has any right to criticise other countries removing their natural forests and feel also, that there's a lot worse reasons for doing so than cultivating palm oil. After all, we chopped all ours down years ago. There's just something a bit sad in knowing that the fauna is suffering with the change in flora.

It started to really chuck it down as we reached Sukau. The reason we had wanted to reach there as quick as we could was to be in time for the 4pm river cruise. Would we want to still go in this weather? Luckily the indecisives would have that decision made for them - heavy rain = no river trip as the wildlife isn't keen on the rain either, apparently. The rain eased off just in time so off we went. We saw plenty of hornbills, a few crocodiles; large and small, monkeys and although at quite a distance, orangutans genuinely in the wild. Our lodge, which was really quite charming, if basic, filled our bellies before we set off again on a night cruise. How these dudes spot tiny wildlife at night, even with a torch left us bemused. Birds the size of an average supermarket egg? No problem. Again, we saw a few different sized crocodiles, a thin snake curled around an equally thin branch that we just couldn't fathom how our guide had spotted, but the highlight was the birds. We did see a very large owl before we set off, rather incongruously perched on a rusty JCB, but the rest of our feathered sightings were of the small to very small variety but equally, of the colourful to the extremely colourful. We were curious that they didn't move even when we were less than a foot or 2 away. We could only assume rather sadly, that they were frozen by the light.

I have to just try and relate the most bizarre incident that occurred in the toilet on our return. Agi had already been for a pee but when it was my turn I noticed this creature emerging from under the toilet rim. I don't know how to describe it. I've never seen anything like it. The best I can do is a tentacle of some sort, varying its size, stretching from 1 to 2 1/2 inches with superglue over one end. Nothing else could explain why we couldn't detach it from the rim and send it on its way down the toilet. We tried the humane method, encouraging it with a prod of our fly swatter. It just extended to its full length. We tried the slightly less humane option of squirting some water on it. No joy. I'm not proud of myself but this thing was starting to freak me out. I figured it would likely stay on a wet surface but I really didn't fancy the remotest possibility that it would make for our bed in the middle of the night. I armed myself with a flip flop, whack! Wriggle, wriggle. Whack, whack. Wriggle, wriggle, wriggle and so it went on. This critter was truly indestructible. Full blast with the mini shower head, normal use - ass washing, accompanied by prods with fly swatter finally sent it into the bowl, from whence we assumed it came. I made several checks to make sure it hadn't returned. We figured it must've been some kind of leech variant. Never having encountered one, both of us thought its shape wasn't what we expected of leeches but its stick ability was. Aggers rightly concluded that her right buttock must've been perilously close to getting attacked.

Night entertainment concluded, we headed out for our early

morning and final boat trip. The highlight was 2 families of Proboscis monkeys, close enough to see their impressive hooters with the naked eye. We headed back to Lahad Datu, content with our wildlife sightings. Lahad Datu is yet to receive its new airport. Work is due to start next year but I'm afraid that won't entice us to return when it's completed. It really didn't have anything going for it and the smell of raw sewage forced us to curtail our wander around town. At least the current airport is conveniently located in the town and was of the tiny variety we so prefer. The turbulence on descent into KK was as bad as I've experienced. Poor Agi was all clammy hands again. Once on the ground the rain wasn't quite as bad as we expected.

We'd gone for the luxury option once more - roof top pool, but no buffet breakfast. Our taxi driver was so delighted to have his first foreign passengers that he requested a selfie with us. How could we refuse? The icing on this cake was the runway view, not only from the rooftop but also our 7th floor room. Spotters delight. The view in the other direction of the islands was none too shabby either. We headed to Tanjung Aru beach for a superb sunset, scarcely believable with the weather all around us, and some rather delicious food for our last evening in Borneo. In the morning we were greeted with a spectacular moon setting followed by some extremely welcome sunshine. After a few dips in the pool and breakfast we headed out to the airport for our first Scoot experience. I do hope our journey back to Europe with them will get off to a better start. There's nothing wrong with the flight but the check in was a joke. Having checked in on line we were forced to queue for almost an hour to receive our boarding passes. We left KK 40 minutes late so are just about to miss our connecting flight in Singapore, having received very little cooperation from the crew so far, to help us. Whatever slight chance we had, just disappeared as we appear to have aborted our landing and entered the hold. Let's see how Scoot choose to look after us, or not, seeing as they allowed us to book the 1-hour connection.

# CHAPTER 16

While we go round and round in circles waiting, we can only assume, for the stormy weather to pass away from Changi Airport (no announcement from the crew), let's talk Spoons. Ireland, done! But what a fine selection of pubs. It's tricky to choose which was best. From purely the pub itself perspective then the recently opened An Geata Arundel in Waterford wins, but from location it's difficult to beat Dublin's The South Strand. It's only gone and plonked itself in Forbes Street! Out of the 7 pubs we visited the other 2 in Dublin were extremely attractive. We stayed in a charming Airbnb on the coast in Tramore not far from Waterford and enjoyed a lovely chat and a G&T with our hosts. Our Spoons collecting, like the airports, was taking us to places which may have otherwise remained off our radar. As I believe I recounted, I dragged my dear old mother and sister to Waterford airport many years ago. Aggers was quite keen to pass by the now pretty defunct airport, so we did. Waterford was a fine city but our time was limited, well, the truth was, it was raining on and off, so we lounged around in the pub for a few hours.

We enjoyed a splendid drive back through the Wicklow mountains. I even remembered the waterfall where I took a picture of my sister, all those years ago. Our 2nd night's accommodation came about quite bizarrely. We were looking for somewhere to stay in Dun Laoghaire, on the outskirts of Dublin. We had identified a potential B&B on Google but the reality was that it no longer seemed to exist. A kind chap from an adjacent residence asked if he could help me. He confirmed to me that the B&B was, indeed, no longer. His house looked suspiciously like a B&B to me so I enquired. His initial response was no, followed by used to be, then, what are you after? Well, just a bed for the night. OK, so no breakfast but the room was decent as was the price - for Ireland, and we knew where we could get breakfast! In Forbes Street!

We headed down to The Forty Foot, overlooking The Irish Sea, for a couple of pints and dinner: pub 796, in case you're counting. We had decided where and when we wanted to hit 800. The planning for this had been done in Yorkshire. Our 3rd and final pub in Dublin would be number 799. That number was notched after a visit to the Guinness Museum. It was fairly interesting but a bit gimmicky. The pint included in the admission ticket was very refreshing and the views over Dublin pretty decent. We've both been to Dublin before but a long time ago and with not much time to explore. We both opined that Dublin is a bit overrated, although it has its charm. The Wetherspoons within are certainly top drawer though. After a couple of relaxing and enjoyable days with friend Colin and family it was time to hit the 800 mark. In case you're wondering about Colin's health, he was on a break from treatment and in good spirits. Very sadly, we have just learnt that the results of his recent scan were not as promising as first thought. He and his ladies will still join us for a couple of days of pre-Xmas festivities in Krakow, hopefully.

Aggers' mum is also a keen Spooner so we were keen to include her in our 800 celebrations. When completing the SWCP we had chosen to leave 4 pubs for her planned visit to Cornwall. We would breakfast in George's Meeting House in Exeter. I decided it might be quite nice to surprise Aga with some kind of recognition in the pub. I called them and it would be fair to say that their response was only just above lukewarm. All I wanted was a number 800 and a bottle of bubbly on the table. I was advised to send an email to the manager, which I did. I knew Tim Martin lived in Exeter, had a quick Google and learned that George's Meeting House was his local. If you don't ask you don't get, so I asked my Wetherspoon magazine contact if she thought Tim may be interested in joining us for a swift half. She said she'd pass our offer onto her editor. We never heard back and he didn't pitch up so who knows whether he got the invite to his pub, or not. I wasn't too bothered as his appearance is not one of a particularly endearing chap. However, since number 800, we have listened to his turn on Desert Island Discs. Never judge a book by its cover. He sounded like a very nice man, actually; almost humble and very self-deprecating.

I also hadn't received a response from the pub. To be honest, I'd pretty much forgotten about it so I was as surprised as Agnieszka when there, in the far corner of this charming pub, was a large 800 sign, sprinkles on the table with a bottle of Prosecco in a bucket and 4 glasses. It looked pretty good actually and Agi was chuffed. Let's be honest, it doesn't take much to cut up 3 bits of cardboard into numbers. I've never remotely kept tabs on how much we've spent in Spoons but including every visit, not just new pub visits and hotels, I wouldn't be surprised if it's not that far shy of £10k when we're done. Bloody hell, I'm glad I've never thought about it until this minute. If we finish next spring/summer as we hope to that could equate to £4 per day, every single day, for the last 7 years. That's not counting all the revenue we've generated by dragging friends and family along, having a leaving party in Croydon and an engagement party in Putney. They could have given us the Prosecco on the house!! I don't feel so guilty now taking the coffee mugs from our hotel room in Camborne to nab some free coffees.

The shift manager came over to introduce herself and said she'd been worried we'd changed our plans. I had said in the email I sent that we would be there around 8.00 for opening. I then remembered that they didn't serve alcohol until 9.00. Also, it was a bit ambitious to get to Exeter from home by 8.00. As it was, we left at 5.45 and didn't arrive until 9.45. I explained to the manageress on duty that, as I'd had no response to my email, I figured they weren't doing anything, so hadn't bothered with updating them on our ETA. There was an old boy at the table in front of ours who cheerfully said, "so you're the lovely folks who've nabbed my regular spot". He told us that his wife of many years had not long passed away so he was spending more time in his local. We offered him a glass of bubbly to wash down with his Guinness which he happily accepted. He seemed genuinely chuffed when we asked him to join in some of our photos. The pub, originally a chapel, built in the 1760s, was a fitting choice for our landmark and was a very fine pub indeed. The proud staff told us that their pub was far superior to The Chevalier Inn, our last of 4 in Exeter. It was, but The Chevalier was better than they made out. Considering Exeter got a bit of a battering during WW2, the centre was pleasant. Miraculously, the cathedral and surrounding area had remained intact and was most attractive.

We continued our journey southwest to Tavistock for pub 802. A very pleasant town and another fine Spoon. Liskeard couldn't quite match it in both respects but that was Devon and Cornwall Spoons completed. We enjoyed an absolutely splendid week in a lovely cottage in Mevagissey. The weather was divine and it was a pleasure to return to several of the places we had walked through not so long ago. Returning to a few Spoons I estimated that Bogusia (the mother-in-law) was well past 50 Wetherspoons, not a bad effort at all.

Now, I'm sure you've worked out that we weren't in the hold in Changi whilst I wrote all that. We finally landed in a very grey and moody looking Singapore, 15 minutes after our flight was due to have left for Ipoh. To be fair to Scoot, as we taxied in, the captain asked all other passengers to remain seated while 2 passengers (us) disembarked for a connecting flight. We were both astonished that every one of the passengers, seated in the 28 rows ahead of us, did indeed stay seated. I'm not convinced that there would be a similar response on Wizzair or Ryanair - not that either would give a damn about connecting flights in any case. The cabin crew had told us the gate where our flight would depart. We needed to catch a train to it! Unless our onward flight had also been delayed by the weather we knew it was futile to rush. We were put out of (or into) our misery pretty swiftly by a chap on a buggy. He seemed to be aware of our predicament, told us the flight to Ipoh had already left, so dropped us at the transfer desk.

Now, I'm sure you're wondering why I haven't bored you with

my anxiety at missing the flight to a new airport? No? Well, I'll tell you anyway. I didn't have any. Why? Because I'd already checked before we left KK and knew there was a flight to Ipoh early the next morning. Having less time in Ipoh, wasn't much of a problem. Not doing the airport would clearly be very upsetting. When I booked these flights I'd said to Aga that it would be nice for her to see Singapore airport in daylight. What neither of us figured was just how much of it we would both see. Changi is often raved about as one of the best large airports. On my last visit, 10 years ago, I wondered what all the fuss was about. Admittedly, it was going through a major upgrade. It really is a monster and now, quite impressive.

The transfer desk was also aware of us and issued us with new boarding passes for the flight the following morning. They also gave us an invitation to one of the airport lounges where, they regretted to inform us, we would be spending the next 15 hours! I don't think so! According to them all the airport hotels were full. So what? We didn't need to stay at the airport. They said they would contact the Scoot rep but that she may not be with us for up to an hour. We said we'd go and check out the lounge in the meantime. Before we could the Scoot rep appeared. She started by saying that they had originally held the flight for us, but when the weather caused us to be further delayed, they had no option but to let it leave without us. Therefore, it wasn't their fault so they didn't have to provide us with a bed. I politely countered with the facts that if they hadn't arrived in KK 20 minutes late and inexplicably, added another 20 minutes to the delay on the turnaround, we would have made the connection. She didn't deny that but said she would have to see if they could find an hotel within their spending limits. Agnes told her that the Ibis was available for around £60, pretty good for Singapore. The Scoot agent was concerned that this was only a 2-star hotel. We said we didn't care about that. We just didn't want to sit upright all night. We could've said, 2-star hotel for 2-star airline but that wouldn't have been helpful.

She said she would need some time and that we should go

to the lounge to while away our time. The lounge didn't look inviting for a night's kip but it did have alcohol and some pretty decent scran. We tucked into beer, wine, laksa, noodles, G&Ts, top notch cappuccinos and happily lost track of time. All that was missing was some cheese and chocolate. At some point a few hours into our feasting, a note was delivered to us, informing us that we would be accommodated at the, on airport, Holiday Inn Crowne Plaza. Aggers had seen this on booking.com for a bargain £275. Now, I'm sure that through their parent company, Singapore Airlines, Scoot has a preferable rate, but, still, we'd offered to stay at the Ibis. We weren't complaining and it certainly sounded like a better option than Wizzair had given us in Bergamo. Scoot even gave us £30 for food at HICP. Clearly, they didn't count on us stuffing our faces in the lounge while we waited. As we queued to register and enter the lounge some guy just wandered in casually. We decided to do the same. We had a pass, if confronted. We weren't, so we were hoping that we could abuse their hospitality on our layover from Kuala Lumpur en route to Berlin in a few days. Should be fine, as the invitation had no date on it, only a flight number, which we could change. After all, Scoot won't have been charged for this visit, so they would only be taking the original hit. I'll let you know how it goes. If the on-board fare is the same on long haul flights as short haul, we will definitely need some sustenance before we travel.

We headed through the enormous but thankfully empty immigration hall and over to the hotel. It was all so slick, and bizarre to think that Changi and Bakelalan do a similar thing. Admittedly, Bakelalan does not have international flights but you get my drift, maybe? Aggers had read up on Changi's much talked about Jewel. I had no idea what it was. I'm not sure I'm much wiser now. Think Blue Water, Westfield, whatever they're called, on steroids. I believe the highlight is the extremely impressive waterfall. Anyway, Agnes was both impressed and satisfied with what she had seen. I was a bit overwhelmed. It was all quite futuristic. We headed back to the hotel to spend our £30 allowance on some desserts. You don't get much for that amount in HICP Changi, but it was nice to have a bite of chocolate, some mango mousse and, most interestingly some durian ice cream.

If you're not familiar with this fruit, it stinks. It's banned from hotels and aircraft for that reason. It's really quite expensive but we had tried it. It's not bad, but not a patch on our favourite: jackfruit. We also tried mangosteen. Nice, not as smelly but still banned in most hotels, as is smoking. Why do so many rooms stink of smoke then and not durian? Clearly smokers think they are above the rules, whereas I can only conclude durian lovers are more respectful. Or, perhaps the latter know that there's no getting through a hotel reception without giving the game away. Anyway, the ice cream definitely had some flavour, but no whiff.

This was definitely the classiest hotel we'd stayed in since our working days. The room was horny, for sure. Thank you Scoot. You didn't need to but it was yet another example of what can happen if you stand your ground. I'm certain many customers would have known no better and accepted Scoot's initial offering of a night, bolt upright, in the airport lounge. We just wanted a bed. We weren't fussy where or which type. The bed they eventually gave us was exceptionally comfortable. It was all like old times on a work jolly for both of us. We headed back over to the airport terminal in plenty of time for our 7.15 flight to Ipoh. We were already thinking that we probably hadn't missed much of an evening in Ipoh. Aggers had booked an Airbnb for our arrival less than 24 hours earlier. She was a bit disappointed when the host showed no empathy with our missed flight situation and initially declined to refund us. However, a little gentle and diplomatic cajoling and she had all our money back. We really were in credit. The significant lack of alcohol for the majority of this trip has been quite refreshing and no hardship but we'd both had a pretty merry and fun afternoon/evening indulging ourselves.

It was very, very grey and raining on arrival in Ipoh but we had caught glimpses of a pleasant and for me, quite unexpected landscape - lots of limestone jungle clad hills. The guide book and a few people we spoke to raved about Ipoh. It was a very nice city with lots of history. Reminded us a bit of Songkhla, with drizzle replacing cats and dogs, but we only really needed a couple of hours to wander the streets and lanes of the old town. I particularly liked Concubine Lane - hadn't heard that word in a while. We headed over to the splendid, old train station. I have to say that our British ancestors really did know how to construct fine buildings, even if some of their other antics left a bit to be desired. Unfortunately we were told that all trains to Butterworth for the next 2 days were full. Thankfully, we're not collecting train stations otherwise that would've been the equivalent of sitting in the airport departure lounge and never getting airborne. We reluctantly booked a bus and headed off to try the local white coffee.

There's a story attached to white coffee in this area, but you'll have to Google white coffee Ipoh if you're interested. It was very pleasant as were our surroundings, so much so that we kind of lost time and perspective on our need to get out to the bus station. We'd drifted into school run time and, not only were taxis very scarce, their price offerings had tripled from when we'd looked earlier. It kind of stuck in the throat to pay more for the 12 km ride to the out of city bus station than for both tickets for the 150+ km bus journey, but that was the least of our worries. The traffic had built up and was terrible, both for our driver to reach us and for our journey. It made me realise again just how little we've had to endure one of most folk's pet hates. Our driver was stuck but on text, advised Aggers not to worry, he was superman and we would catch our bus, no problem.

He may've been superman in another life, but clearly not this one. With unerring consistency he managed to choose the slowest moving lane and slow down just enough to hit every red light. On reflection, I did get a bit arsey with him but it really was very frustrating. He finally got us to the bus station with 5 minutes for us to locate our bus, telling us that it would probably be late anyway. He was irritatingly cheerful and I was a little annoyed with myself for getting so agitated. It wasn't the fact that we were likely to miss the bus and that we may have to wait a while and pay again. It was simply because there was no need for that situation to have materialised if, a) we hadn't lost track of time in the first place, and b) he had been just 10% superman.

He was right though. Not only did the bus leave 40 minutes late it took 3 1/2 hours to complete the journey scheduled for 2. Not that I minded too much. The scenery was intermittently, much more interesting than I recalled from doing the same journey from Kuala Lumpur 30 years previously and I had a good old listen to TMS (BBC cricket commentary for the uninitiated) from Pakistan along the way, whilst Aggers mainly, caught up with her sleep deficit after our busy night and early start in Changi. We timed our arrival well for the ferry over to George Town, Penang, but it had felt like a long day and we were grateful that it was only a few minutes' walk to our pretty decent hotel.

# CHAPTER 17

The very mild OCD in me (I'm not mocking that very serious affliction in its strongest guise) is compelling me to ensure this book consists of 25 chapters; the same as BID. Easy to achieve but I'd like it to happen naturally and not be contrived. How many chapters will I need to write about 16/19 airports (hopefully to become 15/17 before the end of this chapter), 75ish pubs, 2 footy grounds and, potentially, another walk and a bit? I could pan it out with a whole bunch of digressions but the problem is that I'm not sure what I've already told you and how much more you can take! Besides, this is a book about me finishing, is it not, and the journeys to get there.

I've never really understood why Penang, Phuket and Bali remained on many travellers' and tourists' wish lists for as long as they did, and quite likely, still are. Even after Langkawi, Koh Samui and Lombok came onto the radars of those less intrepid adventurers, as alternatives to those ruined islands, if only until they also became buggered up, people fancy them and even return. It's just an opinion you understand. Personally, I far preferred the first 2 alternatives in the early 90s (never made it to Lombok yet) so, let's be absolutely clear: there was only one reason we were going to Penang: a cheeky little offering from there to Malacca with Malindo/Batik Air. I had been looking at our options to get back to West Malaysia from Borneo and was determined to venture further than a standard KK-KL routing. If we did that, in cautious mode, how soon would we want to be on the mainland in order for panic and anxiety not to come into play regarding our homeward bound flight?

In order to steal some business from Malaysia Airlines, I can only assume, it was £30 cheaper to fly KL-Singapore-Berlin than Singapore-Berlin. We had no desire to visit KL again so

Malacca not only provided a new airport opportunity, it also gave a more stress-free option to be close to KLIA (KL's big, now not so new, replacement for Subang). In a strange decision by UNESCO; Penang and Malacca were lumped together in 2007/8 as 1 Heritage Site. It's not like they're neighbours, is it? Somebody with the power to, maybe decided that neither had enough going for them to feature alone, but combined, they could.

I've just admitted to myself that I feel that same irritation creeping in as I did towards the end of our India trip. This one is considerably shorter so I can only deduce that it is brought on by the amount of travelling in a relatively short space of time. Or have the things that have irritated me in the last 24 hours not happened previously? We don't like air-conditioning in general, although we have to admit that it has provided moments of relief in the last month or so. Was Penang Airport actually blasting out any more ice than KK? Or were we just done with that feeling of being frozen when it's 30 degrees outside? What I can say is that I'm going to relay 2 incidents that really wound me up and which hadn't happened before. I've written quite frequently, lately, about the goodwill of many people and the kind, friendly nature of most that we have engaged with, however briefly, so it certainly won't even things up by a long stretch, that's for sure; 8-2 to the positives.

Firstly, though the positives - sorry -positive, of Penang. They have done a good stint, apparently since UNESCO recognition, of preserving and tarting up their historic buildings in George Town. It's really quite an atmospheric place to wander around and the addition of some classy murals adds to the enjoyment. The city, and island in general, is far too busy for our taste though, both with tourists and also the local population. The traffic is horrendous. We decided to take a bus to Balik Palau in the south west of the island, so we would not have only experienced George Town. A big mistake that we needed to turn into a positive decision. The only positive of the bus journey was the bizarrely incongruous sight of a huge monitor lizard (we're talking 8ft nose to tail) out for a stroll in the middle of a residential area. We had seen a biggy on the road between Sukau and Lahad Datu. That was not so unexpected and certainly not as huge as this critter. We crawled through dense population surrounded by some of the ugliest high-rise apartments we've ever seen. We were grateful that the weather was not great, being stuck on the bus for so long. It took an hour and 20 minutes to cover about 20 kms. It dawned on me that the buses were not that regular and that we really didn't want to go back the same way we had come, so we decided to take a taxi up the west side of the island to Ferringhi Beach, the only one of any note on the whole island. The beach itself is OK but, only OK, so seriously, why would you fly 12 hours from Europe to it? The condos behind it personified the worst of mass tourism. We walked the beach and got out of there, pronto.

Before we had left George Town, we had to find a new bed for the night. Almost every room was taken due to the Penang Marathon taking place in what was already the busy holiday season. On our city sightseeing we passed The Small Inn. We nipped inside this budget option (their description, not ours. It actually said so in brackets after its name outside). The chap told us that they did have a room, wrote my name, Furpes, in pencil on his room list, told us to come back at 2pm and pay him the 50 Ringitt (£9) then. I don't get these "gut feelings" often but when I do, I think they're generally proven to be correct. Aggers thinks so, at least. We went for some breakfast and I suggested that we relocated our bags before heading out of town as there was no chance of us being there at 2pm. Aggers didn't see the point of doing the walk twice - our bags were currently left in the hotel we had stayed in which was opposite the bus station. So, we didn't, which was logical.

I called The Small Inn at 2pm to say that we would not be there until later but please not to give our room away. My gut feeling was only enhanced when the chap on the other end insisted that I was there yesterday and was I calling because I wanted to spend more time with my wife! I thought he had finally understood me when he said for us to be there by 4pm.

That wasn't going to happen either. I almost begged him not to rub my name out before 6pm. He put the phone down rather abruptly so we were none the wiser but I was pretty sure he wasn't the same chap who'd reserved us the room in the morning.

Sure enough, when we arrived, we were told they were full and, on inspection of their very basic room list, I could see that Furpes had been rubbed out on room 302 and replaced by Chin Hock (or some other Chinese customer). To say that the guy was disinterested and dismissive would be quite an understatement. Yes, George Town hotels were all full, but that was our problem, not his. I don't have a temper but I have developed an unsavoury habit of swearing at locals when I think they don't understand me. I think it started in Colombia. It's not acceptable and I need to stop it. The only thing I would say is that on this occasion, "pretty please, I'm going to feel really tired later, please could you find me shelter for my wife and I" wouldn't cut it. "Get me a f*cking room you little sh*t" may resonate more in this instance. He called his boss and put me on the line. I reiterated the chain of events, somewhat more calmly. Something must've nibbled at his conscience. He said to give him a few moments.

Pretty quickly the dude at the desk (to give him a title, such as front desk manager, for example, would really be pushing it) said we could have a decommissioned room on the 4th floor, if we didn't mind that the toilet door was broken. We were quite desperate (my 7 Couchsurfing requests earlier that morning had yielded just 1 (negative) response so this was of no consequence to us. The room was fine, to be fair, but what wasn't fine was the guy walking all over our bed. If you refer to India in BID, then you'll understand why. I've seen all the piss over the gents' floors (alright, no different from Wetherspoon) here so even I didn't fancy sleeping on that bed once he'd left his prints. You see, it wasn't only the toilet door that was broken. None of the lights worked. We told him that wasn't an issue either, we had phone torches. With a bit of guidance from the recently 'qualified' electrician Agnieszka Czekanska, he did manage to get us some lighting, but not before trampling over our towels too. It helped to have light bulbs if you had the power switched on!

We went downstairs to pay. For the privilege of staying in an out of use room we would pay 50% more than if they hadn't rubbed my name out. I couldn't muster any more anger for him. He even had the audacity to tell us that he had already decided to discount the room for us from 90 Ringitt to 77, even though it was a bigger room. How can you discount a room that isn't for sale!? We paid our inflated price and got out of there. Our mood was lifted momentarily, well, actually it was fine really anyway, so was further enhanced by a delightful coffee stop. We finally found a suitable dinner venue, but with inexplicably dumb service. One of our Malay friends in Sabah had described her fellow natives as simple. I offered that they thought differently. She didn't agree. I don't want to sound condescending or patronising but the waitress and waiter (he may've even been the manager) were most definitely of our friend's version of simple. We did finally get our correct order but could've paid a third of what was due if I hadn't corrected him. I don't agree with accepting undercharging (unless it's a nasty corporation) as much as I don't overcharging. We could have had a free taxi ride to the beach. The driver couldn't understand why I wasn't exiting his vehicle on arrival. I asked him if he would like some money. He said that we had already paid on the app. I corrected him. I like a bargain but only when it's due.

We left early the next morning for the airport on another tortuously slow bus ride. It was 7.45 on a Sunday morning and already the roads were jammed, which is odd, seeing as very few establishments were open. We found one which was and purchased 2 local coffees in plastic bags for the journey. Coffee in a plastic bag? A new one for us, but, by golly, was it good. Like rocket fuel, it was that strong. To cap off our not so savoury Penang experience the jobsworth security officer at the airport insisted that we could only have one boarding pass on each mobile. Since when, love? What a load of drivel. To compound this stupidity, she was a member of the "I've got a face mask on so I insist on touching your phone and passport" brigade. We had been spoiled with our flying in Sarawak: basically no security at most airports. When there was, if you held your phone/passport away from the mask wearer's grasp they seemed to understand and smile.

We expected the mask wearing to be pretty rabid out here and in the main, it has been. However, only twice have we been asked to cover up. As I've mentioned before, we would understand if the wearers also practised social distancing and kept their hands to themselves, but they don't. Mask goes down for a cough and a spit, or just a chat on the phone, so what's the point, but I'm sure they're here to stay in this part of the world. So, you can wear your masks and we'll keep your hands away, if you don't mind. This woman at security though, could only be politely described as an officious, obnoxious bitch. She got the right hump when we took a step back from her attempts to get her hands on our stuff and gave us a right evil stare. Aggers decided to give her one back. This was turning into a stand-off. Security bitch then decided to up the ante with a fake cough into her mask. I suggested to Agnes that it was time to walk away. I wanted out of there, not to be detained by this woman.

Once we left the icebox of a terminal and boarded our Malindo Air (or was it Batik Air? They'd swallowed up Malindo but hadn't painted the plane yet) ATR some kind of equilibrium was restored. This was further enhanced when we landed at a deserted Malacca airport. Even though quite a bit of money had been spent on upgrading the terminal and lengthening the runway, it had failed to attract any airlines other than ours. Penang and Pekanbaru (Indonesia) account for the 10 flights per week! Back in my working days I had often been approached by Malaccan hoteliers wanting a slice of our not inconsiderable business to Sabah, Penang and Langkawi. From a personal/selfish point of view I wasn't interested. I'm sure you know why. Faced with 2-3 hours bus ride, coupled with no beach, neither were our customers. A missed opportunity? Well, maybe for some of our clientele but not me, in the end. The airport addiction finally got me here and, what a pleasant surprise. Plenty of history, an extremely attractive riverside scene and some decent eating (and even drinking) establishments. In spite of the rather grey weather, and some areas being very busy and noisy - fair enough, it's their holiday - currently, we were happy to be spending our final days here before heading back to a very, very cold Northern Europe. Main objective achieved: 23 new airports (29 for Aga), and a bloody nice time too. I now need to turn my attention to getting Agnes to parity, and not over, on our way to 500/1000 but before I do, let me tell you about our final European adventure of 2022 before we escaped to warmer climes.

# CHAPTER 18

Some may argue that Liverpool never deserved to receive either UNESCO World Heritage status, or be awarded European City of Culture in 2008. The former is apparently in jeopardy due to the planned relocation of Everton FC, close to the Mersey. The latter gives me justification to name it as the start point of our recent European tour. Aggers had been keen to visit Liverpool for a while. My opinion of the city had been significantly enhanced to that of the late 70s footy only version, when I worked for the government there for a month in 2015. Well, I use the term work quite loosely, but it was their fault not mine.

No points for guessing why we went, primarily: Just a small matter of 20 Spoons in the vicinity. I had managed to bag a very attractive train fare, at an equally attractive departure time from Euston, £12 for Aggers (£8 for me with my old man discount). Slightly more research was needed to find the best solution for our onward travel to Greece after a few days in the North West. It was time to tick off the, so far, elusive Kavala and Kasos airports. We had held tickets for both but our efforts had been thwarted by cancellation and Covid, respectively. I was surprised we managed to get such a good deal on the train to Liverpool as my attempts for Sheffield had proven to be futile. We had an hour connection in Crewe (what a shame that the Spoon there had long been closed) but the kind guard on the earlier train allowed us to hop on, meaning we were in Liverpool just 3 hours after leaving London.

Before we left Euston we popped into the St Pancras Spoon and were chuffed to see that the delayed winter magazine had finally hit the tables, featuring yours truly. What we were less enthralled with was the first of many messages reaching us, just after we left Euston, informing us that 32 Wetherspoons had been put up for sale. I frantically checked the list. Our friends who claim indifference to our Spoon collecting were not so indifferent after all. One in Merseyside, no problem, I'm sure it wasn't going to close in the next 48 hours. One in Durham, a bit more of an issue. When we visit a Wetherspoon in jeopardy, we always feel for the locals. Even if the property is taken over by a brewery or another pub chain they'll be pulling way more out of their pockets for whatever their tipple is. If the Wetherspoon becomes a shop - most likely, a mosque or a synagogue - less likely, or just a derelict space, whether it's a social gathering or a lonely soul their haven will be no longer. Whatever you say about Wetherspoon; the media and individuals do tend to enjoy giving them a good bashing, there's a helluva lot of customers out there who are extremely grateful for their existence.

Our first port of call was the splendid North Western, located in Lime Street station. Full of understandably, mainly railway history, it was very busy for a Wednesday afternoon and not many of the clientele looked like they were about to embark on a railway journey. They had a splendid selection of real ales so we stayed a little longer than planned before dumping our bags in the previously mentioned Adelphi Hotel. We spent the afternoon and early evening sightseeing and ticking off 4 more centrally located pubs (The Captain Alexander, The Lime Kiln, The Welkin and The Richard John Blackler), all OK to good, but not memorable.

We saved one central pub for coffees the next morning, The Fall Well, before heading under the Mersey for a tour around Birkenhead, etc. We had hoped to go across the famous river but we had just missed a ferry by a whisker and the next one was in an hour. I had, mistakenly, presumed that they were far more frequent than that. So, we caught a far less romantic and interesting train to a not particularly interesting 2nd pub of the morning, The Brass Balance. Aggers wasn't overwhelmed by Liverpool. I still think it's much nicer, and far less threatening than I found it on my first visit. Let me explain the threatening element. As was the norm back in the day, whoever out of Liverpool or Everton was due to play a home game on the day of the Grand National would do so at 11 or 1130 am, in order not to clash with the famous horse race. In 1977 this would be Liverpool v Leeds. There was a huge negative to this but also a positive. The negative was that for a 16-year-old boy the only way to get there was to catch the last train from London on Friday night, which arrived in Liverpool at 0230 Saturday. It certainly wasn't in my budget (based on a paper round and a few weekday evening shifts in Keymarkets - a long defunct supermarket chain) to stay in somewhere with a bed for the evening.

While the few older and wiser members of the London Leeds Supporters Club ventured off into what remained of the Friday night scouse scene, 92 (Steve Crawley) and I snuggled up in an unmanned ticket inspector's box until daylight. You would have to be of a certain age: similar or older than me to remember these. If there was a waiting room in Lime Street back then, it certainly wasn't open. We weren't that naive. These ticket boxes were built to fit one employee, with a stool for comfort. What this one did have was a heater, and a folding door. It was early April so we Southern Softies were either underdressed or the weather was unseasonably chilly, or both, or, well, we were just a couple of Southern Softies. It's 45 years ago so I can't remember every detail, funnily enough, but I do remember being very grateful for the heater being left on and us not getting moved on by some Penang security officer type, jobsworth. Leeds lost 3-1. It may as well have been 3-0 as, extremely rarely, we left before the final whistle, with very good reason, so only heard the muted cheer from outside the ground which, we later found out, was the Leeds consolation goal.

The positive of this foray was the possibility the early kick off presented to tick off a new ground. That's why we left a few minutes early so we could catch the train to London but stop off at Crewe Alexandra v AFC Bournemouth for the standard 3pm kick off. "Real" footy fans, apparently, don't have a second team. I do, so I'm not a real fan in some of the fanatics' eyes then. The Alex are mine, and have been as long as I can remember, for the sole reason that my mum used to have family friends whom they visited in Gresty Road: Crewe's ground name before sponsorship got in the way. I doubt my mum ever went to a match, but the fact she stayed across the road from the ground, randomly prompted my low level support of The Railwaymen (their other nickname).

All this seems a long time ago and even further away from our current setting (6717.84 miles from The Captain Alexander, Liverpool, according to the Wetherspoon app! - as the crow flies). Far from getting bored or complacent with the food and beverage choices on offer in Malaysia we are going to miss them as much as the warm weather. I certainly haven't been pining for a Wetherspoon breakfast wrap, fish & chips or anything else from other outlets, for that matter. We found an absolute gem in Malacca yesterday for brunch. The laksa, roti and iced coffees were amongst the best yet. So good that we have returned this morning. We've added fresh mango lassis to our order this morning in an extravagant last day splurge. The street scene is ideal for people watching and directly opposite a blind and disabled lady plays for a very long time on her violin, sat on her veranda. Judging by the number of passers by dropping notes into her donation box, she and her family must be relatively well off. She smiles a lot which helps with my feelings of sadness for her predicament. She said thank you when I dropped a note in her box yesterday. Could she smell my foreigner's odour? I'm 99.99% certain her conditions are genuine. She even played a number yesterday that I could singalong to, it being the tune accompanying a very common Leeds anti-Chelsea chant.

We have relocated for the rather glutinous and unnecessary second half of brunch by the river. We can justify this on 3 accounts: we are unlikely to eat again for 10 hours, whether compliments of Scoot or not, we have 50 Ringitt to spend and we want to try Ramen Kosong with Asam Padas sauce followed by cendol durian. The former because Aggers spied it 48 hours ago and has been after it ever since. The latter because we had a cendol mango on arrival and it was very, very tasty. We also shared a durian pancake last night and the after effects were as tasty as the initial digestion. The cendol is a strange but scrummy mix of coconut milk, red beans, ice cream, palm oil sugar, green noodle jelly and chosen fruit. Very filling too.

Meanwhile, our Spoon adventure over/under the Mersey threw up a very pleasant, if unexpected beach walk from Hoylake to West Kirby. The Dee Hotel was top drawer too. Our plans had to change slightly. I can't remember what alerted me but something did. As we checked our transportation from The Clairville, Wallasey to New Brighton, I decided to call ahead to The Master Mariner. No answer. Further research informed us that it had been closed for a full refurbishment since March. 8 months later, it seems unlikely it will reopen, considering Spoon's planned closures, of which a further 7 were announced after we left UK. One of which is on our to do list, in Peebles, Scottish Borders. This has prompted consideration of a winter trip to beat this and the Durham pending closures. Watch this space (well the next chapter to be pedantic and precise)! The endangered New Brighton Spoon had encountered some unexpected and expensive problems during the refurbishment, hence my scepticism re permanent closure in the current economic climate. We can only do what is laid before us. In fact, there was another pub closure, but we had expected it for a while. Not only did the Wetherspoon at Doncaster/Sheffield Airport close, the actual airport itself did. The prospect of taking a flight from one airport to a destination, which we've both done, just to visit a pub wasn't the most appealing aspect of our collecting. We had considered just buying the cheapest ticket, having a consequently rather expensive pint and heading back out of the airport to carry on visiting South Yorkshire pubs. Now the decision was out of our hands, thankfully.

With brief visits to The Mockbeggar Hall, Moreton and the fairly new Hoylake Lights, funnily enough in Hoylake, done prior to Kirby we had a rather longwinded journey via Heswall Spoon to Chester for an overnight in another fine Wetherspoon hotel. What a lovely city Chester is. Better than York in our opinion. The Square Bottle and The Bull and Stirrup Hotel certainly were better than York's offerings. The weather was a bit inclement and it was getting dark but we just about managed a circuit on the remains of the city wall before having a night cap in the other Spoon in the city. We broke our fast and took coffees the next morning in the remaining 2 pubs south of the Mersey, The John Masefield in New Ferry and The Wheatsheaf in Ellesmere Port, before heading back under it to do the last 3 on Merseyside; The Wild Rose, The Raven and The Thomas Frost. Without a car we could enjoy a decent pint in each. All 3 were "proper" pubs and appeared to be doing a fine trade. Job done (as Billy Davies - Preston North End manager at the time - once incorrectly - said!)! And theoretically neither was ours as we only managed 19 of the 20 planned, but we'd done what we could and would winter on a fairly respectable 822.

After much searching the final plan for the continuation of our European adventure had resulted in a new airport for Aggers, first up. During my days at Dan Air I took a training course as a loadmaster, for the simple reason it involved training on a post office flight from Gatwick to Liverpool. 40 years ago, many of the airports now offering a significant number of low-cost flights had little or no regular passenger flights. Liverpool was one of them, so getting that one in at such an early stage was quite a bonus. I also took much shorter, non-commercial flights from Gatwick to Southend (for a Dan Air aircraft to be repainted), Stansted (for a Dan Air aircraft to be positioned there for the summer charters) and Lasham (for a Dan Air aircraft to undergo a heavy-duty maintenance check). Lasham, near RAF Odiham in Hampshire is primarily used for a large gliding club but still, to this day takes in commercial aircraft for storage or maintenance. After my initial visit to Stansted I never imagined I would return, let alone as often as I have.

Liverpool offers a number of destinations these days, many to Eastern Europe. I chose Cluj Napoca, in Romania, at a similar price to our train tickets! I should be used to it by now, but it still amazes me what unbelievably great value some European flights offer. We were flying for 3 hours for less than we could return to London! Before we headed to Cluj though, we had a day to spend with our Liverpool-based Polish friends. Although they had lived there for almost a year, they wanted us to decide on where to spend the day. During our pub travels we had passed through Port Sunlight station several times. We read a little bit about this "village". It sounded interesting and most certainly was. If you're interested, I'm sure you'll Google it, but suffice to say, it really is worth a visit if you're ever in Liverpool, or Chester, for that matter. Not only were our friends chuffed with their day out but we, yet again, thanked Tim Martin for giving up law to open a pub. Funnily enough, on our walk back from the park of the same name: Port Sunlight, not Tim Martin, I got chatting to a local couple who asked what brought us to Liverpool. I came clean. Imagine my surprise when the lady said she spent some of her childhood living next door to our hero. He was very tall back then, she informed me. Her husband alerted me to Tim's appearance on Desert Island Discs. Our visit to Port Sunlight was massively enhanced by one of its older residents. This lady was standing outside her house, bidding farewell to a friend. I asked her if she minded if I asked her a question. "Of course not, but I'm not standing out here, you better come in. You look trustworthy, are you?" What an interesting response. Not only was my initial question answered but we got a right old history lesson on not only Port Sunlight, but on her life as well. What an interesting one it had been too. We also had a guided tour of her home. And I thought I could talk!

We weren't disappointed that our flight from Liverpool was delayed a couple of hours. We had been indecisive about booking an hotel for our 0230 arrival in Cluj. With a new arrival time nearer 0430, there seemed little point. We hoped the flight would be further delayed but it wasn't. We whiled away an hour or so on arrival at Cluj airport, and then set off on a very uninspiring, chilly walk to the city centre. One problem with travelling so light is the lack of warm clothes if our main destination doesn't warrant them. Liverpool had been pretty mild, if quite wet. It had stopped raining by the time we left

Cluj airport but mild it was not. We had landed in Cluj on our first Romania trip but not visited the city. The guide books are quite glowing about it. Maybe it's not at its best at 7 am on a grey Sunday morning but we didn't feel disappointed to be getting a train out of there a couple of hours later. We were off to Suceava to rectify that airport's current status with us. You may recall a few chapters and months back that the Italian Air Traffic Controllers put paid to our flight there from Bergamo.

The 6 and 1/2-hour train journey passed through pleasant scenery but we arrived in heavy rain. Suceava doesn't have a great deal to offer, apart from a fairly interesting monastery up a hill, which we managed to do dry, dodging the frequent showers. The airport was a shambles. It doesn't have room for 180 passengers let alone more than one flight at a time. Wizzair is planning to expand its offerings so who knows where the passengers are expected to wait. Anyway, at least it hadn't taken long to right that wrong, so this time we had a planned night stop in Bergamo before our flight to Crotone the next afternoon. Our plan, as I said, was to head to Greece but our roundabout route provided a couple of unexpected and delightful diversions.

I'd seen Crotone on Ryanair's flight search but knew nothing other than that it was in Italy. I was also aware of the existence of Reggio di Calabria. Where I had never heard of were Pizzo and Scilla. What a couple of gems. Crotone was none too shabby either with a pleasant coastal promenade. We took the train the next morning via Lamezia to Pizzo. The late summer/early autumn weather was idyllic and the small, crowd free town an absolute delight. I'm sure it's very busy in the height of summer but, just like many Greek islands, virtually deserted and void of tourists by early October. The train ride down the coast from Lamezia all the way to Reggio must rate as one of the most scenic in Europe. We couldn't decide which we preferred; Pizzo or Scilla. They were similar but different if you get my drift. We even managed to book a place with a pool in Pizzo, which it was warm enough to use. There was only one thing disturbing my complete peace of mind: our future travel plans. Not only did we not have a destination planned for our end of year winter break, rather more pressing we didn't have a flight home before we would embark on that little jaunt.

I really needed to apply myself but I certainly wasn't going to be doing it during the day and the lure of an ice-cold beer whilst watching the sunset, followed by a bottle of wine over dinner, lulled me into a feeling of relaxation which was not conducive to intense flight planning. The long-haul trip we're currently concluding proved to be the easier to bring to fruition. The route home, less so. I couldn't find a flight back from anywhere in Greece to either UK or Poland for less than £200 each. That's what I was hoping to spend to get us to Thailand! I'd also tried to get us back from Turkey with the same lack of success. Normally, I do all the flight planning myself but on this occasion, Aggers - on sensing my growing frustration; she could hardly avoid it - decided to try and help out. She found a dirt-cheap flight with Ryanair from Bourgas to Krakow and another one, for me, onwards to Gatwick. I had booked us as far as Rhodes but no further so all we had to do now was get ourselves to Bulgaria. That plan was fairly swiftly implemented after the time taken to come up with it, initially.

Now I could completely enjoy our surroundings and the present with that nagging feeling dealt with. Aggers was completely relaxed and unperturbed by our lack of plans throughout. I came to the conclusion once more, that I need to have something to fret about. Once the plan was in place I could concentrate on worrying about its execution. I had a few days off first as our immediate schedule had some room for any disruption which may come our way. After a few really blissful days we headed north to Rome from the tiny and quiet Reggio di Calabria Airport. Both Crotone and Reggio only have a couple of domestic departures so both fell into the pleasurable airport experience category. Having both done Lamezia separately, that was the foot of Italy done but we certainly wouldn't be adverse to a non-airport inspired return.

After our night stop on the outskirts of Rome and the aforementioned historic walk to the airport we were off to

Thessaloniki. We didn't hang around there as we were keen to reach Kavala that evening. I'm not sure why but Kavala, like Kalamata, had long been on my radar. I regularly got them mixed up, unable to remember which was the Peloponnese and which on the northern mainland, until we visited Kalamata last year. My desire to add Kavala to our lists was only heightened by last year's failed attempt. The advantage of this though was that we had 5 nights in the area rather than the single one planned last year. We decided to head over on the short ferry ride from nearby Keramoti to the island of Thassos. Kavala was a pretty pleasant city but after a morning wander we were keen for some island life. Whilst Thassos does attract UK and German charter passengers, the UK flights to Kavala had finished for the year and the Germans were winding down too. The island had a very out of season feel to it, which as you know by now, is our cup of tea. It wasn't up there with a lot of other islands we'd give a 9/10 but it was certainly pleasant enough, 7 maybe? We chose to spend our last night back on the mainland in very laid back Keramoti. It was difficult to imagine hordes of TUI bucket and spaders passing through just a few weeks earlier. Although obviously, the main reason to return the night before our Kavala flight was because I wasn't remotely interested in entertaining the extremely unlikely possibility of being stranded on Thassos, whilst watching our plane climb above us, without us, there was another reason: there was a very long beach which looked very inviting for a leisurely stroll. So that's what we did.

We had another, slightly less leisurely stroll the next morning to Kavala Airport. I managed to convince Aggers that the 25-euro taxi fare could be better spent on beer and wine. What a girl! She readily agreed to the 2 1/2-hour hike. It was flat all the way and, apart from a tad more traffic than we anticipated, quite pleasant. Kavala done, just Kasos to go for me in Greece. I was, not for the first time, questioning the lengths I would go to in order to notch one specific airport. There's plenty to choose from to get to the magic figure but I seem to get fixated. Kasos being really quite a small island has few flights or ferries. About 5 or 6 flights per week via Karpathos to Rhodes and a couple of ferries making numerous stops from Athens and on to Rhodes and return. I had worked out the best way to do this was to arrive via a mere 14-hour ferry ride from Santorini and then to leave on the flight to Rhodes. It was good to get Santorini airport in for Aggers and we weren't averse to returning to that island. Now we had a plan onwards from Rhodes it was imperative that things ran smoothly.

In coming up with the Bourgas option to return home, Agi had bagged herself a side trip to Cappadocia: firmly and longstanding on her wish list. I was not averse to the idea, so long as I could add a couple of new airports. I expected another positive return, seeing as the Chinese were still not travelling, so crowds should be manageable. We needed the ferry and flight to run in and out of Kasos to schedule so we could make our onward connections from Rhodes to Marmaris, Izmir and Kayseri. There was no room for delays. The weather was fine on our arrival in Santorini (via Athens from Kavala) but the forecast was not. It proceeded to start raining the afternoon before our ferry departure and what we had hoped would be a sun-drenched ferry ride turned into a very lumpy, bumpy affair indeed. It really was banging about after we left Heraklion for Kasos via Sitia. I think I've already mentioned the downpour just prior to our arrival in Heraklion and the unfortunate consequences. We were quite relieved to make it to Kasos, particularly as our host there had text me saying he'd heard the boat would be stopping in Crete due to the weather. Fortunately, I only got this message after we'd left Sitia. Imagine the panic that would've overwhelmed me if we'd still been in port.

Our host, originally from Zimbabwe(!), greeted us at the tiny port, which was not unwelcome as it was nearly midnight. The accommodation he provided looked like we had entered a time tunnel; and we hadn't travelled forward. It was charming, if in a slightly weird configuration. He had kindly left us bread for the morning but even more considerately a bottle of wine and some cold beers. The tiny town was as cute as many other islands' horas and some well signed walking trails added to our enjoyable day, finished off with our complimentary wine and beers on our patio. The weather was OK: partly sunny, could have been better but the forecast for the morning was for very strong winds. We learned that the ferry had already been cancelled. What's the saying? A little knowledge is a dangerous thing? Well, my Dan Air days had taught me a fair amount about crosswinds and aircraft limitations but they didn't have any ATRs nor did they fly to Kasos. Not that I could remember the specifics for what they did fly and where. I listened to the howling wind throughout the night. Some of the gusts sounded really quite strong. I didn't fancy our chances. I googled ATR crosswind limits, in the morning, and felt just a little less pessimistic. I tried to track the incoming flight from Rhodes on Flightradar24 but there was no information. We walked for all of 10 minutes out from town to the airport. Was the wind actually dropping or were we imagining it? Soon the beautiful sight of the ATR42 appeared in the distance. The landing was textbook, considering the conditions. Never in doubt. Our flight to Karpathos and onwards to Rhodes was remarkably smooth and the weather in Rhodes tremendous. It was nice to be back in the old town. All we had to do before meeting up with an ex-work colleague of Aga's was get our ferry tickets to Marmaris. After a brief panic, caused by being told incorrectly in an agency that the ferry was full the next morning, we were free to have an afternoon of drinking, eating and socialising with people other than each other. We are very blessed that we spend virtually every minute of every day in each other's company with barely any disagreements but we both appreciate our interactions with others.

We caught a bus from Marmaris to Izmir the next morning and were both very pleasantly surprised with one of Turkey's major cities. I had visited both Izmir's old and current airport but not the city. We were both intrigued to find a fair number of European tourists there. Clearly they were better informed than us. After a night in Izmir and a quick flight the next morning, a rather bizarre bus journey from Kayseri Airport finally took us to the city centre and a mightily impressive fortress. If it wasn't for the assistance of a very kind local I'm not sure how long it would've taken us to get on our way to the out of city bus terminal but we were soon on our way to Cappadocia. It was superb.

After a rather fabulous time in Goreme, Urgup and the surrounding areas, including some awesome valley walks we headed off to Konya for an overnight before a flight the following morning to Istanbul. I think I've described our bus driver for the journey to Bourgas but, just to confirm it really was the wild West encapsulated. I know I recalled my airport addition of Bourgas in BID but it was quite cool to experience the town/city some 30+ years later. Not a bad place at all. Another catch up airport for Aggers, in addition to Izmir and yet another successful mission drew to a close.

We managed to successfully blag our way into the lounge at Singapore - thank you Scoot: the airline that does everything in their powers to avoid an on time departure. If that sounds a little harsh then the fact that they arrived 20 minutes late into KK and managed to depart 40 minutes late was starting to repeat a pattern. There's no urgency to get passengers sat down so they can depart, a la Ryanair etc. Our prebooked, prepaid seats from Singapore to Berlin were no longer available. Well, so long as we get our £46 back we don't care. We're sat together, by a window and inexplicably departing 15 minutes late. It's a mere detail. If 2023 proves to be as hugely enjoyable, satisfying and exciting as 2022 then we will continue to consider ourselves to be blessed. Let's see how the next 13 hours passes. One passing observation: KLIA is a simply huge international airport. It felt so weird to see several passengers barefoot in such an environment. We didn't learn where they were from or what their beliefs were but it really was quite a weird sight. Compared to Luton and Stansted KLIA is vast, yet I'm not convinced it handles more passengers per acre. One thing we won't miss from Malaysia is the spitting, throat clearing and insane mask wearing. Other than that, God bless you Malaysia.

# CHAPTER 19

I said we would do Berlin Brandenburg properly at some point and so we did. Scoot landed on the new runway and parked at the new terminal. Any lingering doubt that we shouldn't have counted it as a new airport when we landed on the old Schonefeld runway and disembarked into the old Schonefeld terminal banished. Our flight was made more comfortable when I suggested to our very lanky aisle passenger that he may wish to avail himself of one of the vacant emergency exit, unlimited legroom seats, which you pay a small fortune to prebook. Win, win. He was very happy and so were we. To be honest, apart from the lack of in-flight entertainment and food, both of which we provided ourselves, the latter pre-boarding, there's no difference between Scoot and full-service airlines on board, in economy. The all-important legroom is the same, if not more generous.

Now I'm up to date on writing about our attempt to finish, I can concentrate on making it happen. My mate, Jim the pilot, has described it as "an honour" to fly us to our 500/1000th. If he looks after us like he did both of us to Santiago and me on numerous occasions previously, we'd be daft to turn that offer down. New airports have been ticked off in ultimate luxury thanks to Jim including Entebbe (with the most memorable flight deck landing at sunrise over Lake Victoria), Dhaka, Beijing, San Francisco, Sao Paulo, amongst others, let alone all those that didn't add to the total. Even though I gave him a nice helicopter flight from Redhill to Southampton with his dad for his 30th (Leeds partially spoiled the day unsurprisingly, losing 3-2), I owe him big time. And then there's all those "comp" tickets to witness Leeds' glorious and more frequent inglorious moments. Cheers, Jim!

We have a few options in USA to make that happen: Memphis,

Nashville and New Orleans, being of significant interest. But let's not get ahead of ourselves. We need to visit 14/16 new airports before we're at that point. Should Malaysia Airlines be interested to fly us back to Sarawak we will have a dilemma. If they offer us a guaranteed comfy seat then we'll have some serious thinking to do.

Just 14 to go means, for starters, that there's no need to be looking for a Norway/India/Colombia style trip. What will be Agi's 2 to level up? There are a few short haul routes I'm still keen on but, if need be, they can be done at leisure after the goal is reached. After surprisingly little indecision and not quite as much time spent planning as I envisaged a plan was hatched.

Now, here we are back where it all started. No, not the first ever airport: Gatwick in 1969, or the first ever football ground: Selhurst Park, in the same year. No, not on the North Downs Way, before I even knew National Trails existed. Finally, no, not even in my first Wetherspoon, either before I knew that's where I was or once we were on that mission. No, we are back in Goa, where I first put pen to paper, so to speak, almost exactly 3 years ago. So, we have ended up on an India trip but shorter and many fewer airports than last time. Not only are we back on Patnem beach, but, after a little indecision, we even chose to stay in the same beach huts as last time. I recognised the lady at the bar, told her we had been here 3 years ago and she promptly offered us a 20% discount. She, unsurprisingly, didn't remember me but she did remember Agnieszka. Fair enough. She does have a fairly memorable face. In my opinion, not in a way that that nasty commentor on one of our articles meant either.

We're pretty sure that, apart from staying in the airport handy hostel in Bangkok, this is the first time either of us have performed such a return, not including work enforced ones. We vowed we would return to Goa and, thanks to the remarkable consideration and kindness of the Indian Airport Authorities in opening a new airport here, literally a couple of weeks ago, we had our excuse. To be fair, I was already planning to use the old Goa airport as one of the two required by Agnes to draw level with me, such was the strength of our desire to return.

I'm neither looking for nor expecting a sympathy vote but sometimes travel planning and implementing it can be quite tiring in its own way. We love our current life, appreciate our good fortune in being able to live it, but we both fancied a week of not doing much. I'll probably end up planning airports 995-999, whilst we do nothing, but that shouldn't be too tricky. First though, I'm sure you're gagging to know how we arrived in Goa, and how many airports were involved. I would suggest to skip to the next chapter if you're not. However, if that's the case, I'd love to know who would be reading chapter 19 in the first place!

We ended up foregoing a winter Spoons trip for a number of reasons, primarily because even our madness has limits. That's not to say that we didn't avail ourselves on several occasions of Spoon's unbelievably generous breakfast sale offer for the first 2 weeks of January: £2.49 for a breakfast wrap with unlimited coffees, amongst others!! Come on, how could you not? Especially when you won't have another for at least 5 weeks. Had we embarked on a collecting trip it would have involved a 1000-mile minimum round trip in 4 days. Why? Well, because the point of even considering it was because the 2 pubs on the endangered list which we haven't visited, happen to be in Durham and north of the border in Peebles. We decided to chance that they won't be sold by spring. If they are, so be it. Obviously, if they do close before we get to them I'm sure I won't be so blasé but as Aggers often says, "it is what it is". And from me, "all things in perspective".

We plumped for India for the next adventure because a) we loved it, b) other long-haul fares continue to be unfavourably high, c) it has lots of airports, d) it offered some interesting, obviously new airport, options en route, e) it's cheap and great value and f) the Indian authorities had returned to their senses and reintroduced the e-visa system. We could have easily reached our airport goals in India but had already decided on a plan for that before settling on India next. Also we only had a

30 day visa so didn't want to cram 15 (17) into that time frame. Even 12 (14) after I had found a route to notch 3 on the way.

Many people have the same opinion of Ryanair/Wizzair etc as they do of Wetherspoon: exceedingly low. Not us, as you know. I wouldn't say I am a Wizzair fan. I would say I am a Wetherspoon fan. Having got us from Catania to Abu Dhabi for €25 they now decided to tempt us with Gatwick via Vienna to Dammam, Saudi Arabia for £25!! How could I badmouth them? It's insane isn't it? Let me break that down for you: Gatwick to Vienna £8.77 each, Vienna to Dammam £16.23 each. Yes, we had to book a place to stay in Vienna but we found, what turned out to be, a very acceptable room for just under £35. Not only was it a bloody bargain but we were off to a new country too.

The visa situation for Saudi Arabia (KSA from now on) was a little unclear. If we had to apply for a full visa this would cost £105 on arrival or £120 in advance. Potentially not worth it, for us, if we were only staying 3 days. KSA visa website not only stated that a transit visa was available for 96 hours for around £25, it allowed you to apply, so we did, and it took our money. As we had no acknowledgement, we called Ministry of Foreign Affairs (MOFA) in KSA. At least they answered promptly but their advice was incorrect. Yes, we could definitely get a transit visa on arrival if need be, but we should call the KSA Embassy in London to check the status of our application. During the 4 days we waited for the latter to answer the phone, the KSA tourist board's UK representative, also confirmed that we could apply for a transit visa, either on line or on arrival. When the embassy in London finally answered the phone they stated that transit visas were no longer available as they had proved too popular! Someone in authority clearly felt that too many cheeky brits were getting a sneaky, brief, look at their Kingdom on the cheap. My comments about why they still had a form "live" to apply, had taken our money and that their bosses said we could do it fell on deaf ears: "no, we refund you, allow 3-4 weeks, bye". Not the most welcoming start to a country that had been predominantly off limits until a couple of years ago. We certainly weren't expecting a bottle of red on arrival, a la

Georgia, but we hoped that we would be allowed to board the plane from Vienna and that the welcome on arrival, if we did, wouldn't be quite so frosty.

As it was we checked with the Wizzair representative ground staff on arrival at Vienna about their interpretation of the visa situation for KSA. The supervisor confirmed that they would let us board without a visa. Why was it then, that, having received our boarding passes at check in, with no request for a visa, that the gate agent, initially, denied us boarding, stating we needed a visa? We could see on her screen, quite clearly, that it stated visa on arrival for EU and UK citizens. Keeping with the general non swearing policy of my books .... but really? She even said that she had been boarding flights to KSA since September. 4 months later and she appeared still not to know the basics. She should get a job with a tourist board or airport information. She'd fit right in.

I had booked the flights and onwards to India so invoked the "win some, lose some" mantra and accepted that our getting to India via KSA was not going to be such a bargain after all - still pretty, bloody cheap though. And if Leeds United had had the same win/lose ratio as us for the last few years they would have done the quadruple of Premier League, Champions League, FA & League Cup each year! Add in the Club World Cup for good measure. Alright all you footy lovers, I know Leeds was in the championship when we started our travels but you get my point!?

So, off to KSA we jolly well went. I'm sure the vast majority of low-cost airline customers buy at least a few of the multitude of extras on offer. We don't, as I'm sure I'll have mentioned at least once, but I guess if you're off on your annual or bi-annual trip you'll at least pay to sit together and for some form of baggage. We don't object to them doing this, charging extra for everything but a random seat and a small bag. If they didn't we wouldn't get the ridiculous prices we do. Not wishing to tempt fate but we have virtually always sat together in spite of Wizz and Ryan allocating us 32E and 9B etc. As we managed to on the 5-hour flight to Dammam. We normally blag a row of

3 to ourselves ..... as we did on the 5 hour flight to Dammam. We took our own refreshments, not just to save money but, because my homemade cheddar and boursin sandwiches are far superior to any Wizz offerings.

Surprisingly, there was an abundance of accommodation in KSA for around the £30-40 mark but that would be a bit dull, wouldn't it? Having finally hosted our first couchsurfer, on New Year's Day (and very successful it was too) why not give it a bash in KSA? We received 2 maybes to the 5 requests I sent for Dammam and 1 turned into a yes. What a totally charming and hospitable chap Omar was. Super-efficient in communication to start with - there's a good few Airbnbs that could learn a thing or 2 from him. We took his advice to hire a car due to the severe lack of public transport in KSA. We fancied the train ride to Riyadh but it was full for the next 5 days and the bus wasn't going to be cheaper than car hire, when factoring in taxis to get between cities and airports. Particularly as it seems, so far, that the rental car company has failed to charge us the £50 one way drop off fee. Win some, lose some. We did win that one, in the end. (50) Quids in!

Of course we had to buy a full 1-year tourist visa on arrival. Naturally there was a nice long queue for the privilege. At least we were paying £105 each for 3 days. Some poor sods were paying it for 3 hours! I think a little gentle mutiny was gathering pace when we left, as numerous passengers, well 10-15, were in this situation. Safety in numbers? I wouldn't count on it. Now we have the option to return to KSA as often as we wish for 90 days at a time for the next year. Every cloud, and all that. Would/will we return? Aggers is keener than me but I think there's a reasonable possibility if they don't change their visa rules again.

The most rewarding and important aspect of this visit was undoubtedly the people. First though, after finally getting through immigration the next obstacle was renting the car. The agent insisted we needed a KSA mobile number so he could send us a code. Never heard that one before. We called Omar. He explained he thought it was a scam and consequently, didn't want us to use his number. Fair enough, but no code, no rental was our current situation. The agent continued to fill out the paperwork, then handed us the keys. What about the obligatory code? He'd decided to use his phone number for it! The car was not old but covered in dents and scratches. It soon became apparent why; lane control, speed limits - not as such. Undertaking, cutting up, erratic last-minute manoeuvres - very popular indeed.

Omar had been patiently waiting for us at a nearby coffee shop. What a smiley guy. He briefly showed us his home and then offered to take us on a night tour of Dammam. It was surprisingly nippy so we were happy that most of the 2-hour tour was in his swanky Beemer. It's a funny old set up. Dammam, Dhahran and Al Khobar seem to be 3 cities merging into 1, with no apparent centre. I may very well be wrong but that was our impression. Construction is everywhere and seems never-ending. As I regularly say, I'm not writing a guidebook, so I should move on before I do. However, seeing as KSA is in its infancy of allowing tourists in, I will wager that it remains a mystery to most.

Omar recommended us a very tasty and cheap breakfast spot the next morning as he was at work. We had decided to stay another night with him as, he was nice and it seemed a bit rude to pitch up, have a city tour and bugger off the next morning. We amused ourselves during the day by driving the length of the Corniche from the Bahrain Causeway. Most of it is geared up to walking and cycling but I'd opine that not much of that goes on for at least 3-4 months of the year. We had to keep reminding ourselves how unbearably hot this place could be. Although it was sunny it wasn't troubling north of 20 degrees on the mercury. We were longing for India, or more specifically Goa.

On his return from work Omar took us to a splendid local restaurant where we sat on the floor in a private room and tucked into chicken and rice with our fingers. Afterwards he took us to a Shisha bar to meet 6 locals he'd met through Couchsurfing. What a friendly bunch. We learnt a lot about life in KSA from them and also that the alternative route we had planned to Riyadh was a good shout. We bade a fond farewell to Omar the next morning and followed the coast road south before heading inland to Al Ahsa oasis. Finally, we saw true desert, en route, not churned up by man, or covered in huge industrial complexes, apart from the road through it. It's a splendid sight. The oasis itself is the largest in the world. Wiki tells us that it has 2.5m palm trees. Also, that it consists of 22 villages and 4 cities, one of which: Al Hofuf, which we visited, is in the top 15 in KSA, population wise. Apparently, only 25% of the oasis has been developed and the "empty quarter" still makes up 75% of it. To be honest, in our brief stay, it looked the other way around. We didn't have enough time to explore fully so I'm sure I'm wrong.

Al Hofuf was more how you would expect a city to look with a compact centre, a few historical buildings and an excellent souk. Well worth the detour rather than zooming along the main highway for 250 miles. The onward journey to Riyadh was rotten. The roads incredibly potholed and unfinished, making UK roads look decent in comparison. I'm sure the main road is fine but our route took us on an unfinished dual carriageway which resulted in the bizarre situation of both sides being used in both directions, overtake/undertake at your peril as most drivers did. I think KSA drivers are currently number 1 in my league of worst drivers. Many countries are more chaotic but for outright bad driving......

Whereas Omar could not have been more precise and detailed in our arrival instructions, Amer, our host in Riyadh, was a man of very few words on WhatsApp. He gave us the house number and road name and said he'd leave the key as he was at work. We never did find the key as we couldn't find his house. We found the road but, alas, all the house numbers were in Arabic, naturally! The street was fairly deserted and we had no Internet. What to do? We found a chap sat in his car and asked if he could point us to number 7312. He could but there was no sign of where a key could be. This kind individual then did no more than invite us into his house, via his rather splendid owl cage, introduce us to his sister, mother and wife and ply us with tea, biscuits and a rather delicious homemade custard cake. Turns out he and his sister were Syrian but born and raised in KSA. Even though his wife was Saudi, no chance of him ever getting a Saudi passport. They were so hospitable and seemed to take it on the chin that hardly any country would let them visit, on account of them having Syrian passports. Once again, we counted our blessings.

After an hour or so of their hospitality and conversation we made contact with Amer. On first sight he looked rather conservative, and a man of as few words in person as on WhatsApp. This was just a cover. Dressed in his traditional white thobe and head gear he initially, hid well that he was clearly a bit of a party guy and liked the ladies, a lot. He had a diminutive but equally friendly Filipino girlfriend - still strictly forbidden to live "in sin", but, hey, if you don't get caught...... He was extremely well travelled, not short of a bob or two and owned 4 companies, or was it 5? Why on earth was he on Couchsurfing? He even had a room with 2 bunk beds in it, set up for bigger groups of couchsurfers. We had a very sparsely furnished room but, by heck, was the bed comfortable. We had been on separate couches at Omar's, not that they were uncomfortable but this was a very nice bed indeed.

Amer took us to a splendid local restaurant. No way would we ever have stumbled across this place if we were holed up in an apartment or hotel, let alone eaten there - the menu was only in Arabic. It was very down to earth, like a large working men's cafe, cheap as chips, but the food was superb. The next morning we took breakfast in Amer's home with Claire, his girlfriend and their delightful kitten. It was time to say goodbye and head out to Riyadh Airport. It was disappointing that we had arrived in Dammam after sunset. Apparently the airport is the largest in the world by land size, by some considerable distance. Riyadh did hold this title previously, but has now slipped to second. These Saudi dudes are certainly building for the future and they have a ton of space to do so. The road infrastructure out to Riyadh Airport is quite something. Riyadh felt like a more lived in city than Dammam. Not so much just huge shopping malls and buildings popping up randomly. Will we come back to KSA before our one-year visa expires? I was going to say, you'll never know, even if you are remotely interested, but clever Agnes has had a website designed completely free by some students so, feel free to check on www.aatravels.info one day.

It was time to head off to India. We, obviously, could have flown directly from Riyadh to Mumbai, but why would you, when for an extra £7 you could take a daylight flight to Kuwait, have a 5-hour layover, to arrive in Mumbai at a not massively social 0305? Of course, that's what we did. We didn't imagine ourselves holidaying in Kuwait, so may as well tick off the airport. I did, not for the first time, question my sanity, when our delayed flight arrived in Mumbai with us both feeling pretty knackered.

# CHAPTER 20

At least the Indian visa process was as smooth as a baby's .... and our arrival into Mumbai pretty painless. Mr Modi had recently retracted the ridiculous visa fee and restrictions he had implemented otherwise India wouldn't have been in our thoughts. Mumbai Airport has changed beyond recognition both internally and externally since my previous visit in 1986. It was far less chaotic. In fact, to describe it as chaotic in any shape or form would be a complete exaggeration: an untruth. Mumbai, itself, seemed no more chaotic than any other reasonably sized city we'd encountered on our previous India trip. You wouldn't have to be a cricket fan to be impressed by the Oval Maidan. In the centre of the city and one of the few green, well, sun bleached, large open spaces it is surrounded by fabulous architecture. It's also peaceful by Indian city centre standards, even with the incredible number of cricket matches taking place, one, almost literally on top of the other. There was a match taking place, each end of the park with cricketers in regulation whites, umpires and a proper sized playing area. In between, literally hundreds of games were utilising not much more space than the other 2 combined.

It may've been because it was a weekend that things seemed manageable. Don't get me wrong it was very noisy and very busy in places. I came to the conclusion, rather belatedly (no idea why it didn't occur to me 3 years ago) that they really should remove the horn from all motorised vehicles in India. As it is used constantly, nobody can have any idea if they are the ones being hooted. The noise pollution would drop dramatically. It's a way of life to the locals but I'm not sure if I would ever get used to the constant beep, beep, beep. You could argue what would happen when a horn is genuinely needed. I would counter with, the same as now; nothing, as nobody has a clue who is hooting who. I would opine that Indians are fantastic drivers. How there are not more accidents is a tribute to them.

We had settled on the FabExpress Orange Suites for our 2 nights in Mumbai. It had very, very good reviews and was conveniently located to the airport and a train station for the city centre. We paid £26 per night plus an extra £1 for breakfast. Quite expensive by Indian standards but this was Mumbai and, don't forget, it had very good ratings. As I didn't think we would arrive there much before 0600, I was reluctant to pay for that night's accommodation, of course I was. I hoped we may be able to pay a little extra on arrival for an early check in. I think the receptionist - actually let's not create a false impression here - the boy asleep on the couch, was pissed off at being woken up. The last thing he was going to do was be of any assistance or do anything other than the bare minimum. Fair enough, we would come back at 1200 to check in. The entrance to the hotel was similar to that in my second terraced house in Croydon where a minimal ground floor space immediately gave way to some stairs. Somehow they had managed to squeeze a desk and a sofa in there, whilst still allowing just enough space for guests to get past. I was beginning to have doubts about this place but it had very, very good reviews. I went upstairs for a pee and stumbled, firstly across the tiny kitchen, where I saw a rat the size of a cat but this didn't trouble me unduly. All big cities have rats don't they, and this establishment had very, very good reviews.

We headed down to the train station and caught a commuter train to Churchgate. 80p for the equivalent of a travel card. OK, doesn't cover buses or metro, most of the latter is still to be built, but not a bad deal for the whole of Mumbai railway. Call me childish (I am), but I love the fact that the doors remain open still and the locals still hang out of them, whether the train is busy or not. Passengers jump off before the train has stopped, just as I used to as a kid, and an adult for that matter - broke my nose once doing it as an adult, but that would only be included as a story if I was digressing. I reckon the only thing that has changed since; as an 8-year-old, I had a little book on worldwide trains which included pictures of Bombay's in the 60s, is the announcements not to hang out of the doors or jump off before the train "has come to a complete standstill". Not that my book told me whether there were any or not, but seeing as UK wasn't treating us all like morons back then with the most pathetic announcements, I doubt India was either.

We caught some of the sights. I never knew Mumbai had a UNESCO listed Art Deco area. It also has some fabulous colonial era buildings. We retired to the Leopold Cafe, made famous in Shantaram: a must read for fans of India; well, at least the first 75% and last 5%. Unfortunately, I had been nursing a dodgy stomach since the day after we returned from Malaysia. It came and went but I thought something was in there that shouldn't have been. I think I must be amongst the very few who ran to the toilet in India before they'd even eaten a morsel. We stayed a little longer than intended, while I acquainted myself with Leopold's facilities. Once I felt I was done and there was a potential window of opportunity to head back to FabExpress Orange Suites, we did so, via the chemist and some Indian style Imodium tablets. We also managed to secure an Indian sim with far less difficulty than 3 years ago.

The dude who we found asleep on the sofa must've been on a double shift as he was behind the desk now. No wonder he was very grumpy. I'm not going to bore you with the saga of trying to pay for this hotel on line. Suffice to say, their system is shit. This is a chain of 600+ hotels in India. We had received a threatening email from them just after we booked, during our transit in Kuwait, saying that we had to pay 25 or 100% upfront or the booking would be cancelled. We called them as we couldn't pay on line. "Sorry, your booking is cancelled and the hotel is full." "But we only booked it 15 minutes ago". Line went dead, so we called Booking.com who promised to get back to us, but never did. Bear with me, there is a good reason why I'm going into so much detail here. Our booking, without deposit, was fine. The room was fine, bed comfortable, bathroom OK. Rested, we headed over to Juhu beach, about a

45-minute walk from us. Bloody heck, everywhere was now very, very, very busy. LP describes the ocean as toxic. We weren't tempted without their warning.

When we headed back to FabExpress Orange Suites we were, understandably knackered. The Indian Imodium seemed to be working so we both had a pretty decent sleep. The constant scampering of rats over our roof was a bit eerie but I couldn't see any place they could get in the room. We declined the breakfast in room option, even though we'd splashed out a £1 for it. I hadn't told Aggers about the cat rat in the kitchen yet but the trays lying around in the corridor with half-finished breakfast didn't entice us. Now, I'm a regular 10 giver on Booking.com reviews. I often remark how places we stay in have been given quite low marks and we think they're 9 or 10. It's all about expectations, right? Seeing as the 10 most recent reviews of FabExpress Orange Suites were 10/exceptional it did not meet our expectations. We felt a 7 would be kind. We repeated our journey to Leopold Cafe. It was Sunday morning and it was packed, maybe on account of the Bombay marathon taking place that day. We strolled along Marine Drive and then took a train via Dhobi Ghat viewpoint (world's biggest outdoor laundry - worth a look) to Hahi Ali Dargah Mosque. Only we didn't get to the Mosque. The queues were like Wembley Way on match day. It was very, very, very busy.

Whilst on one of our strolls in Cappadocia in October we were asked for directions by a young Indian couple. We ended up having a chat, mainly about cricket, and swapped numbers, as you do. I thought I was passionate about cricket but I think Nikhil was on another level. The video he sent of him celebrating India beating Pakistan in the T20 World Cup was hilarious. I couldn't help but tease him when England tonked India in the semi-final. He took it well and offered to buy Aggers a new sari (she doesn't have an old one) and to take us to the finest seafood restaurant in Mumbai should England beat Pakistan and we were ever to visit his home city. Well we did both. He and his wife, Dhwani didn't take us to the finest seafood restaurant in Mumbai but they did take us to the

Bombay Presidency Golf Club. It was incongruously situated amid a busy, poor area of the city: such a vivid contrast between life outside the golf club and inside. Nikhil had to lend me a pair of trousers to get past the no shorts rule. Absurd. My dress shorts were quite smart but unacceptable: slip some tracksuit bottoms over them = welcome sir. We enjoyed a most pleasant evening, with some tasty food, Indian gin, but most importantly, the company of this very nice couple. For once, I was the one steering the conversation away from cricket.

Our second night at the FabExpress Orange Suites was rather unpleasant. In addition to the rat music, our room seemed to have become very popular with the mozzies. It didn't matter how many we terminated, more appeared. Consequently, we slept for about 3 hours. We could not establish where they were coming from but our review for this establishment was heading further south, towards the 5 mark. Rather jaded, we set off back to Mumbai Airport for our flight to Mopa, the brand-new airport in North Goa. As expected, it was a rather bland experience but the live band in the arrivals hall spiced things up a little. There was a new electric bus service to Panaji, capital of Goa state, which was pretty impressive and cheap, so on we hopped. Rather sacrilegiously, we visited neither Panaji nor Old Goa on our previous visit. We put that right this time. We stayed in a charming little guest house with 5 rooms, in the old, colonial section of Panaji, run by an older Goan couple who educated us on the latter stages of Portuguese rule and its legacy. This district of Panaji was very pleasing on the eye and we enjoyed some very tasty curries at last - £2.90 for 2 dishes and 4 breads - very kind on the budget and my stomach seemed to approve too. We took a bus the next morning to Old Goa and walked round the rather fabulous remains of it, consisting almost exclusively, from what we saw, of some splendid old churches, one of which is reputedly the largest in Asia.

We could have travelled all the way to South Goa from Mopa by electric buses, but there wasn't one due for the 40-minute ride to Margao/Madgaon from Panaji. We did catch one from Margao/Madgaon to Canacona though. No disrespect to India/

Goa but we were impressed. We're half way through our stay in Patnem and have done very little apart from walk the beaches, about 7 miles each day. That is other than meeting up with another friend who appreciated the lure of Goa. On what seems to have become an annual event - a Reigate hill stomp - my long-term walking friend Julia got quite excited when we said we would be off to India. So would she. Goa too. She would be staying with her friend on nearby Agonda beach - another splendid Goan beach. We enjoyed a couple of most pleasant evenings on the beach. Julia has one of those jobs I wouldn't mind - guiding train/rail enthusiasts around the world - so is never short of a story.

We could both see ourselves coming back here again one day. Maybe some other friends will be here. It's that pleasant. Not too much research to do at the moment for the rest of the trip. We mastered the online train booking system with a few frustrations. So, I've been writing and reading whilst Aggers, in between trying, very kindly, to research how I get round to publishing BID amongst other things, has been busy writing her review on the FabExpress Orange Suites. So now I'll get to the real reason why I've been banging on about this dump, and its reviews. Normally we would book via Booking.com on my account. Since BA have kindly been offering 8 Avios for every £1 spent on their link to Booking.com we have occasionally used Agnes' account. Once you've finished your stay via Booking.com they ALWAYS send an email for you to review the property. If you don't do so they send you a few reminders. I'm sure I said in BID that I'm not into reviews but I've changed. I particularly enjoy praising a place that others have slated. We do tend to go for establishments with no lower than 6, and preferably 7 out of 10, since we got a bit into reviews.

Agi asked me how she posted a review. She hadn't had an email. I suggested she contacted Booking.com. Imagine our surprise when they told her that she had already posted a review and to view it on the FabExpress Orange Suites pages on their website. Sure enough, there it was: Agnes, UK, 10, Exceptional!!! Not the worst case of identity theft or data breaching ever, but.......the cheeky bastards! And certainly not the first case of falsified reviews but our first experience. There's something pretty unsavoury about any establishment bigging themselves up, but to do it in other people's names, well, that's not just low, it's deceitful in the extreme. I'm not going to read all 848 reviews but the 10s seem quite a recent trend. The best bit is that they've even replied to some of their fake 10s with classic comments such as "thanks for taking time out to rate us.... " and "we would like to thank you for giving us such an amazing rating.....".

I was concerned that my initial feelings of anger and incredulity were turning to admiration for the bare faced cheek of it. I'm sure some of you will be saying, "come on A&A wake up and smell the coffee, this goes on all the time, kids", but as Alan Partridge says, " a lie is a lie". The trust has gone now. I think they've even posted the odd 1 about themselves to make people like us think, well 30 reviews giving a 10 must be right, over the 2 giving a 1. I may have been jumping to conclusions but I don't think so. I also jumped to the conclusion that Fab hotels weren't only posting fake reviews on this hotel alone but I really couldn't be bothered to look into it that much.

Which brings me onto Booking.com's response when we brought this matter to their attention: repeat last 10 words of previous sentence! Add on some prescripted drivel such as "have a nice day, sorry for any inconvenience, stay safe", a rather outdated "would like to wish you a happy new year" and the simply pathetic "take care in these unprecedented times". Move on. What's unprecedented about January 2023? Nothing. Same old. Perhaps look into the matter. Contact a bunch of the 10 givers and confirm whether they did genuinely find it "exceptional". There are a few genuine 3-5s with comments that must've slipped through the net. We had the time to not let this rest, so we vowed we wouldn't (we did). They needed to remove the hotel from their listings. I didn't think a yellow card was sufficient. Straight red! Ban them for 3 months. Agnieszka did manage to change her review: This hotel posted a fake review with a score 10 under my name! I had to make an effort to change the review. I would guess that all reviews without comments and with high scores are fake, and made by the hotel!!! It's a disgrace and we have reported them to Booking.com. Very unwelcoming reception staff, hopeless on-line payment procedure which results in the hotel threatening to cancel your confirmed booking (also reported to Booking.com), room full of mosquitos, rats crawling all over the roof of our room and in the kitchen, is the reality. Admittedly, it was very handy for the airport but that is the only plus. We barely slept the second night due to the mosquitoes and rats. AVOID - untrustworthy and dishonest.."

With a score of 1 (you can't do 0!). It is preceded by 12 straight 10s and currently followed by 2 exceptional 10s.

I had a sneaky suspicion that Fab Hotels were not the only ones in India employing this underhand tactic to increase business. We're off on our travels next week so I'll keep you posted. If Booking.com didn't come up with a reasonable resolution we planned to take our story to the popular daily which is the Metro. We finally achieved our ambition, well mine not Agi's, of recognition in my favourite rag. On Boxing Day, no less, we featured in their on-line edition. I think it was the best article yet as it mentioned all 4 obsessions and focused equally on pubs and airports, as we do. There was no paper edition for 2 weeks over Xmas/New Year so I still had that to aim for in 2023.

Such was the success of this article, thankfully we had no idea as it didn't seem you could leave comments, that we even had a follow up piece on the start of this current trip. This appeared ahead of yet another story on Prince Harry. Famous or what!? Not too sure how the bottles of beer would have gone down in the collage of Saudi Arabia pictures but I reckoned the Metro would have loved a fake review story (it seemed they didn't, as it happened!). We were becoming media whores but we didn't care. In the meantime, we planned to lap up the rest of our lazy days in Patnem before our short tour of South India.

# CHAPTER 21

It is good to be back on the road. I didn't feel that sentiment immediately for 2 reasons: we were just loving our lazy time on the beach in Patnem and could, quite easily, have turned our 1 week of doing very little, into 1 month. The idea of what constitutes a best beach is very subjective and must take into consideration many criteria. That's why all these "10 best beaches in the world" articles are BS in my humble opinion. We both consider ourselves very fortunate to have visited some absolute stunners in our time. You don't have to leave the British Isles to see some beauts. You can even find most folks' idea of the idyllic beach - crystal clear, turquoise waters with unblemished white sand stretching for miles in good old blighty. Admittedly that crystal clear, turquoise water is close to freezing but that's why you've got a good chance of having the place to yourself.

We've done our share of those far-flung stunning, deserted beaches in the past but feel for a longer stay we want a choice of places to eat and drink at nice prices. The sand is not perfect at Patnem, the water is far from crystal clear. In fact, the unusual presence of a bunch of jellyfish put us off going fully into the sea. But, the backdrop and scenery in general is idyllic as was the climate. The beaches are fabulous for walking and offer variety. It's quiet, but not too quiet. At the moment, we certainly think that, if we're looking for more beach time in the winter we may look no further. Very out of character. Is this what not having an addictive collection will result in?

I'm not sure if the 2nd reason is part of the first really: I just felt a bit sad to be leaving Patnem, because of the above. Did I feel I was getting older? Not really. Was my travel enthusiasm waning? No. What I could only put it down to, this 2nd reason for not buzzing about leaving, was that I'd decided to add an unseasonal cough and cold to my ailments. Very rare for me. Agnes had it when we left for Vienna. Had I taken this long to catch it from her? I very much doubt it. Anyway, that's all a bit boring isn't it?

After a long day yesterday; 13 1/2 hours, travelling not very far: 150 miles, my enthusiasm is back though. Even whilst it was being tested yesterday, we marvelled at how many passengers our bus conductor managed to squeeze in. Is it much different from a packed Victoria Line tube? Probably not, but it was impressive nonetheless. Our 7-hour train ride to Miraj Junction was painless enough apart from the most horrendous stink of pure pooh which came and went too regularly for my constitution. The open nature of the carriage failed to disperse it. At one point I started to wonder if I was the guilty party.

On a lighter note, when I returned from a brief leg stretch, I found a lady occupying my seat opposite Aggers. She had approached Aggers for a chat. Problem was she spoke and understood little English, but she wobbled a good head and smiled a lot. She did vacate my seat but pretty promptly asked if she could share Agnes'. We'd chatted the limited chat for a while and were encountering a few silences so we figured we were done. She probably didn't understand Aggers, when she politely said that she had some writing to do. Unperturbed, or oblivious, she almost sat on Agi, rather than next to her. She wasn't tall at all, but there was plenty of her! This action was met with hilarious laughter from her 4 travelling companions. It felt like, maybe, she was doing it for a dare. We sat, mainly in smiling silence, for about half an hour, before she decided to give Agi her space back and move back to her own seat.

For those of you not familiar with Indian train travel I'll try to describe our carriage: for the princely sum of around £2 each we had booked non a/c sleeper class - I think the most common. This train was making a 29-hour journey so the horizontal position would clearly be desirable at times. The layout is 3 layers facing each other on one side of the gangway and 2 in the direction of the train, on the other side, repeated in an open carriage. It can feel a bit claustrophobic, but actually in our, admittedly limited, experience, there seems to be a lot of spare seats, even though availability is very limited on the booking website. Food and drink vendors constantly pass through with many offerings, although we've yet to be tempted. We had no need to use our upper bunk, so converted the lower bunk into 2 facing seats, pretty handy really.

We climbed slowly, but steadily, from Margao station. The scenery was pretty impressive, with one waterfall, striking in particular. Once things flattened out it was a fairly uninspiring journey. There was no direct train from Margao to Kolhapur, our destination, so we had to change at Miraj Junction for the last hour of the journey. Indian Railways (IRTC) website does not allow booking of more than one sector so it was their fault, not mine, that I booked the connecting journey for the next day. If I could have made the booking as one, it wouldn't have happened. I may have blamed them but couldn't be bothered to see if I could get a refund before I made another new booking for the correct, same day, connection. Aggers was concerned that I may be becoming a little careless with our money. I had wasted a £1. Or rather IRTC had taken a £1 off me for their mistake.

I didn't think it would've been a problem to try and use the original ticket, but for the sake of a quid? As it was, when we pulled into Miraj 15 minutes early I spotted a train opposite with a board on the side including Kolhapur in its routing. Only problem was that before we could ascertain whether it had come from Kolhapur or was going, it gave one long blast of its horn and was off. We fancied jumping over the tracks and hopping onto a moving train Indian style, enabling a pretty impressive 30 second, seamless connection, but not if it was heading in the wrong direction. So we headed out into downtown Miraj, treated ourselves to a few snacks and caught a train scheduled 40 minutes before the one we had tickets for. We were very surprised that our tickets had not once been checked on the long ride from Margao to Miraj. From memory, they had always been checked numerous times 3 years ago.

What was happening to bureaucracy in IRTC? We weren't surprised therefore, when there was no ticket check on the shorter, commuter-like hop to Kolhapur.

Our overnight accommodation in Kolhapur restored our faith somewhat in Booking.com reviews and Indian hoteliers' integrity. A small, 5 room, family-run affair did what it said. The critter on reception was such a sweet young chap. I don't wish to sound condescending but I'm not sure a British version of such a person exists. He was delighted to inform us that 1 room was occupied by an English man, who would be staying 4 nights. I know we tend to cut our time in places quite short but 4 nights in Kolhapur? It's not a bad town/city at all, seemed quite well to do in places, but it only had one sight worthy of mention in LP. It just so happened that when we decided to leave for our visit to Mahalaxmi Temple, our fellow Brit Richard, was just setting off too. Our receptionist could probably do a reasonable job working for a dating agency. He paired us up (I know, that's not totally accurate as we were a threesome but you get my drift) in a way that it felt that we had no choice.

We stopped for a fab breakfast on the way, the largest dosa we'd ever encountered, and it turned out Richard was Welsh actually. One of the more two-sided conversationalists we've encountered recently. He's been coming to India for 3-6 months every winter for the last 40 years, bar Covid years. Very relaxed guy who looked my age to me, but had a decade on me. We headed off to the temple and quickly regained our celebrity status of 3 years past. We'd had a few selfie requests so far, but now it was in full swing. Richard, who we bumped into several times, admitted that he felt deflated one day, on his travels, when he didn't get a single request.

Kolhapur had some other fine architecture to admire but by midday, we were off to achieve the sole aim of our visit. I had figured that the new terminal due to be open would have been delayed by Covid but turns out it's still a shell. Kolhapur needs it but for us, we were happy we could still utilise the tiny old terminal, together with procedures that felt like you were in a time tunnel too. Multiple checks of documents, even 2 security checks.... for a domestic flight. I counted no less than 14 ground staff surrounding the Indigo ATR72-600 as we boarded. That's roughly 1 per 5 pax ratio. Our friends in Europe would be more like 1 per 50! What did they all do?

Now I'm into the nervous 90s. That's only going to resonate if you're a cricket follower. Agnieszka is still a couple behind and, as a non-cricketer and altogether more relaxed collector, will not feel this anxiety. For you non cricket types, the "nervous 90s" refers to a batsman when he has a score of between 90-99 and he is heading for 100. If you know so little about cricket that that still leaves you blank, you could either get a friend to explain further, or move on, as I'm about to. I'm actually not nervous about just having taken off from Kolhapur putting me on 990 and being close to landing in Tirupati taking me to, yes you've guessed, 991. Many batsmen claim they don't suffer from the nervous 90s. Also I think only one cricketer, a young Indian chap, quite recently, could claim to have been in the nervous 990s (I'm gonna have to check that when we're down on the ground). He may be the only one to have had nervous 490s upwards. In cricketing terms I believe we are primarily talking about the 90s, rather than 190s up. I'm on my own then. We have room for delays/cancellations through the 990s/490s and the airports we have planned do not have high terrain or suffer from adverse weather frequently. So, all is calm for now.

We had our first negative encounter on this trip on arrival in Tirupati (yes, there was a young Indian cricketer who scored an unbelievable 1009 not out, when he was 15 1/2 years old, 7 years ago). Tirupati has its new terminal, and quite pleasant it is too. Like most Indian airports we've encountered though, it's not memorable. It's a way from the city and with no rickshaws in sight, we tried Uber. It still amazes me how the rickshaw drivers in India are on it. This guy accepted our request but whilst not busy, Tirupati's access road and parking areas have been built for future expansion so he couldn't find us. He was shouting away in Hindi or Tamil to Aggers on the phone, which was a bit pointless. We spotted him so all was good.... for now. He kept jabbering away, the whole trip, about what, we know not, but he became more and more animated, bordering on aggressive.

When we got to our "hotel" he demanded cash. My phone was telling me that Uber had taken £3.50 on my Amex for the ride. I wasn't paying him twice. We took an instant dislike to him, for starters. We beckoned him into the hotel where we hoped the receptionist would speak English. She was charming, mild-mannered and softly spoken. She felt obliged to apologise for the behaviour of her fellow countryman. He was shouting at her in just the same manner as he did to us. Turns out he didn't want to wait a week for the money to come through via Uber. Why didn't he say!? He probably did 25 times. We were bored with this fight now. Of course, he didn't have any change, but, out of principle, I wasn't giving him a 40% tip. Luckily, our friendly receptionist helped out. He ran off without a word. Miserable git.

Tirupati was crazily busy and noisy even by Indian standards. Obviously, we primarily came to tick off the airport but we were also rather interested in experiencing the chaos that was guaranteed at not just India's, but one of the globe's largest pilgrimage destinations. Venkateshwara Temple is the biggy for those of the Hindu persuasion. Apparently 60,000 devotees pass through daily. It's one of those places that sound rather complicated when you read about it, but the reality is fairly straightforward. There are 3 ways to reach the temple, situated on top of Tirumula Hill. You can be lazy and take a bus or drive to the top - possibly not a bad idea if you're queuing anywhere between 3-8 hours for your 1 minute, if you're lucky, with the avatar of Vishnu. Alternatively the real pilgrimage starts in 2 places at the foot of the hill. Alipiri Metlu is a steady 12 km hike, which we discovered on the bus back down, spends a lot of its route by the busy road. We opted for Srivari Metlu. Officially this route starts with a boring 9 km walk on a road. One can, and we did, skip this by taking a bus to the start of the climb up. After all, as an atheist, I could hardly be claiming to be making a pilgrimage. I fancied the 2388 steps that then took you to the top. I convinced Aggers that we needed the exercise.

There really weren't all that many pilgrims taking this route. I'd say we encountered less than 100. We reached the top in an hour which wasn't bad going. Now to go and see what all the fuss was about. Foreigners and Indians with a spare £3, can go fast track. It all reminded me a bit of Alton Towers/Thorpe Park/ Disney Land etc.. However, first we had to leave our flip flops at the entrance, nowhere near the exit. Once we had walked through the Disney-style walkways and parted with our 300 rupees for fast track, we were then told that we had to hand over our mobiles, which would be taken to, and waiting for us, at the exit.

Now kids, you're not the only ones who don't like to be parted from your phones. I've often remarked on how we managed to organise our travels without them, back in the day, but I didn't really fancy reverting to 80s style travelling. I've become too dependent on my camera, music (not that I listen much), books, maps etc all fitting in my pocket, with space to spare. I didn't have a good feeling about this but how did we get back out now, if we aborted, for starters? I don't like queuing at the best of times but now I couldn't even write to you, dear reader, while I remained stationary for far too long for my liking.

We were given a receipt for our phones, which were placed in a box with about 50 others. I got over myself relatively quickly and after a while we were lucky enough to fall in line with a couple of English-speaking locals. Things got a bit squashy when the freebies joined in with the queue jumpers like us. Our new friends said that those not able or willing to spare £3 had been queuing since 6 am!! We started at 1230. As we gradually shuffled towards the temple entrance for our turn, it became noisier and noisier. Where there had been no staff now there was an abundance, shouting at the pilgrims to keep moving. We didn't need to assume as they shouted in English as well when they saw us. We didn't have a prayer to say but surely for everyone else who did, it was such a noisy, rushed experience. Imagine you've been queuing for 7 hours, you're finally getting your moment, whilst being jostled and shouted out. I don't think I'll ever get religion.

After we'd queued to get out (the whole experience had taken 2 hours, plus the hour up the 2388 steps), not only were we reunited with our phones but also our footwear. We were quite proud of ourselves that we had managed to navigate the process. Call me a heathen, I am, but it so reminded me of the aforementioned theme parks. Obviously there were streets of shops selling all kinds of tat, which we had avoided on our spiritual climb. There were several cranes on site and tons of scaffolding so the overall ambience and scenic value was low. Mind you, I'm certain that's irrelevant to the pilgrims. We much preferred the magnificent temple in Thanjavur, not that we knew that at the time.

We were not disappointed to be leaving Tirupati early the next morning. It's a mess and like many towns and cities we were to pass through on our journey south, blighted further by huge, nowhere near completed, flyovers. We had booked a rather unsociable 0515 train to Bangalore, which became even less palatable when it was delayed 1 hour. The sea of humanity at 0430 in the morning had to be seen to be believed. We could not understand why some folk were coming down the up escalator. Only when we looked up to the bridge could we see that their route to the nearest stairs was blocked solid.

IFYRBID, you may recall our fabulous chance meeting with Lt Col Sudhir Philipose in the northern backwaters of Kerala, which resulted in us spending 2 blissful nights in his "shack" on the most delightful stretch of untouched beach - apart from the naval base 5 miles south! Well, Sudhir had told us he had a villa on the outskirts of Bangalore, close to the airport, should we ever need a place to crash. Well, we did. Of course, we could stay but unfortunately, Lt Col was down entertaining in his "shack" in Kerala. As it transpired Spicejet decided to cancel our flight to 992/490 so we ended up spending 48 hours at the colonel's rather than 24. It was an oasis of calm. We both admitted that we felt the need to escape the bedlam of your average Indian town/city more frequently than 3 years ago.

We may as well have been in Florida, for example, or at least an Indian version. Sudhir's villa was indeed a villa, in a gated community, together with his live in "Man Friday" (and wife) - Sudhir's words, not mine. It was very, very peaceful. Not many of the villas appeared to be occupied. It soon dawned on us that this was an ex-military compound. In addition to the colonels' villas there were also blocks of flats which would have been for the foot soldiers, we assumed. The weather was utterly idyllic. Sudhir invited us to sample his upstairs and downstairs liquor mini bars, which we did, both evenings, without taking the proverbial. Leeds managed not to lose to Accrington Stanley in the FA Cup so, together with some super cuisine in the "officers' mess", our Spicejet enforced day off at Sudhir's was all rather pleasant. It was just a shame that he wasn't there to add to the entertainment and give us the stories behind some of the more bizarre artefacts adorning his hideaway. We couldn't be sure but it seemed that the colonel may have been living there full time, rather than in his other house in Bangalore, the marital home. Maybe we will find out one day.

We took advantage of our free time to devise a rough plan for the remainder of our India jaunt. Well, that was Agi's task, while I planned 995/495-999/499. I had a plan, I even booked some of it. To my horror, I realised, when I booked the second flight, that the first flight I booked was for 20 March instead of 20 February! How the f--k did I manage that? Fortunately, only £50 was at stake but I was gutted, obviously. Naturally, I'd booked the cheapest ticket, with no changes, cancellation, non-refundable, etc. There was a glimmer of hope: when booking with trip.com, as I had, there is a gap, normally, of around 15-20 minutes between booking confirmation and ticket issue. If I could get hold of them before ticket issue, maybe they would have mercy on me. The clock was ticking but, after a couple of failed attempts I got a human and it took her time, but she did. I would receive an email very soon, confirming the refund. Thank you very much.

Shortly, I received an email from trip.com confirming the tickets had been issued! I thought it was too good to be true.

Long story short, I called them again and got the refund. I may have told this story before, not this one, but the one I'm about to tell you. You see, the problem I'm having now is I don't know if I've actually written an anecdote, these days, or if I've just told it so many times it feels like I may have written it in addition to the numerous times I've told it. As I'm not digressing in this book, I have to tell you instead, a related anecdote: my friend Mark had booked a ski trip to France for himself, one of his daughters, myself and my youngest daughter, back in 2015. About a week before we were due to leave, my eldest daughter, fresh from splitting from her fella asked if she could join us. We only had a room for 4 but Mark was OK with it, if Jordan (eldest daughter) was prepared to take a risk. After a successful drive down we arrived at our hotel. Mark and I would go and check in, then we would try and smuggle number 5: Jordan, into the room, at some point. "Mr Doyle, I'm so sorry, your booking is for 12 March, not 12 February and we are fully booked". The receptionist was so apologetic, she seemed like she was taking the blame for it. Mark was basically saying, "how the f--k did I manage that!?" He was very upset with himself.

Even though the receptionist was very concerned that we wouldn't find anywhere to stay as it was half term, I just found the situation rather amusing and pretty much took pleasure in informing the 3 daughters that it wasn't only Jordan who would be looking for somewhere to stay. Mark was a bit shell-shocked and had gone into neutral. I asked the receptionist if she had any suggestions for accommodation in other villages/towns nearby. She said that the hotel owner had a chalet on the edge of town which was vacant but that she thought it would be rather pricey for us. It was. 2,500 euros for 5 nights, her boss informed her. From memory we had paid around 900 euros for 5 nights for 1 room in the hotel. I asked her to put it to her boss that we could either give him 900 euros, or his chalet could remain empty. Reluctantly he agreed. What a result. Rather than Jordan worrying whether she would have a bed to sleep in, she now had a choice of which bedroom she wanted in our 5-bedroom bastard chalet.

The place was huge. We looked faintly ridiculous, the 5 of us at our dinner table for 12. No such negative becoming a huge positive with my flight booking error, but problem solved. I reckon it's the February curse, being 28 days mostly, the days of the week correspond with March. That's my excuse and maybe Mark's too.

All was well as our 992/490 took off from Bangalore 15 minutes early, or 23 hours 45 minutes late, depending on how you look at it. Pondicherry was a very peaceful little airport and a breath of fresh air after Bangalore. Actually, for a biggy, Bangalore is quite nicely laid out but it's busy. We fancied Pondicherry on our last trip but ran out of time. Being a former French colony it offered something different from the rest of India in the old colonial area - some fabulous old buildings and one of the nicest cappuccinos we've had in a while. We had considered 2 nights there before the flight cancellation but as it happened, 1 gave us ample time to see the sights.

Trains in this part of India are a bit sparse so we had little choice but to take a couple of buses to our next formerly European-run enclave, about 4 hours south. Tranquebar, or Tharangambadi as it's now supposed to be called, was run and inhabited by the Danish, until they sold it to the Brits in the mid-1800s. It had a nice old gate, a pretty impressive fort and a few charming old buildings but it all felt very run down. It was only once we had returned to our bang average overnight establishment that I remembered reading that the poor old dear took a bit of a hammering in the 2004 tsunami. I felt a bit rotten for chastising the powers that be for not smartening the place up.

The next morning after a short, but unbelievably rammed, rush hour bus ride to Karaikal to continue for 3 1/2 hours onto Thanjavur/Tanjore we decided we were done with buses. Our last 3 drivers seemed to each increase the madness a tad. Karaikal to Thanjavur dude had 3 different horns, all painfully ear-splitting and used constantly. Only problem was that the train to Karaikudi was due to leave in an hour and a) we needed some nosebag badly and b) we weren't leaving without a visit to the Brihadeeswara Temple. Both were superb, the train was delayed by 1 hour 45 minutes (45 minutes would've been just right) and the train was bliss after the buses.

After a brief overnight on the outskirts of Karaikudi, we hopped on a rickshaw to nearby Kanadukathan, one of the main settlements of the Chettiar people. This is another unique, in our experience, part of India. We had treated ourselves to an upmarket hotel, we didn't have any choice if we wanted to stay in the village itself, and LP was very upbeat in its description of the Chettinadu region. Manage your expectations, as Aggers often repeats to herself. Duly managed we were extremely happy with both our lodging and sightseeing. We were greeted by one of the best receptionists on all of our travels at the Chettinadu Court. I'm sure I've mentioned before how hosts, particularly Airbnb, and often, Couchsurfing, outrightly lie about their interest in meeting new people - that's what they may think, but the reality is regularly b*llocks. They either don't care at all, or just like to meet new people to talk at.

In addition, we regularly meet people in any given sector of the hospitality industry who are clearly in the wrong line of work. Well, let me just say that Miss Kavita was most definitely in the right job and she had had to really push herself to get into the prestigious position of a £4 per day receptionist. She came from a very low caste, started life as a chambermaid, waited 7 years for her future husband's parents to accept her and had learned her English solely from guests. She was a delight to spend time with: helpful, kind, informative, inquisitive, engaging (sorry, sounding like Alan Hansen, again). We learned a lot from her about the caste system in India which seems, particularly in more rural areas to be alive and (un)well, unfortunately. She learned from us that Polish people don't build igloos in the cold winter months.

We finally broke off this particular conversation, found that our room was worth the big bucks (£45 B&B), and that there were many more mansions, for which the Chettinadu region has gained "tentative" UNESCO Heritage status in 2014, than LP alluded to. It was most definitely worth the effort to get there.

The Indians, in general, are very friendly and try their best to help but the head wobbling coupled with the language barrier can be a little confusing. Yes food is available, no it isn't? This bus, that bus? In this instance I'm about to relate, it was slightly different. Chettinadu Court, offered an off-site swimming pool close to its sister property, Chettinadu Mansion. We wandered down to Chettinadu Mansion, a wonderful old building. They directed us to the pool. We couldn't find it. We went back and asked again. We found what we thought could be a pool, hiding behind a large locked gate. We went back again. "Ah, you want key?". Well that might help. We went for our 4th trip. It was only 200 metres each way or so, but even though it was cloudy, it was stiflingly hot. Armed with the key, in we went. The pool was almost half empty, the water green. Apart from a few relatively fresh looking towels the pool looked like it hadn't seen any action in a very long time. It would've been quite a pleasant spot if it received a bit of TLC. It was all quite amusing really. We were having a slow day and had time to spare. News travels fast in Chettinadu. When we returned the key the manager was waiting for us. He assured us that the pool had been used the previous day and would be ready again in a couple of hours. We believed him on neither count. He reckoned the pump was on and cleaning the water as we spoke. I'm no expert, but I did inherit a pool of a similar size for a decade or so, and that pump was most definitely not on and had it been, the water level was way too low for it to circulate. We weren't bothered but I planned to go and have another nose around the next morning after breakfast, just out of curiosity. Unfortunately, the gods had decided to help with filling the pool, with non-stop, unseasonal rain, all the following day. The pool would likely have filled up but I'm sure the water would've remained a pretty unpalatable colour.

We were grateful that we had seen all the sights, and for Chettinadu Court's ample umbrellas, as we headed off to the mansion for breakfast. It was lucky for us that it was a travelling day - 3 buses to our next stop, Rameswaram. This is another of the most important pilgrimages for Hindus. For us we were intrigued by the thin strip of land that continued on to the deserted town of Dhanushkodi (wiped out by a cyclone in 1964) and onwards to within 30 kms of Sri Lanka. Whilst so many town and main roads remain in a state of disrepair, some dude/s had authorised a brand-new road to Arichal Munai, the furthest point on this strip of land, almost 30 kms from Rameswaram. We hired a rickshaw for the morning. It seemed a good idea as the road was mainly deserted and void of any buses. It was therefore, slightly surprising to find 100s of people at Arichal Munai.

Although they seemed to be enjoying the ocean and beach, the spot supposedly has religious meaning to them as one of their gods apparently built a bridge to Sri Lanka. The weather had perked up and was improving by the minute. Finally we had some lovely turquoise sea to stroll by. The constant roadside rubbish was present but not in the normal quantities. Have a look at the map and you'll see just how thin this strip of land is. For us, it was well worth the effort to get there. We feared we would miss it due to the weather and we would have done if Spicejet hadn't knocked us back 24 hours.

I don't wish to sound mean but, as I've mentioned previously, walking in Indian towns and cities is a hazardous pastime. Looking down, left, right, behind, ahead and up simultaneously, is too much multitasking for me. Add in a good downpour and it becomes treacherous. Rameswaram was an absolute mess when we arrived. Never had we seen so much city wildlife: the most cows, pigs, goats and dogs in the potholed streets. Consequently, the most shit! It was difficult to distinguish shit from general mud but we needed to eat. I'm not sure if it's down to the walking style or the flip flops but within minutes the backs of Aggers' legs and her dress looked like she'd been practising her slide tackles at 70s Maine Road, Baseball Ground, Upton Park etc, whilst I was 21st century Elland Road, not a drop of mud on me.

Being a pilgrimage city, loads of the locals were wandering around barefoot in the muck. Mind you, we may as well have been. The rain stopped long enough for us to have a gander and get some pretty decent scran. We decided not to risk leaving the bus journey to 993/491 to the morning of said flight, even though the departure time was 1515 and the bus journey approximately 200 kms. Besides, we'd seen what we wanted to, and we didn't have time to hit Kanyakumari, the southernmost point of India, due to the extra day chez Sudhir. It was just as well as the bus took almost 5 hours to cover the 200 kms. You know me well enough by now, to imagine the level of panic that would have manifested in me, as the clock ticked on that ride.

Tuticorin/Thoothukudi doesn't get a mention in LP. It wasn't difficult to understand why. Apart from a total lack of cows, and I mean none, and temples and a strangely high number of Catholic churches I have nothing to add. We did experience one of the more attentive waiters for our evening meal. He didn't appear to want to leave our table and, at one point, seeming to wish to justify his presence, he repositioned the sauce bottle by, literally, less than half an inch. Not sure that that information would interest any LP readers, or you, for that matter, but we found it quite amusing. We did hope there wouldn't be a need to evacuate our hotel during the night. Having so little opportunity to walk, we wanted to take the stairs to our 4th floor room. The steps to floor 1 were pretty clear, not so to floor 2, but we managed to slither between the obstacles. From floor 2 to 3 we had a mattress blocking our way. Agnes insisted I climb over it first; in case any rats had set up home. 3 to 4 was literally impassable. We took the lift. There was only one emergency exit sign and sure enough, it pointed us to the staircase we'd just abandoned.

Tuticorin Airport - it's funny how most Indians still use the old city names and not the new ones - is about 16 kms out of the city, so we decided to hop on a bus. We've done pretty well so far, getting pointed in the right direction for each bus we've needed first time. For some unknown reason it seemed very difficult for the locals to stick us on the bus which passed the airport turn off. 5th time lucky and we were finally off. With perfect timing we completed the 15-minute walk to the old terminal, just as the heavens opened again. Tuticorin's new terminal was due to open next month but it looks like they're several years behind schedule. The old terminal is only 30 years old but it's quite cute from the outside; very leafy. The new terminal is so far away it doesn't even look like you could reach it from the same runway.

Our 2-hour transfer in Bangalore went without a hitch and when we touched down in Coimbatore, my numbers for this trip were complete. Normally, I try to avoid arriving at a new airport at night, as you may recall, but I'd come to the conclusion that in India, it didn't matter too much. The life size figures of elephants and other wildlife in baggage reclaim provided ample photo opportunities. Indeed it will probably make Coimbatore stay in our memories longer than just another rather bland airport exterior shot.

Our purpose to come to Coimbatore, other than the glaringly obvious, was to visit some of the hill stations favoured by the British Raj and accessible, in a couple of hours, from Coimbatore. The 3 main towns/cities vary in altitude between 1700-2200m above sea level. It was a beautiful climate during the day but pretty cold at night, as was our welcome at JSS Cottages in Coonoor. We had chosen this homestay as the room offered a mountain view and was out of town, in a very quiet location up in the hills. It turned out that the only positive about this place was the setting. It's only a 5-room joint and pretty much resembles someone's home, with a pretty garden.

So..... when we arrived the manageress (we quickly learned that it was she, or she was it) on seeing us come through the gate, scuttled inside. Where was that familiar Indian welcome and smile? Non-existent in this instance, it transpired. It was having a day off for 24 hours. As this place really did fit into the Fawlty Towers category let's call her Sybil. Sybil looked utterly bemused, even perplexed that we had made a booking and wished to check in. She reluctantly showed us to a miserable room with a brick wall view. "Excuse me, where's our mountain view, family room we booked?" "Occupied!" "Well, we booked a mountain view room, so what's your solution?" She didn't have one. If she had just the faintest smile I may have just accepted what we were given, but she had attitude. "This room is not acceptable, it's not what we booked and paid for". She showed us to another room which was slightly less dingy but with a similar window onto brick wall outlook. We accepted it. We didn't want to waste time faffing about. She said the owner would call us, from Chennai.

Basil did call us, "you only paid 2000 rupees (£20), if you don't like it, find somewhere else". Now, that attitude really gets up my nose. Maybe a little apology? Maybe admit you're in the wrong? Maybe even offer a wee refund or dinner on the house (it was advertised as £2pp)? No such thing. "Look Basil, don't pull that one on me. We're only here 24 hours and we're not wasting it, resolving your incompetence. I concede defeat, you win. Can we order dinner with you as Sybil may be able to speak English, she may even understand it but she doesn't comprehend a single word I'm saying?" We were very specific with our order; he repeated it back.

After a very pleasant afternoon visiting a tea plantation and taking one of our longer walks in India, admiring the splendid scenery, we received a phone call from Basil. "Where are you? You ordered dinner at 6. The staff are waiting." It was 6.02 and we were about 30 metres away. Dinner, well what there was of it, arrived just after 6.30. We ordered 2 mushroom masalas, vegetable rice and 2 bread. We got enough plain rice for 4 adults, 1 child's portion of masala and one bread. "Please could we have the other masala and bread we ordered?" "No!" "OK thanks". The fun didn't end there. Whilst I was watching Leeds succumb to defeat, via WhatsApp link with my mate Justin, Aggers came into the room giggling. She had gone to the room we had originally been offered, to borrow the quilt in there to add to ours as it really was chilly. To her amusement there was a rather large pair of ladies' black knickers at the bottom of the bed.

Now, I'm no chambermaid but I fail to see how if you have replaced a white quilt cover and white sheet from the previous occupant with the very same, a black (on white) pair of extra-large knickers would not catch your eye. Would it be wrong of us to assume that the bedding had not been changed? It was time to retire to the slab of concrete masquerading as a mattress under our quilts and humour ourselves on the worst experience of hospitality we had experienced in either of our Indian travels.

To be fair, what food we did have, including breakfast in the garden, was pretty tasty but we weren't quite done with Sybil. Our booking confirmation informed us that JJS accepted credit cards. Of course they didn't. I was 90p short. As we planned to walk back into Coonoor I told Sybil she could either follow us to the nearest ATM or accept my 2200 rupees. Our final bill included dinner hence the cost was 2290. She was very non-committal, so after breakfast I asked her, yet again, for a decision. "Have you ordered rickshaw to take you to ATM to get cash?" Really? You think I'm going to pay extra for your failings? You may think I sound like a right old pompous git, but she was really rather unpleasant. When I had asked her if she didn't mind to clean the sticky muck off the bedside table, she looked at me with an expression that indicated that I was asking her to clear up a pooh I'd just deposited there. She got on the phone to the equally unpalatable and aggressive Basil again. I'd had enough. I wasn't about to enter into an argument with him over 90p. I gave her our 2200 rupees and bade her farewell.

Contrast this with the attitude of a tea seller we had encountered the previous afternoon. We had sampled chocolate tea at the plantation and very tasty it was too. We wanted to take some of that and the even tastier masala tea home with us. Problem was, everywhere only sold 1/2kg bags of the stuff. Far too much for our little hand luggage. Having offered us tastings of 3 different kinds of tea, he then kindly prepared 2 bags of probably 150g each and refused to take a single rupee off us. To insist he did, was clearly going to cause offence. All he wanted was a few selfies with us outside his new and very smart premises.

We had taken 2 buses up from Coimbatore to Coonoor. We continued uphill by buses via Kotagiri to Ooty/Udhagamandalam. Ooty is a lot easier I'd say and that's probably why the locals still use that name rather than Udhagamandalam. We had booked the train back from Coonoor to Mettupalayam but managed to blag a couple of seats from Ooty. This railway is quite well known, as it should be. It covers an altitude difference of almost 2000 metres over, I think, a 50kms stretch. That's some climbing or descending, even for non-train buffs, of which there was a handful, of non-Indian descent. It takes about 3 hours going down and almost 5 going up. We swapped from a diesel engine to a rather posh and modern looking steam one about half way down. Fill your boots, spotters.

The next morning a 5-hour train journey took us to Cochin/Kochi, our final stop and our departure point homeward bound. Apart from the filth on the floor, the frequently overpowering toilet stench and our first cockroach infestation it was a pleasant enough journey, but we were ready to get off and were done with Indian Railways, for now. By the way, in case you're interested or wondering; the train from Ooty consisted of 4 very busy, short, compact, carriages. Contrast this with our 22-carriage monster to Cochin.

We both really liked Cochin, a bit of India Lite really, particularly on the island where Fort Kochi is situated. A lot of history, nice restaurants, little bit touristy in places but very palatable and a very pleasant conclusion to this mini-Indian adventure. Had anything really changed in the 3 years since our previous visit? We didn't think so and we do think it won't be our last visit. IYRBID I finished the India chapters with a story about our last host in Chennai - a rather interesting character. So, I'm going to do the same this time. The rather un-Indian named Clinton Jackson regaled us with how he had travelled the world. Born and bred in Cochin he was working in the port when, at the age of 19, he decided to stowaway on a Greek cargo vessel. Little did he know that it was to very nearly cost him his young life. He wasn't discovered until 7 days later, off the coast of Mozambique, in which time he had had no water whatsoever, let alone food. Once recovered in the on-board medical facility, the ship's captain was more than happy to have another pair of hands on deck. So began his 6-year career in the merchant navy. That's the very short version of Clinton's fascinating life story so far. He's in his late 60s now (government pension £10 per month!!) and runs a delightful homestay with his charming, but sadly deaf for the last 15 years, wife. Together with the, if possible, even tastier cuisine we consumed, a feeling of sadness at leaving prevailed over the occasional desire to get out of India due to the noise, chaos, grubbiness, etc found in many cities.

Cochin airport was new for Aggers. It felt new for me too. I had no recollection of my previous visit about 18 years ago. I had to double check Wikipedia that it wasn't different to the one on my list, my suspicion raised due to its very out of city location. It had actually opened 10 years prior to my notching it and, as bigger, newer airports go, the terminal was really quite characterful. The seating at the gates was extraordinary: the kind of chairs you would have found in your granny's house in the early 70s. We did get a new airline in on our flight to Abu Dhabi: Air Arabia, and they also had very nice seats too, particularly for a low-cost carrier.

Our schedule home involved a short overnight. The reason for our routing was a) obviously money but b) it conveniently brought Agi onto the same 90s as I. She booked what on paper, appeared to be a relatively convenient Airbnb not far from the airport. Our extremely helpful hostess offered to arrange a taxi for us. When it came down to the details the communication with the driver was anything but straightforward. He simply could not grasp our arrival and departure times. Maybe it was his level of English (it turned out it wasn't). Each time we gave him our details, he asked for them again, at least 4 times. Amazingly he did turn up at 1130pm and, no doubt encouraged by receiving payment if he did, returned at 5am the next morning. Our Airbnb turned out to be no less bizarre than our communication with our driver. It consisted of one single hospital bed and a sofa. Agnes was slightly perplexed when our hostess said she hoped it would be clean as the previous guest had not left until 4pm. It transpired that she had no intention of changing the bedding. Maybe that's the culture in the middle east and Indian Subcontinent, but not for us. She said she would go and change the bedding but what she actually did was give our driver, or instruct him to buy a brand-new quilt cover and pillowcase. To be fair, we were justified in insisting on fresh bedding as when we removed the old stuff, it seemed the previous occupant had deposited all her loose hair in the bed.

Anyway, it did the job and barring any major mishaps, we are an hour from landing at Tel Aviv Ben Gurion, cruelly denied to Agi by me on our visit to Israel 4 years ago, bringing her to 494 to my 994. All that remains is an onward flight to Krakow where we will go our separate ways. I have some serious planning, thinking and research to undertake before Agnes joins me a week later in blighty and we head off to the promised land of airports 500/1000.

# CHAPTER 22

Well, that journey did work but Tel Aviv provided a very good example of why some people hate airports. Of course, the security is a bit tighter there but inefficient? Firstly, we asked for and were directed to transit, only to reach it and be told that the transit facility had been closed since Covid. Surely security staff should know whether the transit facility is open or not? Did he seriously think we just wanted a butchers at a transit lounge which we couldn't use!?

We had 2 hours so no need to panic. We sailed through immigration and headed back through to security only to be told we hadn't completed pre-security, security checks. We returned to the aforementioned to be told we were in the wrong terminal. Wizzair informed us that our flight departed from T3, where we had arrived but, no, due to weather (!! It was bright and sunny) the authorities changed terminals at short notice. Damn good job that that transit option wasn't available after all! We needed to catch a bus to T1 which ran every 15 minutes and took 20 minutes. Things were getting a bit tight. We queued for pre-security but it was clear that, if we joined the massive real security queue, we would miss our flight. I was really pleasantly surprised as we excused ourselves and bypassed a good 100+ very patient passengers. Not one protested.

You know we won't give up collecting new airports but we will drastically reduce and, this kind of experience, we won't miss. Probably 80% of our fellow travellers bound for Krakow were orthodox Jews. Just to be absolutely clear, I am referring to the Tel Aviv airport experience as the one we will not miss. Atheist I certainly am, but neither of us are racists. How could you be when you roam the world? Way too hypocritical. So, what an interesting lot they are, the orthodox Jews. They certainly were in no hurry to depart. It really did take the crew an eternity to convince them that, if we were to go anywhere, they would need to sit down. They finally did and off we went. Agi and I said our farewells in Krakow and I continued onto Luton solo. It felt quite weird not having her by my side. We are really blessed that we are able to spend virtually every minute together in harmony and happy, months on end. Sorry, I hope that's not too slushy for you.

Maybe those 2 paragraphs should be in the previous chapter but that's a decision for another day. Right now, we're having a ruddy good time in Morocco and are already in the latter stages of the nervous 90s. We had a plan to get to 499/999 in Morocco, then head to New Orleans for the biggies, as you may recall. This was on the premise that Jim the pilot would manage to be the pilot on our chosen flight and, pretty much, guarantee us to travel and arrive in some comfort at an economy price. Well, not even an economy price. We used our Avios points, which meant we only paid £75 each for the flight. Unfortunately, long story short, this didn't work out. Jim the pilot, wasn't to be Jim the pilot, despite his best efforts, on this occasion. We saw little point in heading to New Orleans, much as we would like to, in early March, if our flight there wasn't to include a return to those comfy seats experienced so often in the past. That's for another day now. The punt cost us £140 in change and cancellation fees but.....you know the rest. In case you don't, in the grand scheme blah, blah, blah.

We had no dilemma with Malaysia Airlines. Much as they may have liked our story, not really that much I'm sure, they weren't interested in taking us to Long Banga on a complimentary basis. Neither of us had any strong feelings about a special airport for the special numbers. I had a fleeting interest in asking Stinky Penguin if he would like to fly us to, or from, Biggin Hill for the special occasion. Not very glamorous, I know, but we could have, and have, walked there and back from home. We went to an airshow there a few years back and I also worked there for a couple of weeks in 2018. I quite liked the idea, but Aggers was lukewarm, at best. There would be the small matters of weather, Stinky's and aircraft availability to consider. Maybe some other time.

I know you must be overwhelmed with curiosity and excitement as to which airport will take the honours but I can't tell you yet. We've done 995/6/7 and booked 998/9 but 500/1000 is still to be decided, although I think the decision is pretty much made. It is, but, as you can imagine, our indecisiveness is on its top game, so in the meantime let me tell you about 995/6/7 (can you please take it as read, from now on that 495/6/7 etc are obviously incorporated?).

After a most pleasant couple of days staying with a very hospitable friend of Aggers' and her family (the friend's family, not Aggers') in Barcelona we headed down to Oujda: 995. Oujda had long been on my hit list since we first visited Morocco together. I've mentioned our previous visits, I'm sure, but Oujda remained unvisited by us. Ryanair have been flying there and not so far away, Nador, for a long time and it would've worked as a long weekend double, only thing being that their flights are currently from Spain and France and I think rarely, if ever, from Stansted. Hence, we never made it before.

I had a tentative plan to then fly back to Spain from Nador and then return to Melilla to continue our Moroccan adventure. It amuses me that the Spanish, government at least, are so uptight about Gibraltar (known by all Poles I've ever met as Giblatar, or however they would spell it, which also amuses me) yet seem quite content to continue to have not 1, but 2, little enclaves of their own in Morocco.

I had a standby ticket to Melilla from Granada around 20-25 years ago, while I was busy adding Jerez (de la Frontera) to my list. Unfortunately, I had overlooked a family appointment, so in an, admittedly pretty rare, act of selflessness, or, as some would say, probably rightly getting my priorities in order, I flew back from Granada to London instead to fulfil my parental duties. Unlike Potosi and Puerto Plata, Melilla hasn't troubled me so much, as I only had the ticket, whereas I'd made it to the departure lounge of the others, as you may remember. Still,

I was keen on this option, until, that is I, slightly belatedly consulted Wikipedia for the list of Moroccan airports. Armed with that information, Skyscanner then provided some good examples of how we could reach our target, without popping back to Spain. I went into full planning mode. Royal Air Maroc (RAM) Express continued to offer a few rare double drops on their domestic routes, the first of which would be 996&7. If we didn't return to Spain, or disappear somewhere else, they offered 3 other double drops. For those of you wondering what I'm talking about, let me explain: if an airline, I'm assuming, doesn't think there's enough business to serve one route from a main base to a couple of smaller destinations, they will combine. For example, Dan Air used to fly Newcastle - Stavanger - Bergen - Newcastle, amongst others (in case any airline aficionados of a certain age are reading, I know we/they more regularly operated Newcastle - Stavanger - Bergen - Stavanger - Newcastle, but I like this example for sentimental reasons.). A bit of a nuisance for some passengers in either direction, but if you were on a return trip from Newcastle, it was fair enough as Bergen passengers would consider it an inconvenience outbound, and Stavanger, inbound, unless they just happened to be airport collectors. I'll be sure to detail RAM Express's offerings as time progresses. In the meantime......

We liked Oujda. LP wasn't too glowing about it but it certainly had enough for an afternoon and overnight to keep us occupied. We also liked the airport. The current terminal is very new and not bland at all. In fact, it looked a bit like a flying saucer. Apart from the fact that, on entering the terminal the Moroccan authorities presented everyone with a form to fill out but no pens, it was a nice start to our last airport inspired trip. Don't worry, I know that's almost certainly BS, but I'd like to continue to con myself for now. Besides, unless I find an excuse to write book 3, you'll never know if I'm cured, or not. Having filled in the form, they then didn't even give it a cursory glance. I only mention this because, having disembarked first, we didn't wish to then join a long queue for immigration. It's just as well we didn't, as the officer was certainly up there with the slowest we've encountered.

In keeping with our habit of avoiding jumping into an airport cab wherever possible, we strolled the mile or just less to the passing main road, in the absence of a public bus. Momentarily this seemed like the wrong call, as there was a distinct lack of buses or taxis eager for our business. Fear not. While we waited for the policeman at the, as we were to discover, very frequent checkpoints, to finish his phone conversation, a car screeched to a halt some 20-30 metres further along. We hadn't even put our thumbs out yet, as we wanted to check with Mr Plod if it was OK to do so. What followed would have fitted in perfectly to a mad, drug-filled, American road trip (Jack Kerouac style, I think), albeit, only a 20 kilometre one. Our driver and his mate were superb actors who should be snapped up by Hollywood, Bollywood or more appropriately, Ouallywood (that's the Moroccan version), if they weren't under the influence of some class As. The eyes were manic, the energy levels unusually high, speech loud and rapid, music pumping, but.....they were very friendly and extremely happy. 20 minutes was enough though. When we escaped from their hospitality, we were immediately reminded, if we needed to be, of just how totally different Morocco is to its nearby European neighbours.

If you want to experience different cultures, scenery and life in general, but either don't want to, or can't afford long-haul, then Morocco is the place. I thought this upon my first visit to Marrakech 30 odd years ago and the 3 visits Aggers and I have made since, only reinforced this opinion. I thought Naples was more like Bombay than other European cities on first visiting, and returning with Agnes 7 years ago, didn't think I was completely wrong. But that's only one different city, not a whole country.

A stroll around Oujda's medina and into its souq felt significantly further away than a 90-minute flight from Barcelona. The next day we timed our first grand taxi ride to perfection. We had not been aware of this mode of transport on our previous visits - one had been a private tour (get us!) and the other two, long weekends involving train and bus travel between major cities, obviously for airport purposes. I'm sure you get the gist of a shared taxi. The norm here are 7 seaters, so yes, you've guessed, we needed 4 fellow passengers. They were already there waiting for us, so we were off, pronto. What was so intriguing to us about the 1-hour ride to the coastal town of Saidia was its proximity to the Algerian border, literally 10 metres away in places.

You'd think there would be little for Algeria and Morocco to fall out about, but you'd be wrong. The land border has been closed for almost 30 years off and on, mainly on, possibly permanently since 1994. I've been doing a bit of googling, mainly to determine if it is fenced throughout. It's a damn long border, most of it in the desert, but it appears it is, together with all kinds of surveillance equipment. Politics, eh? You can fly between the 2 countries, or go by sea, but overland, nope.

LP had warned us that out of the summer season, Saidia was a bit of a ghost town. It wasn't actually as dead as we anticipated, with plenty of beachside eateries open, but nonetheless some roads were eerily quiet. There was about a 200 metre no man's land area to the border fence to the east and miles of pleasant beach westward to the purpose-built resort area. After a simply delightful and humongous 3-hour breakfast in the warm sunshine (it really was that good that we craved not a Wetherspoon breakfast wrap) we took a long stroll along the beach. Plenty of horses added to the already pleasant enough ambience. We knew we were in for some weather in the coming days as we headed east so made the most of the decent sunshine.

Our shared taxi to Nador the next morning wasn't quite as successful. In fact, the driver decided for us that the 4 pax he had, would pay additional for the missing 2. This was explained to us by 1 of our fellow English-speaking customers. He was a fisherman, off to renew his permit. He explained he was originally from a small town called Aoufous, some 375 miles south of Saidia and that he returned in the summer to collect the date harvest. Why am I telling you this you wonder? Well, hang on.... a while.

Nador, certainly on the outskirts, was a bit messy with a ton of construction going on. The ride from Saidia had been scenic, but not spectacular. We weren't disappointed that we'd never made the Oujda/Nador twin centre long weekend. Our destination, Al Hoceima, was not served by shared taxi directly. LP described the coast road as a bit of a stunner. We weren't about to find out. Fortunately, the grand taxi ranks have so far, always been located next to the "Gare Routiere" (sounds sexier than bus station, right? And the buildings, to date, look it too). We were ushered over to this extremely dilapidated version. We were descended upon by a number of ticket touts but none of the buses (coaches to us brits but, I don't think many other countries distinguish between the 2? It's a Greyhound bus for example, not a Greyhound coach) looked like they'd seen active service in a while. We weren't prepared to part with our hard-earned dirhams for an imaginary bus/coach. Shortly, a fluster of activity signalled the arrival of a bus from Oujda which would take us onto Al Hoceima. We bought the tickets and even bagged the front seats, so craved by both of us, Aggers' need being to see the road ahead to avoid travel sickness, mine purely because I'm a nosey bastard.

It soon became apparent that our bus would take a much longer inland route, hence us missing the coastal route. It started raining, quite heavily. It didn't feel like we had climbed noticeably in the first few hours but once we had a distant view of Al Hoceima, in the sunshine, it was clear we had. I don't ever recall seeing an airport from such a distance when on land but there was our intended new airport, way in the distance down on the coast, probably the best part of an hour away.

We, the indecisives, had a decision to make: did we continue the journey into downtown Al Hoceima, or jump off at the airport turn off, some 10 miles earlier? Our main objective was food. Our travels that day had not included any so far. Aggers was getting a bit hangry. I quite like that word/expression as I do "nap trapped", which I recently learned from my eldest daughter, but I'm not so fond of a hangry Agnieszka. My gut feeling (good, eh?) was to go with the latter. Google was inconclusive as to restaurant availability at 3pm so there was an element of risk. We found a few outdoor options, but it was definitely not warm enough for al fresco dining for us. Just when it looked like I was going to pay for my decision, by way of a taxi to, or towards the city, to remove the hanger, our last chance saloon whilst a very basic affair, was just about warm enough to break our fast. The food was pretty decent.

8 days later, we wouldn't be disappointed if we never saw another tajine or couscous dish ever again! As you have hopefully gathered, we are pretty positive on our travels. Morocco is a fabulous country to travel in: the scenery is truly spectacular, the villages, towns and cities nearly all have something to offer. Some of the medinas are among the most interesting sights we've seen anywhere. The people, in general, are just super friendly. The coffee is superb and cheap, as is the orange juice but.....the food. Maybe we've been spoiled by India, Thailand, Malaysia and even Wetherspoon! We're not being ungrateful but choice is not their speciality. We are at a loss as to why they don't cook with spices, and garlic is non-existent. In short, meal times, always to be looked forward to, are just not very interesting so far. We don't anticipate the next 3-4 weeks, if things go to plan, yes, we now have a plan, will prove otherwise.

Back to the positives. After our meal, we enjoyed a relaxing coffee in a warm cafe before the 20-minute walk to Al Hoceima airport. Our decision not to visit the city was also made because we didn't really have time. The inland bus journey had taken 4 hours, just to the airport turn off. The coast road showed 2, according to Google. The airport was beautifully located in between the mountains, with the approach over the sea. The small terminal building was very tastefully designed too. An equaliser for Morocco against India. 1-1. After an early goal for India from Food, Airport-Location drew Morocco level. This could well go to penalties! The incoming flight from Casablanca, 1 of 8 flights per week to frequent this little gem, was kind enough to arrive early. Those passengers, from

Casablanca, due to disembark with us in Tetouan, would no doubt have been happy with our forthcoming 25 minutes early arrival. For us, it meant that we arrived just before full darkness, so we had a better idea of where we had flown to than we expected. Another charmingly located airport and terminal building with character. It was rather strange to pass through passport control both on departure and arrival for a domestic flight. Strange to us, but I think stranger for the immigration officer was us choosing to fly this route. It's 150 miles by road, so likely less by air. I'm sure all the other passengers had come from Casablanca. Aggers had chosen an hotel barely 5 minutes' walk from the airport so we were in bed before we should have even landed in Tetouan. 996/997 done!

All was going well apart from the weather. As per the forecast it was peeing down the next morning. We had no other flights booked and were not planning to be home for another 5 weeks. Time was our friend. The weather was not. We considered sitting it out as we particularly wanted to have a nose around UNESCO status Tetouan, as well as Cueta, Chefchaouen and Meknes before heading south. The problem was we could be sitting it out for 10-14 days if the long-range forecast was to be believed. It was cold, wet, windy and grey; just what we were escaping UK for. We took a taxi to the bus station and when we arrived it stopped raining. We decided to take a chance and go and explore Tetouan. You should too! We would've liked longer and considered overnighting but the rain reappeared after a couple of hours so we decided to move on. It certainly warrants its UNESCO badge though.

We didn't fancy 6-7 hours by bus to Meknes so decided to head for Tangier and the train option. It's only an hour from the Mediterranean coast at Tetouan to Tangier on the Atlantic coast but whilst we were perfectly happy with 7-seater taxi sharing, we saw little need to squeeze the same number into a 5-seater Mercedes saloon. The driver seemed quite pissed off with us as we headed into the bus station but so be it. I was quite keen to revisit Tangier, the first night overseas together for Aggers and me 11 years previously, if not to the day, to the month. It was peeing down so, instead we ran into the super modern train station. This was definitely not the same as when we'd taken the train to Fez in 2012. Neither was the train. A few years ago a high speed line had opened from Tangier to Casablanca. It was 1458. The time, not the year. The next 3 trains, on the hour, only had first class availability. The indecisives made a split-second decision and we were on the 1500 departure. It was indeed, very full and very fast. It was also very comfortable, like a double decker Eurostar. Ironically our first journey to Morocco had started with a first-class Eurostar from Waterloo to Brussels. Agnes never questioned why we were flying from Charleroi to Tangier and not London, back then. I should have realised at that moment that she was the one for me. I didn't and I'm absolutely sure neither of us ever imagined we would be making another journey together from Tangier, married to boot.

Momentarily, I was perplexed by our splashing out on first class tickets; £20 each, instead of £10 but I recovered my composure quicker than I thought possible. We only had 50 minutes on the high-speed train, directly south before our change onto a normal train in Kenitra to head eastwards to Meknes but the on-board display screen informed us we were bombing along at over 300 kms per hour - impressive. The 90-minute ride to Meknes was much more scenic though. It was raining on arrival so we ducked into the nearest restaurant. The food might not be all that, we weren't bored of it just yet, but the pricing, whilst not on a par with India, was pretty agreeable. It had stopped raining so we walked to the medina and our first genuine riad stay of this trip. Both were charming, but it was cold. As much as we wanted to see more of Meknes, another UNESCO recognised city, it was raining the next morning so we contented ourselves with our previous evening's brief wander. There was some fairly major renovation work occurring in the main square so we didn't feel quite so bad about not doing Meknes justice.

It really was time to find the sun and some daytime warmth at least. We were pleasantly surprised that not only were we able to find a shared taxi to take us all the way south to Errachidia; a not insignificant 320 kms south, but that we only had to wait half an hour for 4 like-minded souls. We had been disturbed through the night by the most disgusting guttural sounds by our neighbour in the riad. To top it, when he wasn't clearing his throat he topped up the requirement to do so by smoking. Not only were the walls very thin that the sounds invaded our privacy, so did the smoke. Of course he was a snorer once he'd finished his other activities. By morning I'd had enough. When he lit up again I went out and confronted him. He was quite apologetic but, having agreed not to smoke us out, he continued his best impression of the worst Chinese associated sound effects. We headed down to breakfast. He appeared shortly after. It was impossible to remain angry with him. He was quite a character with an infectious and obviously throaty, laugh. He was fluent in Spanish so had quite a conversation with Agi. Whilst we were getting by on my school boy French it's hardly conducive to interesting conversations. He reminded me a bit of Pavarotti, not that I've met him.

He was heading south, told us we would have to make the journey in stages to Errachidia, and that he could give us a lift to Azrou to get us on our way. Only problem was he wanted us to pay. If we were indecisive, which obviously we were, he made the decision for us. Working on LP estimates which have, so far, proved accurate even though 6 years old, he wanted not much less to take us a fifth of the distance. I was cooling towards him as quickly as I'd warmed.

Even though we knew Morocco gets snow in the mountains, the reality of it was still a shock to us. Even more so to see monkeys on the roadside, receiving food gifts from other passing motorists. Our friendly taxi driver stopped for us to take a few snaps before we gradually descended out of the low cloud into more spectacular scenery. It was a long but rewarding ride to Errachidia. This was just an overnight stopping off point for our onward journey the next day to Aoufous. Nothing to get too excited about. Certainly nothing to warrant us returning one day to tick off the airport. See,

I'm cured already! But pleasant enough and not a cloud in the sky. LP raved about Aoufous, and it didn't disappoint. A 45-minute shared taxi ride deposited us in this delightful oasis town, surrounded by mountains and covered in palm trees. There was very little choice of overnight options but the Gite Tamlii was quite idyllic in most ways. We took a fairly strenuous hike up one of the nearby peaks, only tough going because we opted for flip flops: far from ideal for the terrain. The stroll back through the "Palmeraie" was far more relaxing. What was far from relaxing was my decision to listen to the England cricket team attempt to continue their mind-blowing form in the best form of the game, until 4 am. Those of you interested in test cricket will need no reminding of the result of the 2nd test against New Zealand in February 2023. Those of you not interested wouldn't understand, however long I tried to explain. It was sporting theatre, even though I was only listening, of the very highest drama.

Suitably non rested, me that is - Agi slept throughout - apart from my numerous nerves induced nocturnal toilet visits, we walked back into town to continue our shared taxi adventure to Rissani. Only we didn't, as after we had waited 30 minutes in vain, for some fellow passengers, a bus appeared so off we went, but not before we had one of those crazy coincidences. While we were waiting this chap stops and asks if we remembered him. His face was certainly familiar but from where? It was our Saidia to Nador fisherman friend. He'd decided to head home for a while. We've had a few chance meetings over the years on our travels. I'm sure I've mentioned my cousin from Vancouver catching us unawares on the beach in Mexico. Yet these chance meetings still amaze us. The equivalent would be meeting someone in Paignton, and then again in Whitby, 5 days later, for example, for a UK comparison!

We were greeted on the bus by an extremely friendly reincarnation of Bob Marley. According to him there are a lot of Rastafarians in Morocco but he, to date, was the only one we'd seen. What a cheerful dude he was. It was market day in Rissani but we were bound for Merzouga, gateway to the fabulous dunes, Erg Chebbi. We had done the camel ride and camping stuff in the desert on our luxury, private trip at the even more remote Erg Chegaga. So, marvellous experience that it was, we were content to just stare in awe at the dunes this time. LP had warned that Merzouga could be a tad overrun with tourists and more annoyingly, quad bikes. Maybe it was at other times but both were fairly scarce this day. Indecision took an almighty stranglehold on us as we contemplated our bed for the night.

Despite booking.com resolutely continuing to give a flying about fake reviews we were still giving them our custom. No point in cutting off our noses, etc. So far their prices had been lower than walk in, but we weren't booking in advance that often. We'd had our eyes on one particular spot near the dunes which entailed us walking past many other options. The welcome at this place was not tempting us. Coupled with no view of the dunes, unless you staked out on the rooftop and a miserable whiny German kid at the pool who was old enough to know better, we were pleased we'd left our options open. We didn't feel we were wasting our time as we'd got many different views of the dunes and some much-needed exercise. We headed back to take a look at the slightly strangely named Auberge Camping La Liberte. A vast improvement: a friendly welcome, great 360-degree dune views, authentic, if basic, room. The only thing I did to spoil our stay was tune in to FA Cup 5th Round: Fulham 2 Leeds 0. Not as devastating as the cricket, but still a bit of a downer.

The owners told us in French that 17 motor homes would be joining us that evening. I was pretty sure that I'd understood correctly. We wandered back into Merzouga for some more tajine and couscous and, sure enough 19 French-registered motor homes cruised by. One of us had our dix sept and dix neuf mixed up but we were pretty sure where they were heading. We had seen so many motor homes since we'd come out of the wet and snowy north - Italian, German, Dutch but 80%+ French. It would be hypocritical of us to bemoan their presence, considering our adventures in UK. My initial reaction was that I wanted the Auberge to ourselves but I had to agree with Aggers that the sight of 20 (1 was there on our arrival) motorhomes parked up in "our" courtyard looked quite cool. The French were not noisy, all probably similar age to me, I was happy that our hosts had some good business and I'm not sure if the buffet breakfast would've been so plentiful without them.

We headed back to Rissani the following morning, after a chilly but superb sunrise, followed by aforementioned buffet breakfast. After a sunny wait, we caught a bus to Alnif, a shared taxi to Tazzarine and another one to N'Kob. Like the majority of males I couldn't help but think they'd spelt N'Kob wrong, or that he who named it was dyslexic. The Auberge Kasbah Ennakhile was so splendid, the welcome so warm and the views over the oasis to the 45 kasbahs so magnificent we decided, obviously after some indecision, to stay another night. It was still pretty chilly in the mornings but warm enough during the day to tempt me into the pool. Bloody hell it was cold, seriously icy. We liked N'Kob a lot. LP had waxed lyrical about the 45 kasbahs. Some of them were pretty impressive, others derelict but it was certainly very interesting and completely devoid of any other travellers. Our fellow guests seemed to be on very brief stopovers, in groups, arrived quite late and disappeared pretty early in the mornings.

We've been struggling with our 2 meals per day routine in Morocco. After our sumptuous breakfast the first morning, it's been a pretty standard bread, jams, a boiled egg or thin omelette. Pleasant enough but by 3 o'clock we're ready for dinner and had no alcohol option to keep the hunger at bay. On our second day in N'Kob we lasted until 5pm but then ordered from one of the boys in the Auberge. If I was a 20-year old girl, I'd definitely have had the hots for him. He was quite a character, so cheerful, smiley and quite charming with his broken English. After half an hour though, nothing had appeared, not even any cutlery. Aggers suggested that I check on the whereabouts of our dinner. I did with one of the other chaps. He went to check and charming boy reappeared. You have to think Manuel from Fawlty Towers: "you want food now? You not want 8 o'clock?" It was impossible to do anything other than join in with his laughter.

After a very chilled day, the first with no travel, it really was time to plan 500/1000. That evening, the plan was hatched. We had enjoyed the freedom of not having a bunch of flights to determine our schedule but we needed to book a flight home at the end of the month and you know what happens the longer you leave that! Many folk would read this and think our schedule far too busy but once the cold, wet weather was no longer the determining factor, we were both very happy with our pace. In order to book a flight home, quite logically, we needed to know where from. It's not superstition, or maybe it is, but I've not mentioned any future airport visits planned, if I recall correctly. That's just the way it's worked out so far. We bade our farewells and went in search of transport to Zagora. Not so far away but it would involve a change of taxi at a road junction in Tansikht. From there, left 60 kms to Zagora, or right 100 kms to Ouarzazate, our next destination. Confused? Well, don't be. Why would you proceed 100 kms right to Ouarzazate, when you could go 60 kms in the opposite direction to Zagora and then fly 160 kms from Zagora to Ouarzazate? Well, actually 175 kms as Zagora Airport is 15 kms south of the town. These are road distances but you get the gist, right?

You may have guessed this route is another of RAM Express's double drops. You'd be right, but I bet you can't guess how many flights operate Zagora-Ouarzazate? 1 per week! The airport only has 2 other flights per week, which operate direct to Casablanca, having called at Ouarzazate on the way. There's neither a military base at Zagora (that we could see) nor any private flying. The airport only opened in 2009/10. We could only guess that it had something to do with its proximity to the Algerian border that the authorities had decided to build an airport in the middle of nowhere, as surely, the small amount of passengers wishing to fly to Casablanca could make the 100 mile trip to Ouarzazate?

Anyway, none of our business and we weren't complaining. 498/9 & 998/999 were about to happen. Before they did we actually needed to get to Zagora. There was a checkpoint at the junction in Tansikht, but no taxis. We asked the policeman if it was OK if we put our thumbs out. He had no objections but also suggested that there may be a bus in an hour or so. Within 5-10 minutes we were off. A very friendly prison officer took us all the way to the outskirts of Zagora. His driving habits were a bit odd: very slow, with the occasional random bursts of speed. Like virtually all Moroccans he had about 5 layers of clothes on, when we were in short sleeve shirts and shorts. I'm very keen to know if they shed a few layers in summer. It was already around 26/27 degrees in the afternoons, warming up nicely, but clearly they have different temperature settings to us Europeans. What made this stranger was that he proceeded to close his window on 2 occasions. The first time I figured it was because we were approaching a Mosque and as he was treating us to some very fine local music, he didn't want to offend or turn it down. It was brief, but still long enough for me to get pretty hot. The 2nd time lasted 10-15 minutes whilst there was no sign of life anywhere. I didn't feel it was my place to ask him to open his window. I assumed he'd shut it for a reason. I couldn't open mine as the controls were missing. We didn't talk too much as his English was on a par with my French. The music, which genuinely was very pleasant, negated the need for conversation.

He stopped to buy 4 cigarettes and to put a bit of petrol in his car which didn't even cause the low fuel light to disappear. He said he lived in Agdz, which was 90 kms from Zagora. Did he make this commute every day? If so, why didn't he buy enough fuel to get home? We'll never know. Neither we will know why he turned off onto a dirt road for about 500 metres only to then rejoin the main drag. It was very kind indeed of him to give us a lift, "Mon plaisir" he replied to my "Merci beaucoup". He had already said this at the start of the journey so I figured it may insult him if I offered him money. Again, we'll never know.

We were certainly not disappointed that we stayed an extra night in N'Kob rather than 1 in Zagora. It was fine, but much bigger than K'Nob (sorry, couldn't help myself) and possessed not much charm either. Google showed a 10 kms walking route to the airport. As we had ample time we decided to go for it. After about 500m the route just disappeared: dead end. We returned to the main road and quickly dismissed the idea of heading back into town to grab a cab. We probably just about had time to walk the 15 kms road route but I reckoned we'd get a lift at some point, either hitchhiking or a passing taxi. Wrong on the latter! But fortunately right on the former. There was so little traffic and what there was, either couldn't or didn't fancy giving us a lift. Our dilemma was that the airport was at about 9 or 10 o'clock in our vision. We could see it almost immediately but the road went dead straight, 12 o'clock then, left turn, almost back on itself. Or, put another way, if we cut across the open land we would turn a 15 kms walk into 7 or 8 kms.

I'm glad we trusted our instinct and stuck with the road. What we thought was a hedge away in the distance, turned out to be a pretty large plantation, fenced off. Can you imagine my state of mind if we had missed 998/999 with the next flight in a week? We arrived an hour before departure time and actually loved the walk through the mainly hammada - the term for stony desert, I believe - landscape. The plane arrived early from Casablanca and after a false start through passport control, we were ready for the off. The immigration officer asked Aggers what her name was. Somewhat bemused she correctly stated that it was as per her passport. He handed her back the boarding pass she had given him. It certainly didn't have her name on it. Back to check in for Agnieszka Czekanska's boarding pass. I think I said in India that we liked flying on ATRs. This short flight was what we love about flying and airport collecting. We took off and had to circle around the airport to gain height to get over the mountains before proceeding above the Draa valley to Ouarzazate. Even with that added mileage we still arrived half an hour before schedule. I know airlines build in plenty of leeway to their schedules these days. I'm sure Ryanair etc do it to try and avoid the harsh penalties they can incur for delays in the EU, but a 1-hour schedule for a flight that took 30 minutes is a bit odd.

The scenery beneath us and the snowcapped peaks in the distance were spectacular. The immigration officer in Ouarzazate looked so utterly confused that we hadn't come from Casablanca that it must've been his first experience of a couple of weirdos flying from Zagora. We had no regrets whatsoever. Not only was Ouarzazate also a charming airport, even though it does get the occasional international flight, but it was barely 2 kms to the main square, where our hotel was situated. Aggers had categorically stated that after the 15 kms hike to Zagora Airport, adding on the couple of miles to take us through the town too, that she would not be walking into Ouarzazate. The fact that our early arrival meant it was still light and that she could feel, and maybe share, my euphoria at not only being 1 airport from our goal but also over the spectacular flight, encouraged her to give in to my desire to walk both to and from these 2 new airports.

Was I excited about reaching my target, Agi about her milestone? Not massively, yet. Perhaps not ever. We had 12 days to wait, now 10 as I write. I'd long wanted to visit Ouarzazate airport, just because I like the name. We had driven by the town on our private tour in 2016 but flights were few and far between. I'm not sure when I became aware of its existence but I'm sure it was a good 20-25 years ago. I was happy to have it in my 990s. I'm not going to talk about 1000 until it happens, just in case it doesn't, but it's not far away. It's not the one we wanted it to be, that will be 1001, but I will share a little secret: if all goes to plan I will be on 1005 and Agi 507 when we get home. Ouarzazate (pronounced Wazazat, in case you care and didn't know) is a beautifully located, small city, hence why it has the nickname Ouallywood, as many films have been shot there and it has its own studios. The main square is OK but there's not much else to get excited about. Therefore, we left the next morning, continuing our journey towards the Atlantic Coast with our next overnight in Taliouine, another superbly located town. We both agreed that the scenery to reach there was amongst the best we had seen so far. We found a pretty decent Auberge on the outskirts of town with lovely views of the mountains and nearby abandoned kasbah.

We were enjoying the pace of a few hours travelling each day but most of the time enjoying the clear blue skies and unbroken sunshine. What we did not enjoy was the bus journey to Taroudannt, just 2 hours further west, according to Google. We enquired about a shared taxi. There was one, but we were the first customers. We could've been in for a long wait. We found out that a bus was due in around 30 minutes. When the bus came, we appeared to be still just 2. The cabbie implored us to go with him, but there was no guarantee when. His "now" quickly changed to 5 minutes, when I pushed him further for a time. The bus driver, heading for Agadir, changed his mind several times, whether he was or wasn't stopping in Taroudannt. The price then increased from 30 to 50 dirhams each. That didn't matter. We just wanted to get under way. We sat on the bus for 15 minutes before our driver finally decided to leave. Not 10 minutes into the journey he then proceeded to stop for a 30-minute lunch break. The bus was very hot. All the locals still had 5 layers on. I'm sure there was no a/c so, again, begged the question, what would it be like in summer? Our next stop involved our driver stopping for 10 minutes, moving the bus, I kid you not, 20 metres, stopping for a further 10 minutes, turning the bus around and stopping for another 10 minutes. Maybe the Grand Taxi would've been a better option after all. Apart from stopping at several speed bumps to take them at 2 mph when they were so insignificant they didn't warrant a change of speed, we did finally, make some good time for the remainder of the journey. LP warned against using buses other than CTM. We'd been fine so far, but I think we'll be favouring shared taxis in future.

LP describes Taroudant as a Little Marrakech. Not sure we'd agree on that but it's 7.5 kms of ramparts are pretty impressive. Apart from silver foxes in their motorhomes it was our first stop with quite a few other Europeans for company. This inevitably led to a bit of pestering from locals but very mild really, as was the food, still. Even the OJ and coffee in the main square seemed watered down. On the upside Aggers found us a charming riad for our overnight.

Bonjour Agadir, Au revoir Agadir. That's how it was looking but after some absolutely top-notch indecisiveness, we ended up staying overnight. We'd both done the airport as our arrival point for our private, luxury tour but had headed directly east. I was keen to see what the beach and to a lesser extent, the city, were like, as Dan Air had flown there throughout my career. Now, of course, Ryanair etc go there from everywhere. The beach was pretty OK actually. A very fine, very long one, backed by a pleasant Corniche. We didn't waste our time procrastinating. We sat with a coffee, overlooking the ocean for a few hours, dipping in and out of deciding where to lay our heads.

Aggers wanted to see the almond blossom. According to LP, from the nearby surf resort of Taghazout, you could take a journey into "paradise valley". What LP was pretty vague about was exactly where paradise valley was and also, in relation to the blossom. Not only could we not decide on Agadir or Taghazout. We were also considering Tamraght, in between. All these T places were getting a tad confusing, and that's only the ones on our agenda. There's plenty more. If any of the 3 couchsurfers I'd contacted in Agadir had been able to host us we'd have not had a decision to make. Fortunately, for us, after a few hours, it clouded over, momentarily. The temperature dropped enough for us to get our sh*t together (sorry, I think I've done extremely well on the non-swearing in both books but getting one's act together just sounds lame).

We binned off the 2 Ts and found ourselves a very fine hotel about 20 minutes' walk back from the beach. It clearly catered for European holidaymakers, had a large and pleasant pool area and set us back about £23 with breakfast. Bargain! Logic had prevailed: why go north, to another beach, in the hope, the next day of finding some blossom, when we could continue our route south, with a potential blossom diversion en route? It just took us a while to get to that decision, as usual.

We didn't see much of the city itself. The outskirts, approaching from Taroudant, were enjoying a mass of construction; both buildings and roads. Around our hotel was a modern and pleasant area, still with construction. I reckoned they were building a tram network. Aggers wasn't so sure. We both knew a man who would likely know! Unfortunately, we couldn't get a shared taxi or bus directly to Tafraoute, our alternative blossom viewing destination. We had to take a grand taxi to Tiznit, of course 2 more Ts, and another to Tafraoute. We were very lucky for the 2nd leg. Our 4 fellow passengers were waiting for us. It was a stunning 2-hour drive through the mountains. Tafraoute really was a peach of a setting, in the valley below.

If we'd been somewhat surprised by the 20 motorhomes that descended on us in the desert in Merzouga it was nothing compared to what came into view on our approach into Tafraoute. I'm not exaggerating when I say there were literally 100s of them. We thought we were heading off the beaten track to a village of 5000 inhabitants. We thought we'd missed the annual blossom festival but no, it was due to start the following day for 4 days. Was this why all the motorhomes were there? Apparently not. Apart from Covid intervention they'd been coming for years and staying for weeks, some for months. Obviously mainly French, but German, Dutch, Italian, the odd Belgian and Luxembourger, even a few Brits. We found out that most years 4-500 would make Tafraoute their winter home. Don't get me wrong, it really is a stunning location but, worth the drive from France etc, annually? Well, we're just not the returning type are we, so how can we judge?

Our hotel choice was made pretty swiftly, our decision to stay 2 and then 3 nights could be described as split-second. We never did find the blossom Aggers craved. There seemed little of note going on, on the first 2 festival days that we could tell, but what a delightful spot. Apart from the motorhome crowd on the outskirts of town, our hotel received small groups from Russia, Czech Republic, UK and even Canada, but they all seemed to arrive quite late and leave before sunrise so we pretty much had the stupendous rooftop terrace to ourselves. We enjoyed 2 wonderful 10-mile circular walks in absolutely perfect weather. We did find some blossom on the 2nd walk, but not enough to get overexcited about. Having found this little village/town so alluring we changed our mindset from being surprised that quite a few other tourists made their way there, to being grateful that more didn't. Not wishing to sound patronising but I still find the nature of some fellow Brits we encounter in non-mainstream destinations quite surprising. I can't tell with other languages and to repeat, never judge a book by its cover, but the arrival of an extended family who looked and sounded as if they'd just arrived from a Liverpool Wetherspoon in addition to 3 lads, already our fellow guests, who wouldn't have looked out of place reporting for community service in the same city, got me back on that familiar track of wondering what brings folk to wherever. A natural opportunity to find out didn't materialise on this occasion and I didn't feel a direct approach to be nosey was appropriate, so I'll never know.

We could have stayed another day in Tafraoute but we were down to 4 nights on the coast before heading slightly inland to airport 500/1000. Only 5 more sleeps! Our flight is scheduled for 1135. Whilst it's only 60 kms/1 hour from the coast to our moment of glory, I don't think I would sleep well with that journey to cover. Far safer to be within walking distance. LP does, at least, mention our chosen one but doesn't get too excited. However, as Aggers rightly pointed out, how could we not visit the town of our landmark airport? We didn't have too long to wait for a grand taxi back to Tiznit. We had a quick wander around the medina, brunched, and then continued on our way to Mirleft. I think the town planner there, if there ever was one, must've lied about their credentials on their CV. It really was quite an odd place. The majority of the recent development is set so far back from the coast that it would be a good few 1000 years before the occupants would have to worry about erosion. The original town is even further back. I'm sure they had their reasons. The latter had some appeal and the ocean and coastline were splendid but the haphazard, spread out, gappy nature of the place did not make us regret only booking an apartment for one night.

We enjoyed a walk that reminded us, in some aspects, of the South West Coast Path, and managed to purchase the desired ingredients to cook for ourselves for the first time and take a break from bland restaurant fare. We retired with anticipation of a few days to spend exploring the splendid beaches of the area, renowned "worldwide" for great surfing. What's the saying I'm going to use again? C'mon, you've got it. Yep, that's right, "never assume"! Well, we did, suckered in, yet again, by a mixture of 2 weeks of glorious, unbroken (apart from night time, obviously) sunshine and weather forecasts promising us more of the same for the next 2 weeks. So, where the hell was the sun the next morning? Our rooftop breakfast (my porridge would've been inedible without the bananas) and coffee was hastily rescheduled for indoors. The sun would surely burn this crap off in no time? By 11, it seemed to be the case. We blagged a lift off a couple of Californian surfing dudes to the next beach 10 minutes south, descended to the splendid beach and began to stroll.

Alas, what was occurring? The thick mist that was looking certain to disappear was putting up a right old fight. We headed inland, just a few 100 metres back to the road - glorious sunshine! Almost immediately, we thumbed a lift another 15 kms south towards our overnight stop on Legzira beach with its "dramatic, natural stone arch". A bus does operate along this barren coast road but its schedule was unknown, to us, at least. Our lift provider just happened to be a policeman in the town of number 1000/500 to be. We told him that we would be visiting his town and flying from there, less than 100 miles further south. He rightly thought this was bonkers, told his mate, and they both laughed heartily. I felt I owed him an explanation as to why we were paying £26 each to fly, when we could pay £2.60, roughly, in a shared taxi. His English was pretty good and he got it. They both laughed some more, on learning that we had already flown Zagora to Ouarzazate. He then said, "do you know Guinness?" Like an idiot, I thought he meant were we going to try and find a pint of it to celebrate. Virtually impossible in this neck of the woods. Aggers, nowhere near as stupid as me, knew what he was on about. We told him his town was very likely to be in the national press in UK, the following week. He liked that. I showed him the previous Metro article, he liked that even more. We swapped numbers so I could send him the article, if it were to materialise. All this in a 10-minute lift. They dropped us at the Legzira beach turn off in bright sunshine. Within 50 metres, I kid you not, we were back in the mist. And that's how it pretty much stayed the rest of the day. It wasn't cold, until about 6pm, but visibility was down to 20 metres at times. We could hear the waves, but stood on the beach, we simply could not see them.

We wandered part of the way back up the hill to see if the sun was out up there. It was. Then it wasn't. Swirling mist was not in short supply. I was beginning to think that there was, after all, a very good reason why Mirleft was built as far back from the coast as it was. Our on-line weather forecasts continued to show unbroken sunshine for it. It may very well have been so, in the town. Our next destination, Sidi Ifni, showed the same, but appeared to be closer to the coast. We were grateful that we had only booked one night in Legzira. I'm sure in bright sunshine our basic beachfront hotel would've been pretty appealing. In the mist it was anything but. At this rate we wouldn't be stopping at Sidi Ifni. We're not into misty beach walks. We could only assume Legzira could indeed, be twinned with Durdle Door. The temperature was rising inland a little too much for our taste, 37 degrees, but we'd take that and some shade, over coastal fog.

Should the suspense be proving too much for you, if you haven't already, you can, I'm sure, work out where we were heading, with the help of Google and Wikipedia. I had never heard of these 2 airports (1000/1), before I started planning. In fact, 6 of the airports we hoped to do in Morocco, plus 2 I could ignore, as the collecting was no longer going to be manic, were new to us. You may be wondering why I haven't mentioned any panic about the mist affecting our big day? Well, firstly, even I am logical enough to figure that there is very little chance of thick mist inland in 37 degrees. But, what if the wind got up and all that Saharan sand, that even makes its way to UK occasionally, made flying impossible? Well, airport 1002 to be was also under consideration for a while to be 1000, so there was kind of a plan B. Plus, we had plenty of spare days, if needed, for reschedule. All was calm.

Weather, eh? We were grateful that we had only booked one night in Legzira, I said? We ended up staying 2! We took our time over breakfast, contemplating our next move. By 11 o'clock the mist which had prevailed all day, the previous day, was rapidly disappearing. The natural arch, which was so elusive, became grander by the minute. It bore no similarity to Durdle Door, maybe it was more impressive? The beach certainly was lovely and the ambiance of the tiny settlement so totally different now our friend had outfought our foe.

We didn't rush into booking another night, just in case. Maybe the mist would return as quickly as it departed. Fortunately, that day, it didn't. Sure enough, though, we awoke to more dullness. So, we headed off 15 kms down the road, in the mist, fog and low cloud to Sidi Ifni, a town with a certain charm and different character due to its Spanish history. It actually had an airport which Iberia had served back in the day. Nothing remained of the runway and the bones of the terminal building were just a tad too far out of town to encourage us to inspect more closely. We opined that the town would look more appealing in sunshine and, for a few hours, it did. This weather phenomenon was both interesting and exasperating. We met a gnarled old French man. We had a chat and he said he knew a thing or 2 about weather. Well so did I, from my Dan Air days, so we were no further forward with what he offered. He explained that sometimes the conditions could be the same many miles inland, sometimes completely different. That much we figured.

To write in the past or present tense? Mix and match? Is there a wrong or right way? Seeing as we have made it to the location of 500/1000, but not done the deed and I want to share the anticipation with you now, let's mix it up. I hope I'm not tempting fate by talking about the airport to be! We have hit the "gateway to the Sahara" or another of them. The venue for Morocco's largest camel market; Saturdays only. The airport is a 4 km stroll from our hotel. We have under 24 hours until we are due to take off from Guelmim International Airport! Does this airport, of 9 flights per week, know just how famous it could become!? Yesterday and the day before, the flight to 501/1001 operated on time. That would indicate that, even if it had been foggy, it had cleared by departure time. Tomorrow shouldn't be any different right?

On our short, 60 kms journey inland, we experienced fog, sun, fog and finally sun on arrival. It's going to be just fine. What's the big deal, you ask? I only came up with a target in the last few years. After tomorrow I can go back to calmly collecting airports with no goal. This has been 40+ years' worth of "hard work" for me. Obviously, I say that in jest, no emojis here, so just to be clear. Aggers may have only half the number but she's only been aware of the game for 11 years and only been in the "team" of 2, for 9. I'm quite pleased with myself that we've managed to achieve such a symmetrical, never to be repeated, goal. I'm also impressed that she's done 400 new airports in just over 7 years. 0-400 took me double that! In my defence, I wasn't being led by an airport collector, in his manic phase, at any stage.

Does the location of number 500/1000 really matter to us in the end? We decided not. There's no far flung, exotic airport that we both desire. Morocco has a special meaning to us: our first ever flight together involved 2 new airports and landing in Tangier. We'd never heard of Guelmim. What will we remember about it, other than the airport, whether it gains the coveted 500/1000 trophy or not? Well, after a better than average breakfast, we found an okay hotel. The room was fine but lacked the basics of soap, towel and toilet roll, not a first in Morocco. The receptionist produced 2 towels from her desk, which, unlike normal hotel towels, had unique designs. I reckon they were her own personal supply. She then disappeared to the shop and returned with 96 toilet rolls and insisted I have 2. Yes, I did count them. However, soap was a no no. After all the European motorhomes of Merzouga, Tafraoute and Sidi Ifni, we've yet to see a European face so it feels suitably remote. What we have seen more of is flies, beggars and madmen. Yet again, the words of the wise Irish man stuck with us in Anti Paros, almost 2 1/2 years ago, popped into my head: "It'll be the best euro you'll ever spend". Our trusty green fly swatter has accompanied us on all our overseas travels since then. To be honest, I've maybe not used it as often as he or I thought I would, but I'd racked up a pretty decent score by the time we'd slowly broken our fast, only to get rid of the flies, you understand.

Beggars are such a tricky one, aren't they? Give and you encourage. Don't give and you feel mean. Westerners are fair game but none of those approaching us look to be going hungry. We reserve our donations for those with missing limbs. Perhaps living in Guelmim sends you a bit crazy, or they put something in the tea? There seems a disproportionate number of differently wired people here: a city of 120,000, whatever the reason. You can see I'm struggling and we have no desire to stay longer in Guelmim. Saturday is a long way off to see a lot of camels but, as the sun commences its gradual descent, which we enjoy from the rooftop, we are content. I'm not sure how much I will sleep tonight but bring on tomorrow!

# CHAPTER 23

It's done! And it was fun. Now I can get back to leisurely adding new airports to my 4-figure collection, and adding proportionally more to Agnieszka's impressive 3-figure. I'm 100% sure it is the only time we will have this perfect symmetry. It took some planning too, but felt worth it, so that we both had a very significant milestone to celebrate together.

As we sat on the rooftop of our hotel watching a couple of fighter jets doing their thing over Guelmim as the sun set, we were under no illusion that we would be fogged in, come morning. For you to be under no illusion that our rooftop was no Tafraoute equivalent, let me elaborate: it was positively awash with pigeons' shit, had no seats and was mainly a storage area for broken hotel materials. It did have a grand view, though. We set off on the 4 kms hike to the airport in dense fog. Visibility was varying between 20-100 metres. Walking through the rubble in the unfinished outskirts, in this visibility, to finally meet a wide dual carriageway with only 1 destination, really was a quite surreal experience. Google told us we were 120 metres from the terminal. We knew it to be ridiculously, disproportionately large for the volume of traffic it was currently experiencing, but it remained out of sight.

Aggers had entered into the spirit of the occasion the previous night, not that she'd been anything other than enthusiastic previously. Wikipedia had very little to say about Guelmim Airport. Flightradar 24, another wonderful tool I think I've failed to acknowledge thus far, gave me the basics: 9 flights per week, 3 destinations. What neither did was shed any light on the design of the terminal. Due to Aggers' research, we knew what to expect as it finally, and very swiftly, appeared in front of us. A very impressive design indeed and fitting, in a way, for special numbers. Neither of us had been unduly concerned about the fog, but we couldn't have timed it any better: literally within a minute of arriving, bright sunshine engulfed us. It really was quite bizarre how quickly the dense fog, one minute, became full on sunshine just a few minutes later. We certainly hadn't missed any sights on the walk.

As a security officer approached us, from a distance, crossing the empty car park I, not unreasonably, expected him to tell us to refrain from taking photographs of our landmark airport. Au contraire! Aggers explained to him in Spanish the significance of the moment to us. Not only did he seem to grasp the concept immediately, of what we were doing, he happily obliged when we asked him to take a few snaps; of us, for us. Not only did he snap away, he happily posed with us in our selfie in front of his charming airport building. His Facebook profile now includes his picture, in the Metro's article on our achievement. Yes, we were "headline" news, again.

The departing passport control staff were utterly bemused that we were only flying to Tan Tan and not Casablanca. The rather surly stewardess told us that we must stay on board for Casablanca when we went to disembark in Tan Tan. I reminded her that she had insisted on seeing our boarding passes when we embarked in Guelmim. "But I have never seen this before. Guelmim passengers always continue on to Casablanca!" Not these 2, lady! Tan Tan passport control was equally bemused at the brevity of our journey, as well as our lack of knowing what we were going to do now we were there. Whilst flashy Guelmim looked like it could handle an Emirates A380, at a push, Tan Tan looked like 5 x ATRs per week was its maximum capacity. We were not disappointed that Tan Tan, delightfully remote as it was, had slipped to 501/1001.

We set off on the 8 kms hike on the desolate but immaculate road to town, with distant camels the only break from the stony desert landscape. We figured on potentially getting a ride on reaching the main road but the immigration control staff, their day's work complete, were more than happy to squeeze us in on their way back into town. It is worth mentioning that the Tan Tan staff also did not mind taking photos of us to record our momentous day, happily negating the need for selfies again. Quite in contrast to LP's and UK Government's advice not to take photos in these sensitive areas.

Tan Tan is a one street town, but being on the main N1 route south and north, is quite busy. We celebrated our special day with another fine fresh orange juice and, both feeling quite pleased with ourselves, contemplated our journey south to notch a new country. Well, that depends on whom you speak with!

It was quite a journey to Dakhla in the south of Western Sahara. Seeing as there is no border signage, let alone physical presence of a border, the practicality is that as Morocco claims, Western Sahara does not exist. However, not an inconsiderable number of countries recognise Sahrawi Arab Democratic Republic, to give it its official title, as a legitimate state. I'll leave you, dear reader, to choose whether you wish to look into this longstanding dispute further. No doubt the Sahrawi people have, and do, suffer but we were just left wondering why such a desolate, if beautiful, region was so important to Morocco. Whatever riches the land promised - surely it was about money as usual - would be outweighed by the cost involved in developing the infrastructure and maintaining the military presence. Maybe that's a rather simplistic view. In our simple world we passed by Laayoune airport without adding it to our collection. "How does it make you feel, Alan?" Aggers enquired. "Cured" was my curt and fairly honest response. Fortunately, we are not fixed on country collecting, although, as a list exists, I'm sure we'll stick SADR on there.

We were glad that our airport collecting took us as far south as Dakhla but we certainly wouldn't be returning one day to add Laayoune. For sure, if we had still been some way short of our targets the economic and operational/logistical reasons for not flying in or out of Laayoune would have been overcome and it would feature on our lists. But the obsession has been replaced with a healthy interest. OK, so I readily admit that our route north and home could have been a lot more direct but where would be the fun in that!?

Hitching a ride (he did take some money from us, so not pure hitchhiking) with a 61-year-old hashish smoking - his pipe was literally almost 2 feet long - madman, who delighted in making full use of his truck's cruise control by resting both his legs on his dashboard and hiding us in his sleeping compartment at the numerous police checkpoints, for 150 miles from Tan Tan Plage to Tarfaya was undoubtedly the highlight of our 500+ miles journey south. None of our overnights in Tarfaya, Laayoune or Boujdou were.... highlights. Neither was Dakhla but some of the surrounding desert scenery and the lagoon certainly were..... highlights, of our Moroccan/Western Sahara odyssey. I was surprised to learn that we had travelled over 2,000 miles by grand taxi and bus, in addition to our 3 short flights, from Oujda to Dakhla. It certainly hadn't felt like we had spent so long on the move.

After 5 very relaxing days in an extremely pleasant homestay in Dakhla we notched 502 and 1002 and then the symmetry was well and truly gone. Whilst Casablanca may as well have been a new airport for me (I have no memory of transiting 31 years ago), it wasn't, but it was for Aggers. After so much time in remote locations, the big airport and the big city were a bit of a culture shock. Despite LP not having much to recommend, and an audacious attempt by 2 little fuckers (swearing very much warranted) on a moped to swipe my moneybag off my shoulder (thank you wife for the steel wire reinforced strapping of said neck pouch, resisting their forceful, but ultimately, futile grab), we liked Casablanca. There are enough pleasant and interesting sights to fill an afternoon as we did.

Our first experience of Ramadan was memorable for the sight of literally 100s of devotees praying in nondescript side streets, with no mosque nearby. More so, on returning to our hotel at dusk, having failed in our attempt to find a dinner venue, being offered our buffet breakfast, which due to our early morning departure we would be unable to partake in the following morning, for dinner! We were not alone and not the only ones hungry as heck. No offence meant but I just do not get religion. If these dudes, who sit around drinking coffee and smoking profusely 335 days a year, all day, seriously resist for the other 30, then fair play to them. Casablanca was like a ghost town in places.

We took an early morning flight to Nador, completing that Ryanair long weekend that never happened. Being a significant distance from the city, with no bus service, and LP quoting £25 for a taxi 5 years ago we weren't really sure what we were going to do as we headed away from another very pleasant airport building. We were purposely down to our last 189 dirhams (£15ish) so were quite chuffed when Aggers negotiated a taxi direct to the border with Melilla for just that. The Melilla situation has always interested me since I learnt of its existence before my foiled attempt in 2004. Aggers apparently learnt about it, and Ceuta, at school. I was too busy being bored senseless, reading about Marco Polo. The border crossing was straightforward but the contrast was stark, in the extreme: bikini clad girls, men in shorts, beer and wine in abundance. Within half an hour of completing customs and immigration formalities we were quaffing an ice-cold pint by the beach. Rarely has a pint tasted so divine. My new personal best of 37 days abstinence was at an end.

We really liked Melilla. Apart from its political interest, it has a fine beach, a lovely small old town, some fine architecture in the new town, bars and restaurants in abundance and just a fine ambience. We loved Morocco but it felt good to be back in Europe, even if we were, very much, still in Africa! We enjoyed our first couchsurfing of the trip. As our host was a Spanish Muslim of Moroccan heritage, observing Ramadan, we still had a touch of Morocco with us. He was very difficult to track down during the day but served us a most pleasant breakfast the first evening! I was pretty pleased to add Melilla to our collection, nearly 19 years after my first attempt. Melilla is so small that the airport would have been walkable from anywhere but our host insisted on dropping us.

I had only one vague memory of my previous visit to Almeria, way back in 1987: standing in a street, on my tod, wondering what I was doing there. I was still a year away from overdoing the magic mushrooms so my mental health was pretty stable. It was a passing thought and when I discovered the charm of Seville for the first time the next day, I knew why I was on the trip. I assume I never got to the castle remains in Almeria, or the surrounding area, otherwise I'm sure I would have felt the first leg of that jaunt to be worthwhile in its own right. In contrast to our rather erratic host in Melilla, our man in Almeria was efficiency personified. With almost 150 couchsurfers giving him rave reviews he clearly knew what he was doing. Even though he'd lived in Spain over 30 years, his German attention to detail was actually most welcome. As was his choosing of the tapas to accompany our beer and wine both evenings. I felt a tad sorry for him when, slightly inebriated, he enquired how he could find a companion/lover like Agnieszka. Naturally, I had to tell him that it wasn't possible - she is unique - but that he could check on polishgirls.com for a likely inferior version. He was a similar age to me but had remained single throughout. 3-0 to me (in marriages), probably something I shouldn't be proud of, but a victory over the Germans is a victory, whatever the sport! The weather continued to be just sublime as, after a pretty lazy day in Almeria, we headed up the coast to Cartagena; another charming coastal city, for our last couple of days before heading back to Blighty from airport 507/1005.

I was aware that Murcia had a new airport since 2019. What I wasn't aware of was that it was actually completed in 2012. 6-7 years of political stupidity resulted in brand new Murcia Corvera airport sitting empty while old Murcia San Javier enjoyed a very lengthy stay of execution. In the 11 years since construction the authorities have failed to implement any public transport options, other than taxi, for the 26 km journey to Murcia and 36 km trot to Cartagena. As I would imagine that the majority of Ryanair, Jet2 and easyJet passengers are headed to La Manga, even further away, we opined that this was a pretty poor show. We didn't fancy paying 50 odd euros to get to our 12 euro each flight so decided to have another look at Bla Bla car. Our only previous attempt at this, 4 years earlier, had also been in Spain. We booked a ride from Seville to Malaga. The driver failed to show. After calling him for an hour he finally picked up and with very little apology, said he'd had a late night so wasn't going until the next day, when we could join him. Twat! We'd then had to wait 3 hours, and pay double, for a bus so hadn't really gone down that road since.

This experience was so much better. Not only was our ride early, but rather than drop us at the junction, as we'd agreed, our kind driver took the 5-mile detour to the airport, saving us 40 euros in the process. Murcia Corvera is certainly one for the future, plenty of room to move around, and outdoor seating to enjoy the last warmth, all too often missing. Our mission was over and successfully accomplished. It had also been another delightful holiday. We continue to be very blessed. As we neared the end of this adventure it was time to plan the next. I feel I have proved to myself that I am in control. A 3 1/2-week trip to USA & Canada currently only involves 3 new airports for me, 7 for Agi. I can't promise that I won't try and sneak a couple more in but not a bad effort, eh? 2 of the 3 had a special meaning to me, but before that we had some pubs to visit. It had been 6 months and 3 days since we had troubled the Wetherspoon scoreboard!

# CHAPTER 24

In those 6 months and 3 days, sadly, more than 50 Spoons had been put up for sale. Fortunately, only 2 were on our to do list. Having let sanity prevail in the Xmas/New Year period we, sadly, lost out on one of the 2 Durham pubs. Another, not on the list, in Glasgow had closed, "unexpectedly". Of course, my mild and insignificant OCD would love us to finish our Spoons collection on 900 but that's not going to happen. Hopefully our economy will improve one day and some of the planned new Spoons will come to fruition. I envisage a small, ongoing addition scenario a la 92.

We had one slight issue before we set off: our lovely old Mazda was making a strange noise again. It really doesn't like being left. Even though dear old Malcolm gives it a spin every couple of weeks in our absence, like me, some of its joints appear to be seizing up. Whereas mine, currently thankfully, touch wood, seem to right themselves without any expensive surgery, Mazda seems to be a bit more needy. Common sense would have led us to delay our departure and get Mazda looked at and most likely, admitted once more, for surgery. Honestly, it's not taking kindly to our winter abandonment.

However, when you haven't been in a new Spoon for 6 months and 3 days, common sense is a loser. So, off we set at the crack of dawn to break our fast in deepest Lincolnshire; Bourne to be precise, a very new addition to the Spoon family actually. Never heard of Bourne? Us neither until Spoons came to town. Not an unpleasant town, or pub, for sure, but our stay was fairly brief. We had 5 more pubs and towns to visit before our overnight in...... Grimsby!

There's been a few Spooners in the news recently. We know we're far from alone in this game. Fellow collectors have become regular features in the Wetherspoon magazine, but one that caught my eye in the national on-line media was the dude who's stolen a menu from every pub he's visited. His numbers are very impressive, in excess of 900, but 30 pubs in a day? You really must've spent a while in each one that day, studying the history, sampling the ales! Each to their own, who am I to mock or criticise? Even if you started in a pub that opens at 0700 and finish in one that closes at 0100 that would be almost 2 pubs an hour. Feasible in London but knackering for sure. Whilst I will admit to being a little envious that he has thought of, and has, a memento from each pub, I'd rather stick to our average daily numbers. I even think that's been a bit rushed at times.

On this occasion, seeing as we arrived in Bourne just 5 minutes after opening time we would not be in a rush. Once more, we were pleasantly surprised by the towns we visited. Bourne, Spalding, Boston, Skegness, Louth, Cleethorpes, Grimsby..... reads like an Alan Partridge who's who of Lincolnshire, rather than Norfolk, or where's where. Louth - both the pub and the town were particularly pleasant, especially the latter. Apart from previous Spoons visits in the area, my knowledge was restricted to footy ground collections, 40 odd years ago in Lincoln and Grimsby. Aggers used one of her favourite expressions to describe Boston: excellent hardware. Software? Well, neither of us had ever seen so many mobility scooter shops in - well, our lives! Of course, there are genuine hard luck stories but so many overweight, and quite young in many cases, folk requiring 4 wheels to get them to the shops? I know that, if I keep it in, will not be a popular view but I'm sorry, it really was a shock. And no, they weren't all heading to the Spoon. There were some decidedly unsavoury looking characters hanging around the main square, giving the city a slightly edgy atmosphere, not in keeping with some of the delightful historical buildings.

Skegness, always derided by my generation in the south, was no different to Littlehampton, for example, and probably a vast improvement on Margate or Bognor Regis. As we returned to the coast from Louth, another seaside town's name: Cleethorpes, failed to live up to its grim perception by us southern snobs. Don't knock it until you've tried it. OK, so we didn't try either for much longer than a quick half hour stroll and half a pint in their best public houses but they certainly both outscored their expected marks out of 10 in reality.

We've yet to have anything other than a very nice experience in a Spoon hotel and Grimsby's offering was no different. I'd like to say it was raining on arrival, which deterred us from going for a wander around the town, but it wasn't. I never like to admit I get knackered but, after a 5 am start and 6 Spoons later, it didn't take much persuasion from Aggers, who never tries to hide any feelings of fatigue, that a couple of pints and an earlyish night was a more appealing option. Coupled with the fact that we had received some rather sad and shocking news that afternoon, that the topic of real addiction (not our silly collecting version) had struck very close to home, we would take our learned friend's, from nearby Scunny, observations that Grimsby was still a bit grim in places, rather than see for ourselves.

Our attempts to secure the services of a mechanic hadn't gone quite as well as expected. The best my Scunthorpe mate could come up with was a loose appointment at Kwik Fit. "Just get there nice and early", was the advice. We had to stop at Brigg on the way - yet another surprisingly pleasant town and pub, but hoped to be in Scunthorpe by 9.30. However, in addition to the rather concerning noise, I had noticed a very flat rear tyre before we left home. I'd stuck a bunch of air in it and all seemed well when we finished that evening. Unfortunately, once again, it was looking rather sad for itself as we left Grimsby for Brigg. We tried to put some more air in it but evidently, it was beyond resuscitation.

We had made a short diversion from Grimsby to Brigg via Humberside Airport so I could bore Aggers senseless once more with how I'd ticked that one off (Heathrow-Norwich-Humberside, bus to Scarborough FC v Can't remember, hitch to Middlesborough, Teesside-Heathrow. In case you're interested

- 3 new airports for 1 footy ground), but I don't think it affected our plight. I'm rubbish with cars so I figured we'd be OK to limp to Kwik Fit with this tyre. Wrong, as usual. 3 agonising miles short of our Mazda hospital appointment the burning smell and bumping gave me no option but to pull over. I knew the car had no spare but one of those useless run flat contraptions instead. Even more useless when the tyre has pretty much fallen apart. 3 1/2 hours we waited for the breakdown recovery. Tyre replaced but no spare part available to cure the noise - a wheel bearing, which curiously, had only been replaced 13 months previously. Only one culprit: our wonderful government allowing our roads to wither to such a state of disrepair, costing the taxpayer 100s of pounds in repairs on top of £365 road tax annually, in our case.

We knew we didn't have too many miles left before Mazda would go no further but we had 3 Spoons to do before our evening in Scunthorpe. I used to play Sunday league footy with 2 lads originally from Scunny. They had moved back some 20 years ago but were very keen to reacquaint after I managed to track them down. Sorry to say, but they both agreed, poor Scunthorpe fits the image of a grim northern town held by snobby southerners. We couldn't just stay there all afternoon while Mazda suffered silently. Probably not my best idea ever, but we did a quick hat trick of Goole (OK), Beverley (splendid) and Hull University (odd) before arriving for our 7.30 rendezvous in Scunthorpe (OK pub). We didn't have a plan to fix Mazda and knew we couldn't continue much further with it in its current state. Knocking off/adding 3 new pubs was burying my head in the sand but that's what we did.

I do hope the concept of opening a Wetherspoon pub on a university campus doesn't become a thing. I had phoned ahead as it was approaching Easter time to check they would be open, as most students would not be around, maybe. They would be but, could we find an entrance to the pub? No. Were they answering the phone now? Nope. I was contemplating whether I could seriously be arsed to come back to Hull University during term time, one day. I was veering towards no I couldn't, when we finally found a student who knew exactly where the Spoon was. Phew, dilemma avoided. How could you be on campus and not know, though!!!!? Well, that's the response we'd had to our previous enquiries. Maybe they just didn't want an old grandad in their Students' Union, come Wetherspoon.

Tim Martin, or one of his minions, or whoever struck the deal has probably come up with a good idea. But, not for us. No history and, more importantly, no carpet. We agreed we wouldn't hang around, did that very rare in and out without a purchase, and took a scenic ride over the Humber Bridge back to Scunny. In addition to a very pleasant evening reminiscing about Upper Norwood FC amongst other topics we made some tentative progress with Mazda. Paul thought he had a mechanic who could help us out. Bruce, who, heroically, hadn't missed a Sunday Upper Norwood football match in our/their last 10 years of existence, was holding out that the Kwik Fit fitter may be able to do the job on the side. We'd deal with it in the morning. Our Spoons count was up to 834, most importantly.

As it turned out, the owner of our humble overnight abode helped with the final solution. Paul's mate reluctantly agreed to squeeze us in Thursday morning but we needed the parts! Long story short, as I frequently say but rarely do, having tried to locate a mechanic through friends in Hull, Wetherby, Leeds and York we were no further forward. The nearest part we could find was in Cambridge! We enquired to the owner/manager of the Hotel Clamart if our room was available for the coming night. We were clearly going to be extending our stay in Scunthorpe! It wasn't, but he had a single room for £35. Sorted. He then proceeded to ring round for a wheel bearing for Mazda. Not only did he locate one in Scunthorpe but it was half the price of what we'd found on line.

Armed with the precious new bearing, we headed down to Kwik Fit to ask Nick if he would like to fit it for us. Nick was on a day off! But Mick gave us his number. Nick was on the golf course but, "call Charlie on this number and say Nick sent you". 40 minutes later and Mazda was as good as new - well, wheel bearing and 1 tyre wise, that is. It was looking every bit of its 17 years in all other aspects. We could escape Scunthorpe after all. It had genuinely been looking like Mazda would be out of service until after Easter. After all the help Mr Clamart had given us I couldn't possibly ask for my £35 back. Plus, it was raining, we had time in our schedule and we could catch up with Bruce again, and meet his wife. We settled in for a mammoth 8-hour stint in Scunthorpe's best pub, obviously, before heading north the next morning.

Norton was such a contrast with Stockton, which we had visited the previous year. A charming village/small town v a rather run-down looking place just a few miles south. Our route took us to Billingham, Hartlepool, Peterlee, Seaham and finally, to Sunderland - home to 2 pretty decent Spoons. The logistics of visiting the remaining pubs in the north east and Yorkshire were complicated by the Premier League's decision to move the Leeds v Palace match from Saturday to Sunday. I planned to tick off Harrogate, 91 of current 92, on Good Friday, followed by a trip to Elland Road on Saturday. I tried to convince Aggers that it would be a great idea to slink over to Barrow on Easter Monday to complete the current 92, but 3 footy matches in 4 days was pushing it. Whilst Harrogate offered the much-celebrated Winter Gardens for her to pass the time while I collected number 91, and Leeds' Spoons are certainly worthy of a few hours in my absence, Barrow.... well, the pub is not bad but there was a 4-5 hour round trip involved, so reluctantly, I agreed to leave it until next season.

We breakfasted in Houghton-le-Spring and Spennymoor en route to Harrogate but my anxiety levels were dangerously high. Harrogate v AFC Wimbledon. Just old-fashioned pay on the gate surely? Harrogate's average attendance 2,500ish, capacity 5,500ish. However, I thought I'd just check before retiring Thursday evening. Members only!? New members must purchase a combined ticket for the last 3 home games for £58! No tickets available on the day at the ground! Seriously? I may be desperate to be 92 complete again, but not for £58 to see Harrogate Town v AFC Wimbledon. I texted a couple of my Leeds locals to see if they knew any Harrogate members.

Nope. It was surprising I managed to sleep. 9 am sharp I called the ticket office. If I could provide proof of address they would sell me just the 1 ticket in the club's town centre shop. "OK, but I actually live about 10 miles from Wimbledon. Honestly though, I'm a genuine ground collector, please, (I'm begging you - I felt like adding)". "Problem is, sir, we've had a large number of ground hoppers (is that what they're called these days?) from South London requesting tickets. We could only give Wimbledon 600, you see, due to ground improvements restricting capacity. Can you prove you're genuine and not an away fan?" Thank you very much, Metro Josh! " Well, I had an article written by a national newspaper on my other collections and it mentions that I do the 92. I have a copy on my phone?". "That should be fine then. I'll leave a note for my colleague. It'll be his decision".

Agnes couldn't understand why I was still stressing. I wouldn't be able to chill until I had the ticket in my grubby mitts, which I did, a few hours later. The much-praised Winter Gardens was indeed, a fine pub, but plenty others equally so, in our opinion. After a fine afternoon in the sun, we headed down to Ilkley for our annual meeting with Mr & Mrs Green, followed by a late evening session and overnight with the completely bonkers but delightful Mrs Hamilton of Yeadon.

We headed north again to the utterly charming venues of Knaresborough and Ripon. Harrogate gets all the plaudits and very charming it is too. But these 2 are equally delightful as far as we're concerned. We had plenty of time to wander around both, as well as spending time in the fine pubs, before heading back to Leeds to visit the recently opened Scribbling Mill. We were initially very excited by the news of a new Spoon in Leeds, what with so many closing. However, once we learned that it was in an out-of-town shopping complex our enthusiasm disappeared. It would be a tick exercise only. We hate shops. The pub was surprisingly small and packed with happy shoppers. A very swift half and we were off. Leeds proceeded to ruin Sunday by losing 1-5 to Palace but a good time was had in the Hedley Verity before heading off to Mrs Hamilton for another barking mad evening.

Back north we continued the next day via Bishop Auckland, Durham - sadly just missing out on 1 of this delightful city's 2 Spoons, having just closed a few weeks previously - Chester-le-Street, Concord (the address of The Sir William de Wessyngton is Washington but it's actually in Concord) and South Shields to Cramlington - our base for the next 3 nights. We had a Spoon free day the next day as our hosts had a rather lovely dog and Tim Martin just won't budge on the no dogs rule, (at least that gave us the opportunity for a fabulous long walk on some of the many stunning beaches in the north east), but couldn't resist nipping out to Bedlington and Blyth, briefly, in the evening. Yet again, 2 fine pubs. The next day we started in Ashington, what a letdown. I expected The Rohan Kanhai to be full of cricket memorabilia. Not even 1 picture of the great man it's named after. I'd been looking forward to this pub for some time but, as well as the lack of cricket history, the building was nondescript and new. Spoon redeemed themselves in Morpeth, with a charming old cinema, and the town was equally pleasant. It was time to head back south of the Tyne to hit the 4 remaining pubs in the region. After an extremely swift visit to the Gateshead Metrocentre, even the pub name is bland: Wetherspoons, Whickham: The Harry Clasper, put us back in more favourable surroundings. Our north east collection was completed by Crook and Consett. Never heard of either of them. Our brief visit, both town and pub wise led us to believe they were at polar opposites: Crook and The Horse Shoe Inn were really quite charming, Consett and The Company Row were not.

Having resisted the temptation between Xmas and New Year to visit The Cross Keys in Peebles before it closed, we could now hold out no longer. We were only 2 hours away and, whilst you wouldn't need to be a geographical genius to work out that it wasn't strictly on our way home/south, a quick phone call confirmed that the pub/hotel had been sold. The member of staff didn't feel at liberty to divulge the closing date but recommended we visit sooner rather than later. We needed no further persuading and enjoyed a most pleasant early morning drive via Galashiels (Spoon) to the condemned Spoon. I did check on the app the other day and 3 months later, it's hanging on! It's a shame as it's a lovely old building in a nice town.

As we headed south, on a most scenic drive, we ticked off another fine pub in Dumfries and perhaps more importantly, learnt where Queen of the South FC live. Well, undoubtedly not important to Agi and most of you, but to those enamoured with the classified football results on a Saturday, you may be interested, if you didn't already know, to learn that it (it's so tempting to say they, but it/they is/are one team) resides in Dumfries. And quite a nice ground it is too. I also subjected Agi to detours to Annan Athletic FC and Gretna 2008 FC.

I read an article recently on the BBC about a young guy who had visited all 92 football grounds with his father within 3 years, I think. Bizarrely, he rarely watched a match and, frequently, didn't even gain access to the ground. I'm not planning to add Scottish football grounds to our collections in this manner, but I do gain a certain amount of satisfaction in putting a face to a name, where possible, if you know what I mean? I'm sure I've mentioned this before but, in case you've forgotten, or were wondering, on such a mammoth Spoon run such as this, we have made a purchase in all 42 pubs bar the shopping centre in Gateshead and Hull University. Sometimes this may only involve a shared 1/2 pint, in order for me to drive legally, or a shared coffee, to reduce the need for toilet stops... for me.

Our Spoons crawl was a huge success and, to the continuing astonishment of family, friends and acquaintances, immensely enjoyable. Despite our explanations to them that we love visiting new places in the UK, many of them seem to only focus on their preconceived idea of a Wetherspoon and some, of their dislike of Tim Martin. Their loss, not ours or Tim's, although he likes anybody's custom I imagine. This Spoon trip was concluded 3 months ago. A bit of forward planning means the next will not start until another 8 weeks have passed. Without wishing to wish our lives away, I can't wait. I feel if I was to tell you about what we've done and plan to do in the meantime I'd be going full on diary mode. I've wondered if I will be tempted to write book 3, should we complete our collections, as a continuation of our adventures. Would this be too self-indulgent? No more than this, so far, I hear you say, dear reader. Nonetheless, I feel it would be remiss of me not to mention Billy Bishop Airport.

Whilst trying to find a cheap way from New York to Quebec City (the latter being a new airport for us, in case you were wondering), I stumbled upon a route including an intermediary stop with an unfamiliar 3 letter airport code at a decent price. Toronto has more than one airport? Well I never did! And how handsomely named too. Even better, the airline which would fly us there? Porter Airlines. Now, you've heard about Jim the pilot? And yes, he did very kindly get us upgraded on our flight to New York. But Russ, has never been Russ the pilot. Not because he doesn't get us upgrades. Not because his airline is orange and only has one class. But because I knew Russ before he was a pilot. What Russ has, however, that Jim the pilot doesn't, to the best of my knowledge, is an airline named after him. If you're not paying attention or don't give a damn, I'll spell it out. His name is Russ Porter! I was disappointed that Porter Airlines didn't have personalised sick bags, which I could have pilfered for him. I was disappointed in myself that I didn't think to take a Porter Airlines glass with me for him.

Not only is Billy Bishop Airport well named, in my opinion, it is beyond doubt, superbly located: it sits on an island no more than 100 or so metres from downtown Toronto, reached on foot by a subway. How cool is that? And, it can only take propeller planes too, so it's nice and quiet and small. Wikipedia will tell you who Billy was, should you be interested.

I was also delighted to land at Abbotsford Airport. Why, I hear you ask? On my first visit to Canada in 1976 I visited the Abbotsford Airshow, not a small affair. When I learnt around 25 years ago that scheduled services had commenced, naturally I wanted it. On numerous visits to family there I couldn't justify the significant additional expense and, even more so, inconvenience of incorporating Abbotsford International into any schedule. Finally the time came to slot it in, in a financially and operationally favourable manner. To be honest, it wasn't a very interesting airport but, for me, it did have special significance. I was also keen to add Bellingham to our list, but baulked at £70 each for a 30-minute flight to Seattle. I thought I'd have a quick check the day before we were due to fly home, just in case, very unlikely, I know, there was a last-minute special. Not a chance. Airline pricing never ceases to amaze me: it was going to cost more to fly 30 minutes from Bellingham to Seattle than 8 hours 30 minutes from Seattle to London! Nuts!

Whilst I was happy that our airport numbers were increasing in a less obsessive and manic fashion I felt myself becoming more preoccupied, and to a slightly spooky and scary level, with an aforementioned, well to myself and Agi, desire to visit every airport on the networks of Ryanair, Wizzair and easyJet. I don't have to fly there with them, any old airline will suffice, as Dan Air did for a good chunk of them. I didn't want to go full on cold turkey but this was and is bordering on failed rehab. Our next trip; to Poland, is scheduled to include 4 Ryanair destinations in Sweden, for example. On our way back I couldn't resist a very reasonably priced flight with Wizzair to Kutaisi, which then leads to a slightly longer than necessary journey home via 3 (4 for Aggers) new airports, not served by any of these 3 airlines, through Turkey. I'm getting ahead of myself though. Actually, I have. Our next, post Spoon, European trip is already booked and includes 5 (9 for Aga) Ryanair/Wizzair destinations.

I hope I haven't tempted fate by even mentioning this, because there's the small matter of a visit to Barrow FC to accomplish too before we head off, with hopefully just part of one hand needed to count the Spoons left to complete that little collection, currently at 864 should you be wondering.

Lest we forget the National Trails: someone has been busy renaming the England Coast Path the King Charles the 3rd England Coast Path. Perhaps this will lend some momentum to getting the beast completed and opened. Whilst walking the 20 miles from Allhallows to Gravesend, it allowed us time to contemplate the complexities involved. It's rather disheartening to see the progress made since 2014, when the project started. At the current rate of sections opening I would be in my 90s, at least, before it's completed! We can but walk what is there, so far, and that is what we intend to do. Maybe that could be the core of a 3rd book? For now, I have one more chapter in me, I've decided. Will there be a happy ending?

# CHAPTER 25

I've found myself becoming increasingly impatient to finish our little collections, to the point where I have to keep telling myself to stop wishing my life away. We have just made our way to Poland via a week in Sweden and daily, at the very least, I found myself trying to fast forward to the last day, so that the airports I was after, materialised, without weather or any other, however unlikely, incident jeopardising their addition.

I think I have proved to myself, beyond any reasonable doubt, that I have an addiction to collecting: I think I have become unhealthily obsessed with notching every Wizzair/Ryanair/easyJet served airport. However, yet again, this airport obsession has led us to visit places which, I'm pretty certain, would not have featured in our travel plans. So... perhaps the obsession is not so unhealthy, after all. If I just write for a while, it will keep me off the aforementioned airlines' apps, checking to see if they have added or deleted any routes. Yesterday I was quite disturbed to see that Erbil in Iraq had been added to Wizzair's destination list, 3 times per week from Abu Dhabi. This would really test my resolve. Whilst I welcome the opportunity to add Bishkek and Samarkand, amongst others, I'm not sure that an Iraqi visa will be that easy to come by.

Fortunately, for now, although flight dates show on the app, none are bookable. In a positive frame of mind, if these flights do materialise it would give us the opportunity to add Iraq to our country list, which we're not counting, obviously. I'm sure the decision makers at Wizzair are looking at Tehran too, hopefully. Whilst I wouldn't be disappointed if Erbil disappeared from the list not long after it appeared, I was a bit gutted that Mattala vanished. We were both keen to spend some time in Sri Lanka and, with the airport numbers no longer being such a driver, Wizzair were promising a very palatable price option with a new airport into the bargain. If we planned a bit further in advance, I would have booked the flights before they disappeared. This would no doubt have resulted in Wizzair giving us credit for the cancelled flights from Abu Dhabi to Mattala but I bet, if I was a gambling man, they wouldn't have allowed us to cancel the flights we would have booked with them to Abu Dhabi from Europe. "Things happen for a reason", I hear Aggers saying. So, it's back to the drawing board for the next winter break.

We feared a week in Sweden may play havoc with the budget but it didn't thanks to Aggers' bright idea of hearty and pretty healthy hotel buffet breakfasts. Where we weren't staying with breakfast included, such as the prison (converted, you understand) in Visby, we could purchase it at a very reasonable price indeed in another establishment. Thus, food expenditure was kept at an appetising level! My concern at spending more than I would've liked on completing Ryanair's (and Wizzair's) Swedish offerings did not materialise. Orebro, Visby, Skelleftea and Vaxjo were all worthwhile visiting in their own rights, particularly Visby; highly recommended, even if we left without mastering their pronunciation. In addition, we also hit Kalmar, with SAS; another fine city. There are a few tantalising domestic double drops in Sweden, not operated by our low-cost friends, which could yet result in another visit to this fine country.

Our journey home only included one Wizzair destination, Kutaisi, but another 3 (4 for Agi) in Turkey. Kutaisi had been on our to do list since our Georgia visit in 2015. No free wine on arrival at immigration this time, but still the best looking and most smiling officials. Georgia did not disappoint again. Whilst Kutaisi wasn't the most exciting city ever, it was pleasant enough. We had decided against departing Georgia from Batumi, therefore completing the small set of Georgia's commercial airports, in favour of the rather bizarre Rize-Artvin, not far over the border in Turkey.

We took a train to Batumi. The departure time was rather

unenticing - 0530 (the only other train was at 1800), but the cost of the ticket at 30p each was most palatable - for a 5-hour journey! The distance involved was 150 kilometres. You don't need to have finished top of the class in Maths, nor hopefully need a calculator to work out how incredibly slow we would go. We weren't in a hurry, the old train had had a decent refurb internally and it was very empty. It didn't seem that Georgia Railway were purely profit focused.

We liked Batumi. Unfairly dubbed, in our opinion, "Dubai of the Black Sea" it seemed to have a nicely balanced mixture of old and new - not something immediately apparent in one of our least favourite destinations. If you love Dubai, I guess you'd be disappointed in Batumi. We don't, so we weren't.

Why did I describe Rize-Artvin Airport as bizarre? Well, firstly it is not close to either of these towns/cities. Secondly, it has been built on a huge swathe of reclaimed land, less than 70 miles from already well-established Trabzon Airport, walking distance, for us, from the nondescript town of Pazar, where we overnighted. It is just 20 miles further from Rize to Trabzon Airport than it is from Rize to Rize-Artvin Airport. Not a huge gain for the folk of Rize, you could argue. Fourthly, it's huge. Granted it had barely been open a year when we visited but, planning for a more climate friendly future it certainly isn't. Currently only offering several daily flights to Istanbul, one to Ankara and Muscat a couple of times per week, unless we're missing something in that region, it looks like it could be underutilised for some time to come.

The lack of any information at the fingertips of the information desk employee (as usual - they really are the biggest waste of space, with few exceptions), all food and beverage establishments being closed (when exactly would they be open? When there were no flights due, making them equally as useful as the information desk?) just added to the bizarreness. The location was quite interesting though and the whole experience ensured that number 1015 (521 Agi) will remain in the memory for a while at least.

I need to be careful here as I find myself going into self-indulgent diarising mode. So, suffice to say that our day stop in Ankara was much nicer than expected, as was our stay in Canakkale. Our overnight across the Dardanelles Strait in Kilitbahir has to be mentioned though. We were in the company of a retired Turkish naval captain, who ran the most delightful 3-bedroom B&B. It, and he, reminded both of us of our friend Sudhir in India. What is it about military personnel and their attention to detail in their homes? Granted, we only have 2 examples to date, but the similarities were striking. Indeed, their conversation wasn't worlds apart either, apart from the lack of sexual encounter themed stories from our more reticent Turkish friend. Mind you, he wasn't shy in voicing his prejudices. Virtually his first comment was how much he "hated Arabs". Not what we were expecting to hear in Turkey.

Anyway, the main reason for mentioning him, was breakfast. Butter my arse (as Alan Partridge may have exclaimed)! What looked like a buffet fit for 20 hotel guests was all ours! Neither of us had ever seen anything like it. I counted over 25 different dishes and I'm not exaggerating. If we were in any doubt that it was all for us, there was an identical table laid adjacent for our 2 fellow overnighters. Whether they didn't have the same determination to stuff themselves as us, or that they were simply short of time, we will never know. They were driving from Antalya to Serbia, and had chosen to break their journey with Richard. After all, he did come extremely highly recommended. We spent literally 2 hours over one of the best breakfasts ever whilst they were gone in 20 minutes.

I did manage to plant the seed of doubt, yet again, with Aggers as to the reality of the previous travels I claim to have made. I even surprised myself at my latest bout of stupidity. Our plan was to visit the island of Gokceada. I was intrigued to see how it measured up to the nearby Greek islands. We needed to take a 5-10 minute bus ride to Eceabat and then a longer bus ride to Kabatepe, from whence we would take an hour and a half ferry ride to the island. Due to the time we had taken stuffing our faces it already looked like we were leaving ourselves very little time to spend on the island itself. When we arrived in Eceabat there was a bus with a Kabatepe sign in it. It was open but there was no sign of a driver. After waiting around 30 minutes I was seriously questioning the logic in continuing our journey when, lo and behold, another bus screeched into the opposite side of the square with a sign telling me it was headed for Kabatepe. I shouted to Aggers to run over and join me.

Whether it was the right decision to continue on our way we would know when we arrived in Kabatepe to find out how long until the next ferry. Well that was the theory. I was slightly surprised that the other 3 passengers waiting for the original Kabatepe bus to depart hadn't joined us. Maybe they weren't as quick as me to seize the opportunity. I wasn't unduly alarmed when we headed off, initially back in the direction of Kilitbahir, "must be taking the scenic route" I ventured to Aggers. What a dick! I had only gone and put us on a Kilitbahir bus. I'm sure you can sympathise how easy it would be to confuse Kilitbahir and Kabatepe, particularly for such a seasoned traveller? No? Neither did Aggers. They both began with K, but that was where any similarity ended. Not for me. They both had 4 syllables, as well. Fortunately, it was I who had the stronger desire to visit Gokceada. Any doubts that we didn't really have time to make the journey were laid to rest by virtue of us being back at the start of it an hour later

We, or I, consoled ourselves with the alternative: a quick hop on the ferry back over to Canakkale to buy some beers and hire a moped. The latter proved impossible but, luckily, the former didn't. I wasn't done yet though. We popped into the adjacent tourist office in the harbour to enquire about buses to Edremit, our next obscure airport. Whilst in there I reached into my pocket to find out on my phone how far the bus station was. It's quite scary the level of panic I felt when I realised my phone had decided to remain on the ferry. What was it thinking? As I sprinted the 100-200 metres (well, as close to a sprint as my 63-year-old legs can manage these days) back to the ferry, ignoring the protestations of the ferry staff that I couldn't reboard, I thought I was actually going to cry. Sound pathetic, or are you fully empathising with me? As I continued to sprint through the now empty ferry, my panic levels were rising. It had been fully 10-15 minutes since we'd parted company. Would my phone have had the sense to make its way to lost property or would it have decided to stay put for my return? I'd told it times over not to go off with strangers. The amount of relief I felt when I saw it lying where I had left it was almost perfectly in proportion to my anxiety level on realising my latest bout of stupidity.

It isn't only a phone though, is it, these days? I'm sure I need say no more on the subject. I'm writing a book on it for starters. Well, at least I'm trying to, with the level of turbulence we're going through on our return from our latest European adventure. Such is my desire to complete the Ryanair/Wizzair/easyJet trilogy I got so far ahead of myself that I'd booked this trip fully 3 months ahead, at the same time as the Sweden/Georgia/Turkey 3 centre holiday. One month later and we were booked through until Christmas Day! I'm not going to tempt fate by telling you now where we hope to be off to on the first part of our winter 23/24 jaunt. Suffice to say it involves 7 Wizzair destinations but, as they've already cancelled one route we booked and reinstated one we didn't, who knows what the outcome will be. Throw in the latest horrendous outbreak of war in Palestine and Israel and even I can't get too anxious about whether those 7 materialise or not. It's actually quite difficult to enjoy travel, knowing what suffering others are enduring. Sadly, like the Ukraine/Russia situation we'll end up becoming somewhat numb to it, the longer it goes on.

One benefit of this forward planning was what we paid for the flights. Another habit I've developed, when I remember, is seeing how the prices have changed from when we booked. Our current flight from Brasov to Luton cost us £26 each. Yesterday it was retailing at £236!! Our train journey from Luton to Woldingham costs £32 each! Mental, isn't it. As I had promised Agnes we would visit some places which would only be new to her it was time for me to deliver. After we had arrived in

Bergamo again (becoming quite a little hub for us) via Tampere and Lappeenranta, as you do, we were off to Sardinia. First though, I was intrigued how Lappeenranta remained viable as a commercial operation with just 2 flights per week, both of them on Ryanair to Bergamo. Once we had located the Lappeenranta Tourist Office, bizarrely located in a shopping centre, it became clear. For once, someone was in the right job. The cheerful and helpful lady explained that the Russians would come to Lappeenranta to fly onwards in Europe. We knew Lappeenranta was very close to the border but we didn't realise that it was only 2 hours' drive from St Petersburg. Sure enough our flight was full of Russians. The numbers had unsurprisingly dropped dramatically since the outbreak of war. Only those with dual nationality could cross the border, hence why all other flights had been suspended.

I thought that Tampere and Lappeenranta may remain elusive but I'd managed to snap them up at bargain prices and in a very convenient routing. OK so you can fly London to Bergamo very directly and cheaply but it was only a minor diversion. It was no hardship to return to Sardinia. I remembered virtually nothing of my Dan Air trip 35 years earlier, all 3 airports ticked off courtesy of a double drop in Alghero and Cagliari on the way out and a return from Olbia. Thanks again to Aggers making and keeping connections we were able to meet up with Gigi whom we had met in Mulu Caves the previous winter. He'd told us that he ran a small guesthouse but neither of us could remember where. Just so happened that it was in Alghero and yes he would be back there in a few days and would be delighted to have us stay. He didn't mention that his guesthouse was pretty decent so it came as a rather pleasant surprise. What a very, very classy joint he ran. It was a bit of a shame that we only had one night but it was really nice to catch up with him.

Another guy with life nicely sorted; Sardinia in the glorious Mediterranean summer, bugger off for the winter. He'd told us that after Borneo, he would meet up with his girlfriend in Bali around Xmas/New Year. "How did your Bali trip go,

Gigi?" Aggers enquired. "Well not quite to plan." Gigi replied in what turned out to be in extremely understated fashion. The day after his girlfriend arrived he was only attacked by a shark whilst surfing! Now Gigi, being Italian, no Sardinian (they identify primarily with their island not their bosses on the mainland) was pretty cool and quite the adventurous type so naturally he kept his cool while his frickin' foot was hanging off! He did admit to acknowledging that he was in a spot of bother but panic he did not. I can't remember the details of what followed but after several days in hospital he decided that he would prefer to have the required surgery in his homeland. At least he'd had a couple of months away. His less fortunate girlfriend had a couple of days, if you don't count the hospital days. It was her first backpacking trip and Gigi reckoned she was more scarred than his foot. Luckily his foot had made a pretty reasonable recovery whereas he didn't think his girlfriend had fared so well. It was time to retrace my Dan Air journey from Alghero to Cagliari but this time by train, mainly.

We had a wonderful 5 days in Sardinia, followed by the same in Malta and Gozo, all in the name of Nis! You remember, don't you? Last year we couldn't enter Serbia from Kosovo. So Malta provided a handy gateway. There really is something so utterly charming about the Mediterranean in late summer. The holiday crowds had certainly left Sardinia. Even if Malta was still very busy, certain parts were superb and our experience was enhanced by our Egyptian Couchsurfing host, Sherif and his pal, Omar, I kid you not.

Nis, as a destination, was fine but we chose to head straight down to North Macedonia. I think I mentioned before, that I had undertaken a journey to this neck of the woods during the height of my first bout of depression/anxiety. My distant memory stored images of cobbled streets in Skopje. Nothing of the sort on our arrival. I was really quite relieved when they materialised the next day. Agi already had enough ammunition to doubt my pre-Agnieszka travels. I openly admitted that I could recall nothing of Lake Ohrid apart from the Dan Air flight. We both agreed that North Macedonia is an extremely underrated destination. Apparently Ohrid gets seriously overcrowded in high season but it was an absolute gem for us as was the journey to and from Skopje. If only they'd stop smoking! Them and the Serbs and Romanians, they love it; indoors too.

It was time to return to Romania and finally tick off Constanta. But how to get there from Skopje? Via Luton, obviously. I didn't look into it but I'm certain it wouldn't have been any cheaper or quicker to go overland. Besides, a new opportunity had also presented itself in Romania. 13 hours and 20 minutes after leaving Skopje we were in Constanta and that included a Saturday night partying in the Ibis Hotel Luton Airport. Well, if you count being in bed by midnight and up at 0430 as a party. Agnes had quite rightly baulked at my extremely tentative suggestion that, particularly if our flight arrival was delayed, we could enjoy an evening in one of our (least) favourite airports. Luckily, not only were we on time into Luton, but we arrived 30 minutes early in Constanta Airport - well, what was left of it.

As you know, we're all about terminal buildings and locations when it comes to enjoying a new airport visit. Constanta, literally, didn't have a terminal. It looked as if a stray Russian bomb had destroyed it, I kid you not. We have experienced many airports where a new terminal is being constructed and meanwhile, the old dilapidated one remains in use. Pardubice, a briefly Ryanair served destination being a funny example: the new commercial terminal wasn't open, although fully constructed, so we were bussed to the nearby, and very ancient-looking military barracks for immigration formalities.

Now, some clever folks in Constanta had taken the utterly inexplicable decision to completely bulldoze their old terminal before even laying foundations for a new one. We learnt from a local passenger that she had passed through the fully intact terminal only 3 months earlier. It was only that she had been forewarned that she wasn't as gobsmacked as us. In lieu of anything resembling an airport terminal we were filtered through a shipping container for immigration control. You can imagine how many people you can fit in one of these, allowing for a couple of counters as well. It's certainly nowhere near the 230 Wizzair fit into their A321s! The sun was shining so it was no hardship for us to queue in the open, but winter can be pretty unpleasant in this neck of the woods.

Constanta is hardly a busy airport, 6 flights per week, but what's the record time taken to build a new airport terminal from scratch? I imagine the shipping containers (there were a couple more for departures and baggage) are going to see a fair bit of use for a couple of years at least. I don't know why Constanta had appealed to me for so long. I knew that the city wasn't blessed with endless attractions and that the nearby Black Sea resorts wouldn't be charming. Maybe because it had eluded me in pairing it with any other airport on our 6 previous visits to Romania. The fun continued at the airport as we waited for a non-existent bus service which the locals promised us would materialise. Once the last of our 200+ fellow passengers had disappeared we decided to head out to the main road to see if we could find a passing bus. I tried to wave down a passing minibus but, as it shot past us, the car in front of it screeched to a halt. I hadn't even started hitchhiking but we'd blagged a lift the 25 kms to downtown without even trying. Coupled with the kind chap at the airport who'd given us 10 Lei to help with our fare for the imaginary bus, we were quids in.

We were promised by LP that the non-stop partying in the height of summer in the resorts would be long gone and they weren't wrong. We did manage to find a nice lakeside restaurant and a ridiculously cheap, and open, hotel for the night but the place really was deserted. We headed back to Constanta and again LP was right, even if their book was 7 years old. The old town was still very much a work in progress, but not unpleasant. 3 months after our visit I read an article in the Metro titled "The hidden paradise tipped to top Croatia as this year's hot holiday destination". Imagine my surprise when I read on; you are sh*tting me!! Had the author actually been to Constanta and the nearby beach resorts? Now as you know, we always look for the positives but Constanta a hidden paradise? Alright, a vision of paradise is subjective but I bet even the Romanian Tourist Board would have a giggle at that.

We enjoyed a couple of old-fashioned train journeys to Brasov from Constanta via Bucharest and immediately set off to complete a journey we started 8 years ago! The Transfagarasan Highway was open! Mind you, as we headed out from Brasov we were slightly concerned by the amount of snow on the mountains. Our host Victor assured us, over a couple of glasses of his homemade wine, that the road was most definitely open. It was freezing, first scrape of the windscreen in a while, but the journey did not disappoint in the slightest. LP had suggested that the drive was best undertaken north to south. We had made it to the closed tunnel from the south previously. They were right. It was a stunning drive. However, the welcome in the restaurant overlooking the lake at the summit was as frosty as the weather. User-friendly the staff most certainly were not.

We spent our final day and evening in Brasov, a town we had overlooked on our previous visits and yet another fabulous spot in Romania. Brasov Airport couldn't have contrasted more starkly with Constanta. It only opened 4 months before our visit. Sadly there wasn't a Dan Air plane there. I may've already mentioned the new Romanian airline, stealing its name from my former employer. I'm not sure if I'm happy, sad or indifferent to it. I'm sure you're eager to know why it's Dan Air. Well not far from the original, in terms of initials (Davies and Newman in case you'd forgotten). Apparently they are the initials of the founder, although Google and Wiki are letting me down as I try to confirm.

Anyway, with 12 departures per week, it was our kind of airport. Now, seeing as collecting Ryanair/Wizzair and easyJet wasn't a thing when I started this book-writing lark, best I get back to the original collections. No doubt you're eager to know how we're getting on with Spoons, walking the ECP and Barrow. Well, the latter 2 weren't on the radar when I started But I Digress but I'll update you anyway, as, if you've got this far, you must be interested.

I'm afraid it warrants a chapter 26 so, with a heavy heart, my 2 books will not have the equality in chapter numbers I craved. Let's just say that it's Barrow's and Spoon's faults. While on number 26 let me share this with you: as you know Wizzair and Ryanair love to sit us as far apart as possible unless we pay them not to. We realised some time ago that the later we leave it to check in, the more likely we are to be sat near each other or even together. If the flight is full then the airline has no choice but to put you in the front rows if they haven't sold them. So instead of 9B and 30E we may get 2A and 3B. For our last 2 flights I checked to see what seats I could pay for. In both instances the only seats available were in row 26. On both flights we were allocated seats together in row 26. On the flight before those Agi overheard the cabin crew telling passengers that row 26 was free if they wanted to sit together. Spooky, eh? There is nothing special about row 26 I can assure you.

Just before I start chapter 26 (probably in a couple of months with my track record) let me share something with you, which I know you'll already know if you read this but, please let me have my moment of glory: But I Digress by Alan Forbes is now available on Amazon. In paperback and on kindle. I bloody did it, 3 1/2 years after starting. Not without a few issues and it certainly would never have happened if I had had to do it, the publishing that is. Thank you, Agi! Quite how chapter 25 appeared between chapters 15 and 16 we'll never know. How we still had to make so many corrections after ex-wife, Jackie, had cast her beady eye over it is another mystery. Nobody has bought a hard copy yet, let alone downloaded for free (not surprising considering I've not told a soul yet) but it's done and I have a copy. So, as I was told so many years ago, "everybody has a book in them" and, as I said at the beginning of that book, "if I can do it, anyone can".

Right, so about those pubs and bloody Barrow....

# CHAPTER 26

Well of course I'm not going to go straight to Barrow or Spoons. I'm sure you'd be very surprised if I did. Or maybe I'll shock you. Can I shock you?..... I like wine, sorry digressing (Partridge fans only). Or we could play 'Where's Wally' but take off the W. Well Jeddah airport is the answer but let's come back to that. It's barely been a month since I finished chapter 25 and "But I Digress" is just flying off the shelves; or more accurately the Amazon conveyor belt. Worldwide sales, I kid you not - North America, Europe, Australasia, Asia; done. Antarctica could be a bit tricky but Africa and South America - I live in hope. When we last checked I was approaching the first cricketing milestone for batsmen, 50 not out. So not a complete waste of time but a little way off becoming a best seller. And I've set the royalties as low as I could to encourage sales. Seriously this Amazon app, KDP, is amazing. I'm baffled how I can order a book, which hasn't been printed and it's dispatched the next day. No, I haven't ordered all 50. Author's copies are not included in this total. At least there's no danger of any unwanted copies of my book being pulped!

I've had a lot of time on my hands lately so have had plenty of opportunities to consider the way forward. 26 chapters? Can I stretch it to 30? Should I write a chapter completely plastered/off me 'ead? If so, should I then correct it or delete it back in the land of sobriety? How many more stories can you handle, dear readers? Should I have several appendixes listing the airports, footy grounds, pubs and walks?

More importantly we've just picked up our boarding passes and, although Wizzair had allocated us 12F and 14C, not bad, when we asked if we could be sat together, guess what we got. Yep, you've got it 26A and 26B. Having been told that the flight is very empty why this row again? It's so odd.

OK, so we're nearly off on a mega-Spoon jaunt, a bit of walking and football heaven but it would be remiss of me not to tell you first, how 2 more Spoons were ticked off, even though it was after the large trip. We, well I really as chief planner, had come up with a plan to finish our Spoon collection in London, courtesy of the relatively recently opened Stargazer in the 02, Greenwich. Not an ideal venue but, if we want some friends to join us in our celebrations which we do, then London is the best bet. After all we celebrated our airport and walking milestones solo and I'm unaware of anybody willing to join me in Barrow's ground. So we needed to get Birmingham Airport Wetherspoon out of the way. At least they'd opened a pub in Birmingham New Street Station to make the trip a little more worthwhile. But would we actually fly from Birmingham? We had toyed with the idea of just buying the cheapest ticket, having a pint, then missing the flight and heading home. Just to reiterate that the pub is airside so one needs a flight ticket. That idea didn't sit too well with us so once I was able to chuck a new airport into the equation we were off.

Birmingham Airport security! Well, it may be a temporary situation but what a bloody mess. Almost an hour to get through, putting our pub visit in jeopardy. We would miss the flight if it meant getting the pub in. That's probably a bit over-dramatic as I'm sure we would have had time for a carpet pic only. No need to panic as the station and the airport pubs of Birmingham were added and we were off to sunny Spain, a chance to catch up with Agnes's friend, Vanessa in Palma, who had finally got me writing in Goa. How convenient of Vanessa to live within sensible walking distance of the airport. As I've mentioned before, more than once, we just love the late summer Mediterranean and a wonderful coastal setting for dinner and our airport walk the next morning validated our efforts to complete our Midlands pubs, as if we needed validation.

In keeping with the theme of ticking off the Ryanair destinations we took a flight to Valladolid the next morning. This return route enabled us to catch up with a friend of mine who I'd not seen for 20 years and Agnieszka to add another airport, Oviedo. If you remember the fellow footballer who couldn't get Russ Porter's name right I'd be both impressed and scared. Upper Norwood FC stalwart, Terry Jardine, no less. It may be a bit negligent of me not to have waffled on about UNFC as I have to admit I was obsessed with/addicted to playing for this very low standard Croydon Sunday League team. Let me give you 3 examples: my second surprise visit to Vancouver involved a Sunday afternoon departure and a Saturday afternoon return so I didn't miss a match. We rarely had the option of functional showers so I headed out to Heathrow directly from Sanderstead Rec with my legs caked in mud. (Is this the sign of a true writer? Agnes caught me on my phone in the middle of the night, "what....... are you doing?" "I'm making some notes for the next chapter because I know I'll forget what I've been lying awake thinking about, in the morning. I think I'm a writer." "Right, good night darling.")

In 1995 Leeds were drawn away to Man U in the FA Cup. I would be half way through a 12-day trip to Central America, missing one Norwood game in the process. 14/15 days would have involved the unbearable withdrawal symptoms of missing 3 games. If I came back for the Leeds game on the Saturday I could play for Norwood on the Sunday before picking up on my Central American airport influenced trip (Belize was a right old carry on; 6 fun new airports). Whilst I was mulling over whether I really could justify this to myself, the Leeds game was moved to Sunday for TV. How could I resolve the dilemma of putting Leeds or Upper Norwood first? I couldn't do both now. Easy, stay away.

My ex-business partner was getting married in Sandakan, Malaysian Borneo. As I had been present at his spur of the moment wedding in Barbados (to the same woman) it was rightly decided that I would stay in Blighty and look after the business while others headed off for the celebrations. At the last moment I decided the business would be fine in the capable hands of the staff but I also had football to consider. I played the first half for British Island Airways in the

Wednesday Gatwick League before heading off with muddy legs to Heathrow to arrive late Thursday evening in Kota Kinabalu. My ex-business partner wasn't surprised to see me. He was expecting me. I don't think his mother, also a partner in the business, was impressed that I'd deserted the troops but she was certainly in shock. I had no option but to leave on Saturday after the Friday wedding in Sandakan. I had a match to play Sunday morning at Lloyd Park. I had my boots with me so the early morning arrival into Heathrow allowed me to head straight to Croydon.

I'm actually quite impressed with my stamina when I look back on it. Not a bad effort, straight off a 13-hour flight, let alone the 2 domestic connecting flights beforehand. Thanks to the flexibility of my supervisors at Dan Air I don't think I ever missed a match when I was rostered to work a Sunday day shift. A quick call after the match normally allowed me to head off for a few post-match pints before rolling up for the second half of my 12-hour duty. Playing in between night shifts was never in question.

There were other examples of when the addiction of playing footy resulted in some slightly abnormal behaviour, along with the need to see Leeds at a new ground; I had been invited on a very brief but enticing, business trip to Hong Kong. Only problem was that Leeds, in their lowly League One days, were due to play at Cheltenham. Surely, I couldn't turn down the Hong Kong trip for Cheltenham? Our schedule involved leaving Thursday evening, arriving Friday evening and returning overnight Sunday. The match was moved to Sunday 1pm (from Saturday 3pm). Result! Result as in I could leave the group a day early, arrive back Sunday morning and hotfoot it over to Cheltenham. Result? Of course Leeds lost 1-0 to bloody Cheltenham, but the ground was done. If you're getting the impression that I didn't, and don't like missing out you'd not be in the wrong ballpark. It wasn't the first time I'd been to the Far East for 1 night.

Anyway, it was great to see me old mucker Tel, in charming Valladolid (he's lived down the road in Pamplona for 20 years) and spend a night on the coast in pleasant Gijon. Once again these addictions of ours, mental as they may seem, resulted in another immensely enjoyable jaunt.

"Let me finish" (this chapter), by telling you about a new, to me, app. It's a footy ground collector's dream is myGrounds. I could now bore you with not only the 92, but most of the grounds I've been to around the world - the ground for the Ugandan Cup final which Jim the pilot and I stumbled into in Kampala is one of the few I can't add. I'm not going to do that though, you'll be very pleased to hear but I am going to tell you that I could add 2 grounds I played at, that's how far down the pyramid of non-league football this app goes; Lingfield and Burgess Hill, seeing as you asked. The latter being the venue for the only silverware I ever collected. I was very much in the twilight of my lengthy, if very undistinguished career. Pushing 45 (years old) it should've been no surprise or disappointment to me that I was on the bench for some lowly cup final we - we being Dormansland Rockets - had played a couple of games to reach but I'd managed to avoid being a substitute until the very last few games so waiting to be subbed on, as opposed to dreading being subbed off was a novel experience. As the game approached the end of extra time I'd given up hope of gracing the hallowed turf of Burgess Hill (but I would be able to add the ground to my Grounds, not that I knew that at the time) when in the 119th minute the coach said "Forbsie, you alright to get on and take a penalty?" Of course I was. I didn't touch the ball in the remaining minute so my 1 kick was to be telling. If I say so myself I bloody buried it. I doubt Nigel Martyn would've got near it. This in spite of me hearing some wag - I think there were about 5 'fans' - behind the goal offering his opinion that "subs always miss penalties." Huh! Not this one pal.

Upper Norwood did win the Sportsman Cup, not too difficult in the Croydon Sunday League but finally, after 25+ years I had my hands on a medal, based on footballing merit, albeit having made a minimal contribution. Why am I writing about my football career? Well, it was an addiction and there's a few airport stories it led me to, it filled a good few hours waiting in Jeddah Airport but most importantly, it's another chapter because it's gonna have to be 30 chapters. I just can't handle those numbers in between. What I can handle is a 230-seater Wizzair plane with little more than 30 passengers on board; pretty damn unique these days in our experience. We did wonder who else would be flying Larnaca to Jeddah and the answer is not many. We're off for a quick night in Larnaca so Barrow and Spoons coming to you soon. Can you bear the suspense?

# CHAPTER 27

We had initially given ourselves a 3-week window to finish off the remaining Spoons in Scotland and Wales, 29 in total. We hoped to walk some of the England Coast Path (ECP) depending on the weather and maybe some of the Wales Coast Path, even though this is weirdly not a National Trail, as I believe I've mentioned. It strikes us as so odd that rather than continue the coastal walk there's a rather large gap between Chester and Chepstow - roughly - or Chepstow and Chester. I'm sure there's a reason but it's certainly not an obvious one to us.

We had also factored into this time a potential return to Ireland to visit Colin, whose situation was desperately sadly deteriorating. When we received a message from Kelly, his wife, asking if we could visit to help out we naturally didn't hesitate. We had ample time to do the pubs and any walking plans could wait. Having had a few blips along the way with our Spoons counting, caution was in order. Just as bloomin' well. The tally on Agi's spreadsheet did not match the remaining grey triangles on my Spoon's app. It was looking like I had overzealously turned one to green without being arsed to visit it. Surely we had been to Bedworth? Where's that I would expect all but the best geographers of UK to ask. We'd done Coventry and Nuneaton, between where it is located. We'd travelled north and south in that region on numerous occasions. I checked my diaries to see which one of us was wrong. No sign of Bedworth and clearly neither of us had any recollection of the pub or town.

Research completed we had ourselves an unexpected breakfast stop on our route oop north, and 30 pubs to do, instead of 29. On arrival, we were totally convinced - rightly so - that this was a new pub to us. To be fair, neither pub nor town would've left a lasting impression. The friendly barman told us that a new Spoon was due to open in nearby Kenilworth and that it was hoped to be open in time for the Xmas rush. We weren't over the moon with this news. We afternooned and overnighted with friends just north of Newcastle. Such was the strength of the Indian Summer heatwave we had a BBQ... in Northumberland... in September! Amazing, eh?

I'd long wanted to visit Berwick-upon-Tweed. Firstly because Berwick Rangers, as is the town, is well and truly in England yet they play in the Scottish leagues. Yeah, I know, what about Swansea, Wrexham, Cardiff and Newport, you say? I wonder what Berwick Rangers had against England. Maybe they were too rubbish to get into an English league? I certainly don't think it could be argued that they had more local teams to play in Scotland than England but could be wrong, of course. Secondly, Jim the pilot had started his honeymoon there and had said what a damn nice place it was. Far more recently and thirdly it's the first, or last town at the start or finish of the ECP. Just a shame it didn't have a Spoon or commercial airport. Even though Berwick Rangers had slipped down to the Lowland League I still wanted a quick peak but first we had a wee walk to accomplish.

The early morning mist on the drive up from Cramlington had lifted to reveal another stunning early autumn day. We took a bus a few miles north and made our way to the coast and walked the short distance to the border, 1/2 mile or so, and the start/finish of the ECP. What a bloody let down. There's not even one indication whatsoever that you're about to start or finish a 2,700-mile coastal walk. We were pretty disappointed but it couldn't spoil our mood. The coastline and weather were equally spectacular. Don't get me wrong, there's signage both on the footpath and by the railway track that leaves you in no doubt that you're on the border of England and Scotland. It's just the lack of National Trail signage. Maybe it's coming in the future. You wouldn't want a big fanfare for sure but a little acknowledgement of what you're about to set out on or have just achieved would be nice. For now you'll have to be content with the first/last acorn a few hundred yards south of the border. We walked the first 5 miles of the path south to Berwick, so at least had a few meaningful miles under our belts.

Jim was right: Berwick-upon-Tweed is indeed a very picturesque town in a lovely location. It was time to head north though. We had 2 pubs to visit on our way to our overnight stop; not very interesting Livingston and far more interesting Dunfermline. At least I knew now where Livingston FC hung out - we even parked in the club car park and walked to the pub from there. The pub was in our least favourite location - a shopping centre - but at least it had a beer garden. I knew I had visited Dunfermline on a week-long school trip to Edinburgh but not why. I figured that there must've been a reason and the splendid Abbey was the answer. The pub was much better too with a few tables out front on the pedestrianised thoroughfare, one of the few advantages of Covid; more outdoor areas at many Spoons.

After an overnight with more of Aggers' friends in Carnoustie - golf course ticked - not that I'm counting - we headed on a circular tour south, breakfasting at opening hours in a fine pub in Perth; well actually outside once more, in a pleasing riverside location this time. I now also knew where St Johnstone FC lived and where their name came from. The Kelpies en route to Falkirk were well worth a visit. I'm no art scholar for sure but these giant horses made a very favourable impression. Falkirk and Alloa pubs and football grounds visited, we headed east - via Cowdenbeath FC, I couldn't resist it and wasn't disappointed - to Glenrothes; apparently, according to another Agnieszka acquaintance who joined us there, one of the rougher towns in Scotland. The pub wasn't up there with the best either but it did lay claim to being the first Wetherspoon hotel. Unlike all the pubs we have stayed in this was not an historic building; it looked more like a 70s constructed office block. It had a large outdoor area, the sun was shining brightly and we were unseasonably warm. Our final pub for day 3 wasn't a bad little affair in Kirkcaldy and my knowledge of, but not collecting of, Scottish football grounds was further enhanced by locating Raith Rovers FC. A brief diversion to East Fife FC the previous day had caused us to run out of time to visit St Andrews. A bit like Berwick-upon-Tweed I was keen to visit as my son, Callum, had added it to his golf course collection and sung the praises of the town. I doubt it's going to be graced with a Wetherspoon any time soon but the number of non-golfing tourists (never judge a book by its cover, I know) were proof that there were plenty of other reasons to visit.

We'd done the pubs in Dundee with Bogusia in 2019 but I was very keen to view both football grounds due to their unique proximity to each other. Mission accomplished we needed to increase our daily pub total as we weren't even averaging 3 a day. We took coffees in Cumbernauld; a dire location for the pub but so nice inside, on two levels, that we stayed a lot longer than anticipated. Kirkintilloch provided an equally nice pub and much better environs for breakfast. Wishaw and Motherwell bit the dust next - bang average as were East Kilbride, Rutherglen and Renfrew. The same could not be said for the pub in Cambuslang; straight into the top 20, or potentially top 10. The John Fairweather is of the converted cinema genre and a very fine job they've made of it too. I also added Motherwell FC and Hamilton Academicals FC to my knowledge and (non-existent) list of Scottish football grounds. At least when we drove past Ibrox Park I could tell Agnes that that was one I had actually seen a game of football in. A unique experience: I actually thought Leeds would win. Of course they didn't. The powers that be had decided that Leeds and Rangers fans probably wouldn't mix too well. Therefore no tickets for away fans. Luckily the boss of one of my friends was a director of Rangers and put a couple of tickets his way, at the last minute. I just had time to catch a flight up to watch Leeds somehow manage to lose 2-1. A visit to Celtic Park 7 years later was far more pleasant, being amongst permitted fellow Leeds fans and a 2-1 win. Shame it was only a pre-season friendly!

Our final day of Scottish Wetherspoons started off in the splendid Greenock offering (via Morton FC obviously) with breakfast with yet another Aggers friend. In case you think I don't have any friends we did meet one of mine on the outskirts of Glasgow but the posh northern bird couldn't lower herself to meet in a Wetherspoon. Not completely fair as she and husband did join us several years earlier when we were hanging around Glasgow centre, ticking away. We made our way down the west coast via delightful Largs to not so delightful Saltcoat, Irvine and Prestwick to Ayr - a fabulous church conversion. Ayr FC's ground was undergoing some major works but at least it allowed me to nip inside. We headed north to Kilmarnock. It was dark now but Scottish Spoons were complete and Kilmarnock FC had left the lights on, probably not solely for my benefit. A dearth of sensibly priced beds sent us into the middle of nowhere and our beloved Britannia Hotels' Prestwick offering. It was huge and who knows what it was doing there but it did the job, even if the first room we were given was completely unmade. The older dude on reception was sooo friendly and apologetic that it was impossible to do anything other than chuckle.

In case you're wondering I have done Prestwick Airport and there's a story! 1980 not yet married so first wife Jackie could only travel for free on Dan Air and other charter carriers. We had a 5-week trip to Canada. CP Air had kindly offered me a free ticket to Toronto. We travelled out separately. After 3 weeks with her family in Toronto we headed via the Rockies to visit my folks in Vancouver. For the return my plan was to travel Air Canada on staff standby ticket to Toronto for the CP Air flight back to Gatwick. Jackie would fly directly with Wardair from Vancouver to London. A slight inconvenience was that my flight was at 0700 and hers at 1700 but she decided that she would travel to the airport with me and have a day plane spotting. There were a lot of staff standing by for the Vancouver - Toronto flight; maybe 30+. Names were being called. I figured I would be one of if not the last, if I even stood a chance. I had all but given up hope when my name was called and boarding pass offered to me. Before I could take it, it was gone: "Sorry, no tie, Mr Forbes. We were putting you in first class but staff must wear a tie in this cabin". "Oh sorry. No problem, sir, I've got one in my bag". "I'm sorry there's no time, the doors are closing, you can't travel".

Seriously mate? It'll take me 10 seconds to put the tie on. I didn't say the first bit to him but he wasn't impressed with the timescale I offered him and that was that. Every cloud and all that; at least Jackie would have company for the day. At least I had the sense to carry a back-up Vancouver to London ticket with me. Unfortunately my reluctance to comply with the tie rule for staff was going to set me back around £140, at least that's what has stuck in my memory. A very expensive tie indeed! That wasn't the end of it though. I bade farewell to Jackie again later in the afternoon. Whilst I was sat waiting for pushback, rueing my mistake - it was no secret that some airlines enforced the tie rule, so I couldn't really complain that they got me on the 'no tie, no fly' policy - the expected 'Good afternoon, ladies and gentlemen etc.' was replaced by a rather more curt and unwelcoming, "ladies and gentlemen would you please leave the aircraft as quickly as possible in an orderly fashion". Well, I wasn't expecting that. At least it wasn't just me they wanted to offload.

Jackie hadn't yet boarded her flight so was quite surprised to see me again. Air Canada advised that there was a 'security issue' with the flight. The information was backed up with the sight of the aircraft being towed off into a remote area of the airport. A hoax bomb threat wasn't on the itinerary, neither was me waving Jackie off! Both our flights were routing via Edmonton so when mine finally took off, it was quite ironic that we parked not far from hers on arrival. That was one positive in the negative - Edmonton added to the not very long list, at that time, of new airports. What wasn't a positive was the news that due to the delay, we needed a crew change and this would take place in Montreal. If it had been Dorval not Mirabel, I'd have been pretty chuffed but it wasn't. I do remember being woken on the approach to Mirabel by screaming from what sounded like most of my fellow passengers. Maybe I'd slept through the worst of the turbulence as it didn't seem that bad to me. This was before my habit of dreaming on almost all long-haul flights that the plane was crashing: I may come back to that later.

There was one final positive in this scenario and those of you who haven't thrown the book away in frustration (or turned your device off) may have sussed it; yep, we had a scheduled stop at Prestwick before continuing to Heathrow. In 1980 there was obviously no Ryanair to use Prestwick for Glasgow and I can only assume that the runway at Glasgow was too short to accommodate B747's back then. 43 years later it remains my only visit to Prestwick but I did obviously treat Aggers to a drive past.

My generosity also extended to offering her a not insignificant diversion to Stranraer on our way south. No Spoon there but the location had always interested me. If my memory is intact Dan Air occasionally treated passengers to a Stranraer to Larne ferry if the weather necessitated a diversion on its Gatwick to Belfast service to Glasgow; what a ball ache that must've been. The weather continued to be sublime for us and although we hadn't hesitated for long, we were so pleased to have chosen to trust Mazda for our final Spoons marathon. The roof was always down apart from overnight. Stranraer FC may well be an inconvenience for most away fans but at least its location didn't look like it would freeze your bollocks off as often as a trip to Arbroath or Inverness would, although at least they both had a Spoon to take shelter in.

We reached Dumfries in time to break our fast - outside yet again - in the previously visited pub and even take a swim in Ullswater on our way to Barrow. Everything was going very, very smoothly. We even had the added incentive of an evening in Barrow with Pete; he was ticking off Workington FC - a league club until the early 70s still in the same ground - whilst I would finally be back to 92/92. We had enough time to do some ECP walking, take a leisurely drive down to North Wales, meet up with one of our friends in Llandudno - Anna, visiting from Ottawa - 4 more nights on the road and be home in time for our flight to Dublin. The sun continued to shine brightly (there's no way I would've been in Ullswater if it hadn't), even the coastal route to Barrow was a treat. After the anxiety of Harrogate I had bought myself a ticket for Barrow v Morecambe two weeks previously; I couldn't imagine it selling out but it could be considered a local derby, so I wasn't taking any chances. What could possibly go wrong?

# CHAPTER 28

An eerie haze greeted us as we left the Lake District and headed towards Barrow-in-Furness. To be fair and not too down on Barrow, it had become a little hazy earlier but this was more substantial. As we headed over to Walney Island it was still warm but the sun was really struggling. Aggers joked, "what if they called the game off due to the sand pollution?" Ha ha, not funny, but also unlikely in the extreme. We'd read in the news that a Saharan sandstorm was affecting UK but were surprised it had headed so far north. Maybe it had heard about Barrow-in-Furness and fancied a go at adding to its misery. We had ventured down on our last visit to the Lakes with Bogusia and it really did look a pretty godforsaken place. However, the ECP was complete on Walney Island, all 16 miles of it. It did have a few minor seasonal diversions due to bird life but that was fair enough. I figured that to cover all 16 miles of it in the morning before the match was although doable, going to be a bit rushed. We had the time; it was still warm and it was simple to break the walk into halves. We needed sustenance first so headed with the help of Google, to a small fish and chip shop in the middle of a housing estate.

"What brings you to Barrow?" the cheerful fish and chip lady asked. Fair enough question really. I didn't bother with the ECP and went straight to the football answer. "Eee, that were called off a few day ago" the equally friendly fish and chip fryer called out. "What!!!!! You are (f-ing) kidding me (I only swore internally)?" "Aye, saw it ont' news other day." I frantically checked BBC football fixtures in case somehow, the locals had their wires crossed. After all it definitely wasn't going to be postponed over air quality. What possible reason could there be? The fixture had sure enough, disappeared from the BBC listings. Normally a postponed fixture would be there with P-

P showing. I went to the Barrow AFC website. Not only was it most definitely postponed but it had been a week ago, probably why BBC had removed it. The reason: international call-ups for Morecambe! Seriously, their team is that strong in League 2 (Division 4)? Whist I imagined they may have lost key players on international duty for Papua New Guinea, Bhutan, Syria, Palestine and Mongolia (you need to have 5 players away on international duty to request a postponement), the reality was far less exotic: an assortment of Wales, Scotland and N Ireland U18s and U21s (probably U12s too!).

I was royally shocked, gutted, frustrated, pissed off and even a tiny bit amused - but all things in perspective.... Why hadn't they told me? They had emailed my ticket and I'm sure there weren't too many non-season ticket holders for them to contact. It's not like I was desperate to watch the match, just to be clear. I just wanted Barrow AFC done. If only we'd gone to Barrow on Easter Monday! I knew we would have to return to this neck of the woods if we were to walk the ECP but we'd be looking to do that on longer days which would exclude most of the footy season. We had a plan to finish the Spoons which meant I could finish the book. To be fair when I started writing Barrow wasn't part of the 92 and the remaining pub we had left wasn't open (this is out of time sequence but, like I said, there was a plan). It was just inconvenient and frustrating. Still there was nothing we could do, so we did the obvious; headed to the dodgy looking offie to nab a couple of beers to wash down the fish and chips and lift my mood.

To be fair to Walney Island and Barrow-in-Furness the setting for our dinner on the beach was pretty damn fine. If it wasn't so hazy it would've been almost exotic. Suitably refreshed we headed off for a much nicer than expected 8-mile evening stroll and just finished before darkness descended. Our overnight accommodation was none too shabby either and the proprietor was most kind in letting us cancel our Saturday night stay free of charge. In spite of Peter's very kind offer to join him in watching Workington we preferred to head to North Wales a day earlier. Which is what we did after obviously breakfasting in Barrow's Spoon and completing the remaining 8 miles of Walney Island's contribution to the ECP. The haze had disappeared so the walk was even more enjoyable than the previous evening. The beaches were fabulous in places. Add in the interest of walking around Walney Aerodrome and I'd almost forgotten the real reason we were there. Obviously that's not true but Walney Aerodrome is a bit more significant than it sounds; between 1982 and 1988 there were domestic scheduled services to Manchester, Liverpool, Edinburgh and according to Wikipedia, Carlisle. After all it is a pain to get to Barrow but plans to go international at the start of this century never materialised. There's still plenty of activity though with British Aerospace running what amount to scheduled services for their staff (and customers I expect). For those of you not in the know they make submarines in Barrow, of the nuclear variety I believe.

Before we headed south, I wanted to vent my frustration on Barrow AFC. As the match was off it was unlikely that the ticket office would be open but it was only a small diversion to the ground. It wasn't (open) so I decided to write a letter to them. I was very polite but I wanted them to know that I had been there. I explained why and enquired whether, as they would be my 92/92 one day, they might want to make that day a bit special. How, I know not. I did mention that I had driven up from London for the game which was factually correct. I doubt they'd have been interested in our route. Letter dropped in their post-box and we were off.

First stop Holywell. Considering its proximity to Shotton it was a pretty nice town and we were able to purchase some religious paraphernalia for Colin for our upcoming trip to Dublin from St Winefride's Well and Shrine. The prices for some of the offerings at this "Lourdes of Wales" were jaw-dropping; to an atheist at least. The same couldn't be said for Rhyl. I had read in LP Wales that whilst Llandudno and Colwyn Bay had thrived as holiday destinations Rhyl hadn't. Let's just say it looked like it was catering for the less discerning holidaymakers. Lonely Planet didn't describe it quite as politely. Anyway the Spoon was packed and the parking problematic so we decided on a carpet shot and a quick look around. The weather was still marvellous and we had an appointment in Colwyn Bay. We had looked at accommodation options in the area and they were shocking. Why you would pay north of £250 for a night in Llandudno was a bit beyond us. Aggers finally found what turned out to be a very charming Airbnb, high up overlooking Colwyn Bay with a bit of change from a ton but it was still pretty steep with neither en-suite nor breakfast included.

Colwyn Bay and Old Colwyn and the Spoon were all charming. We met up with our friend Anna from Ottawa who was touring Wales for a couple of weeks, treated her to Spoon's finest fare, strolled on the beach and returned to the balcony of our Airbnb, savouring a bottle of red in that all too rare opportunity of sitting outside, after dark and warm in the UK; the pain of Barrow fading but never to be forgotten. The indecisives were in full throttle the following morning. The weather was due to break in this part of UK and thunderstorms were forecast. Dare we risk a 15-mile stretch of the Wales Coast Path? After much deliberation we settled on a 5-mile circular walk, part of the WCP, around the Great Orme (no I'd never heard of it either but it was a fabulous walk and the storm clouds remained in the distance) but not before we had breakfasted in the much-vaunted Wetherspoon. Llandudno's The Palladium features very high on anybody's Spoon list and even those non-collectors will always ask if we've been there. Save the best until last..... nearly. We had considered to make it our last pub such was the hype but decided that if we did, we would most likely have a very small party. It was a very fine pub but better than Tunbridge Wells, Newport (IOW)? I could go on but won't.

Neither The Black Bull Inn nor Bangor will remain too long in the memory. Maybe because they're sandwiched between Conwy - no Spoon but a fine castle - and Caernarfon - the Tafarn Y Porth not matching the splendour of the town. Bangor looked like it had seen better days but it does enjoy a decent location, so all was not lost. Caernarfon was busy with tourists and no wonder. All I knew was that I remembered many years back watching King Charles being inducted or whatever these royals do, as Prince of Wales and how grand the castle looked. 50 years later it was still looking mighty fine. Whilst the pub itself wouldn't remain memorable what happened over a 1/2 pint will; we had taken to recording our pub visits on the Wetherspoon food and drink app as this allows one to keep a tally, unlike the pub locator app. What should have happened as we added Caernarfon was 819/823 but what was this: 819/824!!! Had one of us, both or more likely me, cocked up again? We had Pwllheli, Birmingham station and airport and The (newly-opened) Stargazer in The 02, for the grand finale, to get us to 823/823. How had the open pubs total increased in the time it had taken to drive from Bangor to Caernarfon? It was definitely 823 as we added that one. If a new pub had opened this day surely it would've opened at 0800?

After searching through almost all geographical locations on the app Aggers solved the mystery; Tim (Martin), you bugger, bloody Newcastle University! We'd just been in Newcastle ffs! Although to date there had only been one Uni campus pub it was on a par with shopping centre pubs in the desirability stakes. As we mulled over whether we should try and fly to or from Dublin to or from Newcastle further investigation revealed that the pub wasn't actually due to open until the coming Friday. Alright so we will have to go back to the north east to walk the ECP - no hardship - but we want to get these pubs done and I want to get this book published before they open another one or Gateshead FC get promoted to the Football League. We had had a lovely, lovely trip but we had now failed on 2 accounts.

We had toyed with the idea of leaving Pwllheli until we walked around that part of Wales but decided that that could be a very long time away. Whilst enjoying dinner then in the Pen Cob, Pwllheli 's bang average - actually below average - Wetherspoon, we thought we'd try and find out if Wetherspoon had any more surprises for us. Butter my arse!! They bloomin' well did and it was even more inconvenient than Newcastle University. Heathrow Terminal 4 may well be very close to home but it is not a low-cost carrier's paradise; in fact there's none. Why did they have to open a pub airside in Heathrow? This was painful, I had to check our options; Paris £50 each. It could be worse but that's gonna be an expensive pint. This pub opened in November but at least there was some good news; another new opening in Euston, January 2024. We were never keen on finishing in The O2 so now we had a much better option and...... if Wetherspoon would be kind enough not to open any more pubs for a few months we would finish on 900! Back of the net! Cashback! Buckaroo!! Yes, that's 75 pubs which have closed since we graced their doorsteps and that number is definitely going to increase. In fact I know it has already. So not all the numbers will please me (multiples of 5 being most relaxing) but 900 would be a splendid closing number.

We liked The Castle Inn in Ruthin so much on our inaugural visit, and the town, that we decided we would include a night in this charming Spoon hotel. We weren't disappointed. We revisited Newtown Spoon for brunch on our way south, overnighted with lovely Chantal in Worcester and decided to revisit our wedding night Spoon for breakfast and to see a bit more of Tewkesbury. The last bit of the plan was well and truly in the bin; it was hammering it down but it was nice to be back in our most memorable pub/hotel. Despite the collecting disappointments it had been a mighty fine trip. Now it was time to head back over to Dublin.

# CHAPTER 29

You don't need me to tell you what an utter, utter bastard cancer is. There can be nobody who hasn't been affected by it. Both my parents died from it, my sister's had it, my dear friend Marion, fellow LUFC supporting friend died from it at 43. That's just the start. We spent a week visiting Colin in a hospice in Athlone. 3 days after we left he passed. We had arrived as a surprise for him on his 53rd birthday. At least that brought a smile to his face and him calling me a "fucken prick" (in the nicest possible sense, hopefully!) brought a smile to mine. The only sign that the old Colin was in there still. My good friend Rob (who lost his first wife to cancer way too young) rightly pointed out that he very much disliked the phrase "they lost their battle with cancer" because it sounds like they weren't trying hard enough. This has stuck with me, which is why I mention it, even if some of you may choose to think it's pedantic. Kelly, his incredibly strong wife, asked me if we were looking forward to our next European jaunt; we were leaving 4 days after we returned from Ireland. It was impossible to look forward to it, whilst seeing others suffer so much and even more so when we received the call the day before we left.

Go we did though as described in chapters 25 and 26; apologies that everything is rather non-chronological but that's how I talk too. After this trip we received confirmation that Agnes's mum's cancer had come back. Clearly there was no way we would proceed with our 2-month winter trip. I told you I didn't like to tell you our plans in advance, but I didn't imagine such devastating news would be the reason they didn't materialise. Colin's therapist had tried to show him how to enjoy life when he could, living within the cancer. I think he did a pretty good job of that. It feels so trivial to write about silly collections when loved ones are suffering but it also feels disrespectful not to mention them, the loved ones that is. We have to continue with our lives whilst pausing to do the best for those we love. I know it will be a few months, if not longer before we become 825/825, me 92/92 and that walks and airport goals have been achieved. I can't say that these things become irrelevant but they naturally do slip way down in the pecking order.

I'm sure you wouldn't mind knowing in the meantime, how that Wizzair/Ryanair and easyJet obsession is coming along and a few other stories. Well, I've actually been enjoying the writing for quite some time now and I've even sold 65 copies of But I Digress. I don't actually know how many of those 65 have or will enjoy reading it but enough have said so to make me push on.

I reckon I've stuck pretty well to my promise to myself to reduce my airport collecting addiction; 17 of the last 21 new airports have been Wizzair and Ryanair destinations and I'm on an unbroken winning streak of 12 as I write. We binned off the proposed routing via Saudi Arabia to Sri Lanka and back via Egypt but figured that in between helping Bogusia we could escape the Polish winter for a while. I actually suggested to Agnes that I should abandon this latest addiction; we had purchased tickets with Wizzair via Larnaca, Jeddah, Medinah and Abu Dhabi to Salalah. From there we would fly with Air Arabia via Sharjah to Colombo and back and onwards to Alexandria. We then had internal flights with Air Cairo (new airline to us) from Cairo to Hurghada and back from Marsa Alam to Cairo. Our final airport tick would be the new Cairo airport, Sphinx courtesy of Wizzair to Rome (we are just descending to Fiumicino now so I will continue later) and onwards to Rzeszow.

A few weeks after we had booked everything Wizzair informed us that our flight to Salalah was cancelled and we could rebook. Well, not to Salalah we couldn't. They were no longer flying to Salalah! We would have to fly to Muscat with them if we wanted to continue with our planned routing. At least this would be a new airport for Aggers but she wasn't so keen on the 12-hour desert run by bus from Muscat to Salalah. Around the same time they reinstated their Abu Dhabi to Sohag (Egypt) service. I'd originally planned to fly from Sharjah to Sohag on our return but didn't see the point if it wasn't part of the collection. You see this is why I was thinking to abandon the plan. Coupled with the fact that 4 of the 5 remaining Ryanair destinations, although in mainland Europe, were awkward and infrequently served, my enthusiasm was on the wane. Aggers, though, was having none of it. After all there's been a few hiccups on the way. How could I expect any less with all this air travel?

By the way, Barrow AFC less than impressed me with their customer service; I heard nothing from them for 2 weeks and hadn't even received a refund so I called them. No, they hadn't seen my letter; they didn't really use the post-box by the ticket office door any longer. Yes, they would refund me and if I contacted them when I knew which game I was coming to they would "see what they could do". Not one word of apology for the inconvenience. Charming! If I wasn't so addicted to collecting, I certainly wouldn't be offering them my custom again. Contrast this with the polite request Agi received from the Barrow Tourist Board asking if they could repost her Instagram story on the Walney Island ECP section.

After a month in Poland, we were in a position where a short trip wasn't inappropriate. We were both very keen to head to Saudi Arabia whilst we still had valid visas. Of course I explored a stack of options but if we wanted to add Medinah and Jeddah to the Wizzair list I was going to have to suck up a pretty hefty Abu Dhabi - Medinah option. I actually feel like it's crossing off the Wizzair list rather than adding to it but I've been adding for 40+ years so it would be a bit odd to start crossing off now. Who would've thought a few years ago that you'd be able to fly from Katowice non-stop to Abu Dhabi but thanks to Wizzair that's what we did. If Abu Dhabi hadn't opened its whopping new terminal a week earlier, we'd have been able to walk to our Airbnb and back but they had. It was pretty impressive but I mourned the loss of that wonderful ceiling in one of the old terminals.

With Medinah Airport added to the list we headed straight to the UNESCO Heritage Site of Hegra close to the town of Al Ula, as we weren't permitted to visit the main attraction in Medinah: the Prophet's Mosque, being non-Muslim. The drive itself became increasingly spectacular with signs of a historical pilgrimage railway still intact to test Peter's knowledge. Whilst grubby on the outskirts the old centre of Al Ula was a delight, even though it was undergoing some serious renovation. The mountain scenery was sublime. We stayed in a couple of pretty overpriced and well below par Airbnb apartments but it was totally worth it for our visit to Hegra - Saudi's "Petra", Elephant Rock and Maraya Concert Hall. The latter became a blag we're pretty proud of; Maraya is the largest mirrored building in the world (at time of writing, Dec 2023). The setting is totally awesome, absolutely magnificent. What isn't so great is the cost and procedure to see it. There are a couple of hotels, one being Banyan Tree to give you an indication of the standard we're talking about, and restaurants within the valley where Maraya is situated. Here's the gig: you've gotta prebook a meal at one of these establishments in order to access the area.

As you've learnt Agnieszka is as far from high maintenance as I could imagine. So when on the rarest of occasions she wants something that might be a bit out of my comfort zone it would be utterly wrong of me not to help her make it happen. I knew nothing about Maraya. She knew a bit and fancied it. Only problem was all the restaurants were fully booked except at the Banyan Tree Hotel. It was minimum £60 for breakfast. You've probably learnt enough about me and my Scottish ancestry to know that's not natural for me (to be fair my Scottish dad was generous to a fault). I was genuinely gutted though when Banyan Tree said they were now also full. We decided to go and check the score on our way out to Hegra. Sure enough barriers prevented any unauthorised entry. Luckily for us the security guard spoke no English and our Arabic is limited to about 4 words. I explained to him in English that no we didn't have a ticket or reservation but that Banyan Tree was expecting us; not strictly true. We assumed that he was repeating no ticket/

reservation = no entry. Luckily for us I couldn't reverse as there was traffic behind us. Unluckily for him that meant raising the barrier. He probably figured we were going to turn straight around and exit. Au contraire! We were in and if anyone stopped us, and spoke English, I had WhatsApp dialogue with Banyan Tree as evidence that we'd tried to make a reservation and that they'd kind of tried to help.

We weren't interested in some fancy breakfast. We just wanted to see the building. It was truly spectacular and, in my little mind, I was minimum £60 in credit. Saudi is truly in its infancy in welcoming tourists but I'd say they're missing a trick here; yes, charge a small entrance fee but the current set up isn't even about the cost. If you can't get a reservation for food you can't see what is a modern marvel of man's creation. I can understand if they want to keep the numbers down but we had the place virtually to ourselves.

We found an alternative exit thus avoiding any potential confrontation with the security guard, if he even remembered us. We had a fabulous tour of Hegra and a delightful walk around Elephant Rock. The weather was ruddy perfect and the scenery on our drive over to the Red Sea coast the next morning continued to excel. We hit the coast at Al Wajh, devoid of any foreigners, ridiculously spacious and quiet but noteworthy on two accounts: firstly the generosity we received in a fairly smart store where we purchased some snacks - dates and humus. The shop boy; I'm sure he wasn't the manager let alone the owner, proceeded to triple what we had bought with gifts. The monetary value was maybe £10-15 but the gesture non-quantifiable. Secondly the remains of the old city were both charming and evocative.

In contrast the drive down the coast to Umluj was pretty bland. I got flashed by speed cameras at one point so figured that my £60 credit from Maraya was about to be balanced out (3 weeks later looks like I got away with one there). We found ourselves an exceptionally nice hotel, for the price, in Umluj and headed out for some nosebag. Offerings were limited so we decided on Saudi's version of the kebab house. Imagine some foreigner wandering into your local kebab shop in UK and their payment being declined. Well that's what happened to us in downtown Umluj. We were guests in their town so, in this establishment at least, taking money for our food was out of the question.

We are not blind to the (human rights) issues in Saudi and are not getting paid to be ambassadors but the kindness and welcome of the people cannot be overlooked. We continued our journey south to Jeddah. Where we could access the coast, notably near Yantub, the colour of the Red Sea was beautiful but the shoreline is not blessed with perfect sandy beaches from what we saw, that's for sure. Having failed in our attempts to couchsurf in Al Ula or Medinah we had 2 hosts in Jeddah. Only problem was one of them was currently in Syria. No problem to him. We could stay in his apartment as long as we wanted. Not really the idea of Couchsurfing but extremely kind. That really would be getting a bed for free, so we chose to stay with Jamal who was very much at home and in Jeddah. What a super nice guy. The hospitality he showed us would be difficult to find in the western world I would say.

Jamal was originally from Egypt, as was our recent Couchsurfing host in Malta if I didn't mention. Even though both these guys were so kind to host us they point blank refused our attempts to return their hospitality in any way. It was clear that it would be offensive to push the issue. Not only did Jamal refuse our offers to buy him dinner but when his friend Ibdullah, joined us the second evening we were told that Ibdullah would be hosting us. I think it's fair to say that the majority of Westerners are totally oblivious to the Islamic tradition of kindness. We would count ourselves amongst the great unaware until very recently. Let's see if this tradition continues in Egypt; a country where the ratio of hassle had far exceeded the hospitality in our limited experience.

Our man at the Metro had said we would be his "journalistic fairy God parents" were we able to provide him with a firsthand experience of footy in Saudi when our trip was originally planned. As it was, the match we had hoped to attend was moved so we wouldn't have been able to go anyway. As luck would have it Jeddah-based Al Ahli had a fixture that would pretty much fit in with our revised plan. Metro Josh was over the moon. So were we when Jamal agreed to accompany us. Even though it was an increasingly frustrating 0-0 the atmosphere, stadium and occasion made it worthwhile even if Josh's superiors at the Metro didn't share his enthusiasm and therefore, our latest media-whoring attempts failed to come to fruition. Another ground to the non-existent overseas collection.

I've done my best not to bore you with descriptive details of the airports we've collected but sometimes they really do warrant a mention. Jeddah does for 3 reasons: firstly the unfathomably complicated journey to return a hire car. We realised we were not being totally retarded in our attempts when we became a convoy (of 3) following a leader vehicle (instructions received from police), having reversed back down a dual carriageway which promised to lead to the car park but in reality, became another dead end. Secondly, rental car safely returned, the new modern terminal, complete with aquarium, is pretty impressive. Thirdly, the 30-minute journey to the old terminal, and the building itself, are both in stark contrast to number 2.

Now I could go into a full recollection of memorable airports, flights, footy grounds, pubs and National Trail sections. I'm seriously sorely tempted but it seems that I don't need the author's version of a stocking filler. Potentially the opposite, so let's move on swiftly to the next addition to the Ryanair/ Wizzair and easyJet additions/reductions. After returning to Katowice via a night and morning in Larnaca (by the way the Wizzair flight from Jeddah to Larnaca was £12 each - crazy, eh?) and some more time in Poland I was cleared to fathom out a route to Egypt, our return still being in place. Hours of research resulted in us heading to Dresden (served by Ryanair from Palma and seasonally, Stansted) to fly with Sundair (nope, me neither) to Hurghada. Hurghada and Marsa Alam had irritated me for a while. After being completely underwhelmed by Sharm El Sheikh around a decade earlier (Aggers also equally so on a solo trip, apart from what lay below) I had no desire to return to the Egyptian Red Sea but with both airports being regularly served by Wizzair and easyJet I had no choice.

At least departing from Dresden was a big bonus. As it transpired not just the extremely pleasant airport but the city was an unexpected pleasure. I knew Dresden had suffered extremely badly in WW2 so figured it wouldn't have much of historical interest. Wrong! Apart from being rather too busy with Xmas Market lovers for our tastes it was neat. As was our Couchsurfing experience there. Unlike Egypt to come and Saudi and Malta previously, I have to admit to my host-finding attempts in Dresden having a not inconsiderable financial motivation. Let's just say that Dresden was looking rather pricey and it didn't float my boat too much to pay more for 1 night there than a whole week's trip to Egypt, flights included. I probably sent off more requests for this 1 night than I had for all our other Couchsurfing attempts, ever. I think any couchsurfer who can say that money has never, ever entered the equation may be kidding themselves. I also think we have now couchsurfed enough times where finances are irrelevant to not feel guilty when they - finances - are.... relevant.

Irrespective, our experience in Dresden was extremely positive and definitely added to the pleasure of our journey to Egypt. Thank you Evgenia and Dmytro. Dresden Airport was an extremely pleasant and quiet experience and Hurghada was pain free too until the haggling with taxi drivers kicked in. Luckily our Couchsurfing host had told us what to pay. I'm sure many before us have paid the 20 euro fare for the 10 minute ride. If like us they only paid 5 I'm sure like us, they later realised what a rip off that was too. And what a frickin' palaver it was to get from 20 to 5. I'd forgotten how expert these dudes were in making you feel like you were ripping them off!

Another chunk of good fortune was that Jamal from Saudi warned us that Egypt, currency wise, was not so far removed from Argentina - official rate 40 Egyptian pounds to 1 UK, black market = 60. It's so cheap anyway but still 50% extra isn't to be sniffed at. Hurghada was neither worse nor better than we hoped for; airport done, basically. Admittedly the weather was rather pleasant as was the colour of the Red Sea but the concept of private beaches makes me vomit, albeit not literally. It's all very well being proud of your city, country etc. but having travelled a fair amount it seemed somewhat patriotically over the top of our Couchsurfing host to insist that Hurghada was the best place to live, in the world! Not to be ungrateful though, Moustafa gave us a better insight into life in Hurghada and way more interestingly his life. He was just 39 and had been married 11 times!! Seriously wtf!!? We were suitably impressed but was this 11 legal marriages and 10 legal divorces? Of course, he assured us. Starting at 17 years old he numbered 4 Russians, 2 Ukrainians, an Italian and with a Puerto Rican being his first conquest. But, he only had children with his 2 Egyptian wives and had always been monogamous! Curiously he did not live with his current wife, their twins and his 2 teenage kids from his other Egyptian marriage. Apparently it was "agreed" that he would live in his bachelor pad, where we stayed, and visit his family as and when he pleased. Tidy little arrangement? You can decide for yourselves.

It struck us as a little bit odd that Marsa Alam Airport is located 50 miles north of the small city from which it takes its name. There's plenty of desert to choose from that's for sure. There seemed little point in adding 100 miles to our journey to go to a place that LP rated as barely worth a mention. It was only the numerous dive sites and resorts that attracted people to the area. We decided to stop for a couple of nights at Quseer, 100 miles south of Hurghada, 50 miles north of Marsa Alam Airport and described by LP as authentic, pretty much devoid of tourists and with a fort and old town to boot. Much more like it for us and I'd found another friendly-sounding couchsurfer. Now you know I like a nice cheap taxi fare. There were no buses as such so Mustafa took us to the Moroccan style Grand Taxi station. Delightful; it was full of old Peugeot (504 I think) estate cars. It wasn't full of potential customers though. Mustafa told us it would cost 50 Egyptian pounds each, less than a £1! You are kidding me. So we could have one of these 7 seater relics to ourselves for just over a fiver if we wanted for 100 miles! We didn't really need to justify to ourselves hanging around for a car to fill up but before we could make this decision Mustafa had found a guy whose car was almost full of cargo so only needed 3 passengers. He would take us straightaway for 150 pounds. I know he was getting paid for the cargo but for us, a £2.50, 100-mile private taxi? I was in heaven. Normally if something's seems too good to be true..... as the saying goes. I showed the dude my 150 Egyptian, he nodded and we were off.

I'm not a car fanatic but I am not averse to a bit of nostalgia. This old beaut rattled along at almost 80 mph on what appeared to be a very new road and if only our driver hadn't been so partial to concentrating on anything but the road it would have been an idyllic journey - mountain scenery on our right and the ocean on our left, late afternoon sunshine (we tried our best to ignore the inevitable rubbish). Aggers and I (she was sitting up front so even more at risk) both admitted to wishing we'd had seat belts once we'd survived and arrived.

Quseer was virtually devoid of tourists. Sadly the same couldn't be said for trash; it was bad, up there with the worst. The place had potential; a really nice bay with a decent length of beach before they got you with the old private beach rule, and an old town full of character which wouldn't have needed too much renovation to be a genuine attraction. Mohammet, our Couchsurfing host was a very cheerful, friendly, easy-going and obviously generous host. Unfortunately his wife wasn't talking to him - or by default us - which was a bit awkward. Something to do with wanting a window shut or other trivial matter. From what we learnt over dinner there may've been just the small matter of him marrying a Russian lady during his current marriage causing some rather more deep-rooted tension. None of our business and he didn't seem overly perturbed. We decided that 1 day and night in Quseer was enough though and Aggers found a ridiculously cheap hotel in Port Ghalib, just 5 miles from Marsa Alam Airport. A morning stroll to the airport was beckoning us.

Quseer's taxi station made Hurghada's look positively bustling.

We reckoned on several hours minimum to fill a Peugeot heading south so quickly settled on a fiver for the 50-mile ride. In my recently more relaxed mode for getting to airports I had been unperturbed about undertaking this journey on the morning of our 1250 flight. However, when our old Peugeot broke down a few miles out of Quseer I doubt I'd have remained as chilled had our flight been in 4 hours' time rather than 20. Our driver implored us not to try and thumb a lift - to be fair there was very little passing traffic - and was true to his word that we wouldn't have to wait long. We didn't know if he was arranging for repairs on his phone or a replacement vehicle but it turned out to be the latter. We were on our way and only hoped he wouldn't be waiting too long himself to be rescued.

It was just as well that Mustafa had warned us that Port Ghalib was a purpose-built resort and not the tiny fishing village we were imagining. We would've had a right old jolt. It now became apparent why Marsa Alam was located where it was. It just wasn't quite so clear why it wasn't called Port Ghalib Airport. After all it was privately owned by the same folk who'd created Port Ghalib and opened the airport just 20 years ago. Shame what I'd read about the airport in Wikipedia didn't mention its proximity to and association with Port Ghalib!

Port Ghalib wasn't horrible it just wasn't, well, very Egyptian. A bit more like Costa del Sol with private beaches. The Polish certainly seem partial to it as there's a ton of charter flights coming from there. At £16 including breakfast our hotel was a steal for 1 night but a 7 or god forbid 14 night package there!? It was a bit of a breezy walk to the airport the next morning but not unenjoyable. Now I know the Egyptians can't afford any further incidents so security is understandably heavy but does it have to be so incredibly unfriendly? I realise I'm maybe going into this trip in a bit too much detail, sorry, so let's just say that not only was security vile it was also pathetically inefficient. I get that they don't see many folk walking up to the airport but once you've established we're not coming to blow up a plane, chill the fuck out!! It's 10 days ago now and I'm still riled by it. "Well, don't fly so much you knobs", I'm hearing and fair enough, but if you're addicted to collecting something you'll understand that's not an option just yet.

The thing is Sphinx Airport the next day was even worse and it's only been fully operational for a year. One of our pet hates is taxi drivers agreeing a price and then trying to up it at some point during the journey. So after several heated exchanges in no common language we ended up walking the last 20 minutes to Sphinx. Same incredulous, arrogant, rude, ignorant security: "why are you walking?" "Err, because our taxi driver wasn't that nice". All things in perspective as always; our new deserted 5-lane highway had reduced to 1 lane at one point. Some poor dude was lying in the road with half his head missing, or at least that's how it looked (I looked away pretty damn swiftly). How he had managed to go into another car and consequently through his windscreen on a road virtually devoid of any traffic we could only conclude involved a mobile phone... just maybe.

Anyway, ignore the security and both Marsa Alam and Sphinx were rather fine buildings and being served by Wizzair and easyJet brought my totals down to 4 easyJet, 4 Ryanair and 8 Wizzair, no repetitions so 16 in total. Not bad, eh? This total will change I imagine and this book long finished, I hope, before they're done, if they ever are. The highlight of our trip though was an unexpected overnight with the closest and uninterrupted view of the Pyramids as you could hope for. Cairo's main airport being to the east of the city, Sphinx northwest and Pyramids southwest made a short detour a no brainer. Of course Agi excelled at her choice again. These dudes running a very simple establishment had made full use of their rooftops that's for sure. We arrived just in time for sunset and had enough time in the morning for sunrise and a sunny rooftop breakfast before heading for the airport. Truly magical. With Alexandria and Sohag airports to do we have an added incentive to go back. Our original plan allowed us a minimum full day in Cairo but the rescheduled didn't so we'd given up on any sighting of these amazing structures. I had visited Cairo some 20 years previous but was as keen as mustard to revisit with Aggers.

So, as we descend into Gatwick, after another 10 days in Poland on Xmas day, apart from the obvious aforementioned cancer related stresses and loss of a dear friend, 2023 had been a bumper year; 1000/500 airport targets reached, 1 footy ground and 73 pubs visited (or 1 footy ground and 4 pubs left) and some reasonable chunks of the ECP walked, which I realise I've not mentioned. Will we need the whole of 2024 to visit 4 pubs and Barrow AFC? I should ruddy well hope not. Chapter 30 should be rather short, shouldn't it..... dear reader?

# CHAPTER 30

So here we are chapter 30, the end is in sight. Can I shock you? I like Barrow, despite what I've previously said. In fact I may be falling in love.

But before I tell you of my infidelity to Aggers let me just tell you quickly how we finished 2023 and saw in 2024. Boxing Day: as our family gathering was moved to 27th how could we best fill our vacancy on the 26th? Yep, you got it; breakfast in a new Wetherspoon. We considered The Stargazer as one to get out of the way now we had an alternative venue to finish in. We were never particularly happy about having this pub in the O2 as our finishing party but had no viable alternative. As it turned out the pub was pretty OK really, with a stack of interesting history adorning the walls. It wasn't such a hardship ultimately. Now, I never like to pay for parking Mazda but realised there was no option if we wanted to be in for breakfast (no trains in UK on Boxing Day). £6 for 2 hours was just about bearable. Imagine my surprise when on feeding the ticket machine within the 2 hours it wanted £36!! Luckily the ticket office was open. Apparently that's what you have to pay for the privilege of taking your kids to Disney on Ice and parking for the duration of the show. Well, I'm glad my kids are long past that stage in life!

What other addiction could we feed? 2 1/2 more miles of the ECP bit the dust around St Mary's Island, Chatham. Considering my sister has lived there for almost 40 years I think I'm qualified to have an opinion on this region of 'The Garden of England' as Kent proudly calls itself. Apart from the historical centre of Rochester the Medway towns look like the compost heap in this particular garden. However, credit where credit's due: the regeneration of St Mary's Island looks pretty well done apart from the inevitable shopping mall. This didn't make much of a dent in the 2704-mile total but every little helps as Tesco says.

A last-minute invite to Essex for NYE prompted Aggers to suggest a spot of North of the Thames side ECP. I don't think I'm in obsessive mode with ECP yet but it's fair to say I'm interested in its progress. As we had earlier in the year when walking from Hythe to Folkestone, we miraculously avoided the downpours around us and walked dry from Benfleet to Thorpe - 12 miles - and very pleasant it was too. As soon as we arrived back in Benfleet on the train from Thorpe it began to absolutely pee down. I think it will be a while before we add to the 36.74% of the ECP we've walked so far (yes, Aggers is in spreadsheet mode) but at least we added another 9 miles on NYD from Tilbury to Stanford-le-Hope, getting 2024 off to a positive start.

I'm actually fascinated with this whole thing; when exactly does the Thames stop being the Thames and become the North Sea? For that matter when precisely does the English Channel become the North Sea? How far up the Thames/Mersey/Severn/Tyne to name but a few do the makers of the ECP go before crossing to the other side? The coastal path without rivers/inlets etc. is quite straightforward but looking at certain areas on the map, Essex for example, it looks quite problematic. Supposedly the ECP should be fully open by the end of 2024. That's the theory. We took a trip south west last summer to continue on from Minehead and made it as far as Burnham. There was a rather frustrating and not particularly interesting 20+ mile stretch going up and back down the River Parrett to Bridgwater but the diversion around the new Hinkley Power Station was very educating. There is a frustrating short gap in the path just north of Weston-Super-Mare to Clevedon. The path currently stops near the Severn Bridges. Is the plan to finish there or to continue towards Gloucester? Who knows? There wasn't much point in us heading down there again until we know and that gap is filled.

Therefore, we concentrated our efforts nearer to home and have done what is open from Worthing to Ramsgate - some very pleasant stretches. Our knowledge of our wonderful island and its coastline and history improving along the way. It was an added bonus to revisit Folkestone Spoon several times; one of the best, a beautifully converted old church. Since then more ECP has opened west of Worthing to Portsmouth and north and then west from Ramsgate to Whitstable. Hopefully if it opens we will have a nice stretch from the southern Welsh border round to the Thames completed. Right, you want to know why I'm falling in love with Barrow, don't you? In pretty quick time for me, I'm going to enlighten you.

Agnieszka was to return to Poland as soon as possible in the new year. I had an NHS appointment I had been waiting 6 months for, finally confirmed for a week later. Should I take this opportunity for a solo trip to Barrow? Or should I wait until we could combine with some more ECP walking? When would that be? This 91/92 situation was becoming more and more troubling. Of course, plenty of indecision. Finally we decided I should go. Agi's primary motivation for this? She's worried I won't stop writing until we've finished the pubs and I've been to Barrow AFC. She's right. Once it was decided I would go back to Barrow imagine the indecision as to how exactly. Throw in the fact that I wanted to go and watch dirty Leeds in Peterborough the next day and the options really were endless. Mazda? Coach to Barrow, then train to Peterborough? Day trip to Barrow, home, day trip to Peterborough? Inexplicably nobody wanted to join me for either match! Having pondered and finally dismissed the cheapest options of night coaches to Lancaster or Penrith I gradually narrowed down the options. After our recent extremely pleasant Couchsurfing experiences overseas I thought I'd give the good folk of Barrow a chance to shine and make my return to Barrow more worthwhile. There weren't too many of them but I banged off a few requests mainly to guys who hadn't been active for 5+ years.

As you know Aga says that things happen for a reason. Well, having settled on a day trip by train (due to no Couchsurfing replies, not really relishing a night on me tod in Barrow and realising that I really didn't need to slum it on a night bus) my attempts repeatedly failed on the payment page. Transaction failed, I'd have to wait and hope that the cheap fare would still exist when I could try again. Well I'll be darned/blow me down with a feather; before I can have another go up pops a message on Couchsurfing:

Hi Alan, thanks for your message. We can indeed host you (I have a wife and son now). We have a spare room you can stay in and I like your story in covering the 92 FL grounds! Barrow has changed for the better in recent years, that's for sure. I must mention that I actually live in Ulverston now which is a small town 20 mins drive/train from Barrow. If I'm available, I'll come to the game with you if OK. I'll also be able to drive you around some of the places of interest. We look forward to hosting you if still keen?
Thanks, Simon.

BOTN! (Back of the net for you non-Partridge fans). I wasn't expecting that. I went back on the Avanti West Coast website and this time my attempt to pay to travel up Friday and back Saturday worked first time. Barrow AFC had done the minimum and at least given me a couple of free tickets. All I had to worry about now was the weather. Plenty of flooding, followed by freezing all over the UK. BBC Weather app informed me that it was actually going to be dry and temperatures preceded with a + rather than a - for Friday and Saturday in Barrow-in-Furness. I dared to dream. As I wandered down to Woldingham station to catch the 0559 to London I questioned again my sanity. All this just to go to a football ground that I'd already been to twice but just missing a vital ingredient; someone kicking a football. As the already ridiculously busy train filled up in East Croydon, I figured I wasn't that mental after all. At least catching the 0559 was offering me a return to Barrow, not just another day at work.

As it happened, I decided to spend a few hours in Lancaster before proceeding to Ulverston as Simon wouldn't be around before 4 pm. Having never set foot in a prison in my life I'd now been in 2 in less than 6 months; part of Lancaster Castle was a prison until just around 12 years ago and was now home to Lancashire Police Museum. My visit to Barrow had only just started but was already turning into a mini holiday. If you're not familiar with Alexei Sayle's 'Strangers on a Train' podcast have a listen: " What's your name and why are you on the train?" he asks in a friendly manner. I fancied reenacting this to the 2 guys who sat opposite me on the 0830 Euston to Glasgow but before I had even finished contemplating this and how it would be received, headphones were on and not a chance of any interaction. Whilst it looked like my overseas Couchsurfing experiences may be replicated in UK, that frequent conversation on public transport didn't stand a chance. Shame as they looked like a couple of Mexican drug lords but I'm sure they weren't speaking Spanish.

Finishing my pleasant interlude in Lancaster with a late breakfast and unlimited coffees in Wetherspoon for the ludicrous January sale price of £2.98 I was off on the scenic ride to Ulverston. It was a beautiful sunny, crisp winter's day and the intricate coastline was looking splendid. My mind drifted to the ECP. How the hell was it going to run along this wetland area? I was happy to see some paved and fairly well-populated sections but other parts showed no signs of a potential route. Hopefully we'll find out later in the year.

I had wrongly assumed that Ulverston wouldn't be much other than an inland version of Barrow. We had passed by as we made our way despondently out of Furness (meaning rump at the headland apparently) on my previously failed attempt but closer inspection revealed a very pleasant town centre. A hike up to the Sir John Barrow Monument not only afforded splendid views of the surrounding area but also an intriguing conversation with a slightly strange character. I couldn't really ask him why he was on the train and where was he going but I could and did ask him, after asking if he minded me asking, why he was wearing a long skirt. To be fair, I only asked him after he pointed out that his skirt was going to prevent him from continuing to the top of the hill. I was vaguely aware that his trousers were very flared even by 1970s' standards but

I was more interested in his teeth - or more precisely tooth - than the fact that his flared trousers were in fact a skirt. Was he wearing the skirt for religious or sexuality reasons? No. Since his wife had died he'd enjoyed wearing skirts at home and he was now trying it out in public. He'd driven up from Devon that morning to visit his stepdaughter. I wondered if she knew he was wandering around in a full-length skirt. Interestingly despite numerous visits to Ulverston he'd never ventured to Barrow. See how much more interesting life is when you get chatting to (strange) strangers. I actually felt like I'd boosted his confidence in wearing a skirt out in public as we bade our farewells. I was having a ruddy good time and I hadn't even met my hosts yet. Only Aggers was missing.

A thoroughly pleasant evening in the company of Simon and his Thai wife (I only mention that she was/is Thai because of the delicious Thai curry she served up) made me feel that even if Barrow AFC v Tranmere Rovers was unexpectedly postponed my trip had already been worthwhile. Not only were they both thoroughly nice and interesting people but Simon was a fellow Leeds fan to boot. Why was I falling in love with Barrow though? Well, the next morning, after an equally flavoursome breakfast, and in beautiful sunny skies, Simon took me on a tour of the area including Roa Island, where a nearby basking seal added to the views over to Walney Island, and charming Furness Abbey. As he was unable to join me for the match due to his own match not being postponed, Simon dropped me at the ground around midday. I was in no danger of missing the 3 pm kick off so I retraced our steps over to Walney Island even revisiting the chippy where the bombshell of the postponement had been dropped. They even remembered me.

Passing through the pedestrianised town centre I knew I wasn't in love with downtown Barrow. Perhaps because I'd been so down on Barrow-in-Furness in general, I was feeling these emotions. The beautiful sunshine definitely helped. It certainly hadn't been love at first sight. Or second. A bit like my experiences in romantic relationships; me and Barrow, sorry Barrow and me have been a slow burner so I reckon we could last, whereas we'd have been done already if we'd fallen for each other immediately. To be fair I've no idea if Barrow feels the same about me. After all I've not been very nice about it previously. Simon opined that Whitehaven was lovely and Workington not so bad either. Well let's see when we revisit on the ECP (that section is already open).

Barrow AFC 1 Tranmere Rovers 0 won't stick long in the memory but Patrick Bamford's wonder goal in Leeds' unexpected comfortable FA Cup victory at Peterborough the next day will and capped off a pretty decent weekend. It really was pretty special, his goal that is. So why have I gone into so much detail about my trip to Barrow when I could have simply said I was back to 92/92 having finally ticked off Barrow? I dunno. Well, it's the last ground I'm ever going to tell you about, isn't it? Ah, hang on a second. This trip made me wonder how many new grounds I've attended on my own. A few, particularly in more recent years when a new ground came along and Leeds weren't likely to play there but one from many years ago springs to mind.

Way back in 1977 British Rail introduced a revolutionary new train, the Inter City 125 on their routes to the West Country and South Wales. 92 found out that they were offering a special fare of £1.25 single to any destination along the route to Swansea. A bargain even back then, even though we got fares from as little as £2.80 return to Manchester for example, through the Leeds United Supporters Club (London Branch) and Leeds was only a fiver return. I'm not sure why it was always more to travel from King's Cross than Euston but it was and makes my £66 seniors' discounted return to Barrow sound a bit pricey. Dave Brunt ran LUSC London Branch when I started following Leeds around the country. He was very, very rotund. I will leave you to finish Dave Brunt the big fat..... as he was fondly known by the members. I feel a major digression coming on but I'm trying to cure myself so Let Me Finish, please. 92 always came up with the non-Leeds new ground options so I just tagged along. Off we went to Cardiff, Bristol (Rovers) and Swansea with just Newport to go, for just a tenner.

Like I've said before it's so mysterious the memories we store; why is the only thing I remember about the Swansea trip the taxi driver getting his Austin Cambridge into 4th (top) gear well before he'd reached 20 mph? Why were we getting a taxi to the ground? I was barely 17, who did I think I was? Anywaaaay I'm waiting at Paddington for the train to Newport and there's no sign of 92. He's cutting it a bit fine. I decide to leg it to a phone box. Mummy (may've been daddy, brother or even sister) 92 answers the phone. Asking if Steve was there, I really wasn't expecting an affirmative. "Ah, Alan Groves. I've overslept, not going to make it". I distinctly remember that not only was I now going solo to Newport on a miserable December day but he didn't even apologise. I can't be sure the weather was miserable but I was. Only now can I look back and think that at least I had a ground in my locker that he didn't.

I'm no trainspotter but I bloody love those old 125s and it only added to the pleasure of our honeymoon some 44 years later to travel on one from Arbroath to Aberdeen. I did have a quick butchers on Wikipedia about the year of their introduction (1976) but I'm sure Peter could explain why the promotion was on when it was. Last time I saw him by the way he was proud to tell me he'd started a new collection; estuary ferries of England. He's on 23 but doesn't know how many to go. Naturally we got on to when does a river become an estuary or vice versa?

Whilst in Welsh territory I also went on my own to Wrexham. I've taken a look back over the 155 grounds to work out why I decided to drive up the A5 all the way from London to North Wales on 25 February 1986. I remember I was getting impatient to finish the original 92. I only increased my total from 51 to 53 in a particularly barren 3-year spell between January 1979 and February 1982. What was I playing at? Courting, getting engaged, buying a house and getting married? - no excuse. I do hope my airport totals and Leeds games weren't as pathetic. I made slow but steady progress over the next 3 years so only had 6 left. Working shifts had many advantages but also left quite a lot of spare time. Jackie and I had split up and I had temporarily moved back to my parents. Ah that's the reason; I didn't want to spend any more time there than I had to. Not that I didn't like my parents but I didn't want to hang around there any more than necessary. So in between a vast increase in my overseas travels I must have had a spare Tuesday (or Wednesday). At least I had a share of a nice car at the time; a brand new Ford Escort XR3 which Jackie's dad had bought for us which coincidentally provided the opportunity to tick off Bristol and Cardiff airports when I went to collect it a couple of years previously. Funny to think that there used to be a Gatwick-Bristol-Cardiff scheduled service but there was. Never been to either since. What is also significant about number 87 is that it remains the only competitive match of the 155 grounds with an attendance under 1,000. Where were the other 10,000 back then who fill up the Racecourse Ground now Wrexham have high profile Hollywood owners? Not to be too harsh on Wrexham, there were some pretty rubbish crowds everywhere in the 80s.

Talking of low crowds I decided when my neck brace finally came off after 3 months I needed to get out. My Leeds mate Greeny was throwing his 50th birthday bash in Skipton. I've no idea how many new grounds I needed back then in 2009 but I saw an opportunity to combine a trip to Skipton with a couple of pre-season friendlies in Accrington and Morecambe. I mention this for one reason apart from that both games unsurprisingly attracted crowds of under 1,000; just a few weeks later whilst half watching the EFL highlights programme my ears pricked up when I heard " and Morecambe in their last season at Christie Park before they move to their new ground.....". You've got to be kidding me. It took me nearly 3 years before I could face returning to Morecambe. At least I made a 3-day trip out of it and had a memorable time in the nearby Lake District. Morecambe wasn't so bad after all either, second time round.

Now I could go on but that really would be pushing it. There's plenty of these 155 grounds that when I visited them for the first time I have little to no memory of the journey or the match. I've been mulling over the idea of having an appendix or appendices. I quite like the idea. So if I do and the grounds are listed then in the almost non-existent possibility of anyone saying: "hey Alsy, Ally, Al, Forbsie tell me what you remember about Hereford v Preston on 11/02/78" for example, I could tell you that I went with my 2 cousins Michael and Curly and that we witnessed one of the dullest (0-0) matches we had ever seen at that time.

I did feel quite chuffed that I was finally football grounds complete. I celebrated with a Barrow Wetherspoon special of fish & chips and a pint of Leffe for £6.18 before heading back south. How can you not love Spoons!? I'm grateful that Everton have put back moving to their new ground until 2025. What I was far less happy about was the news Peter forwarded just 4 days after my Barrow 'high' that Wetherspoon is to open pubs at Haven Holiday Parks!! Seriously? Is there no end to this madness and subsequently this book? They've already announced that the first of these is to open in Filey in March. There could be 38 of them potentially. Will they be open to non-residents or will we have to book into a Haven Holiday Park for the privilege of visiting a Wetherspoon that I imagine will very unlikely be an historic building? Maybe there's a reason not to love Spoons.

We need to get those last 3 pubs done and pronto!

# CHAPTER 31

When I started this writing lark, 4 years ago, I would never have imagined that there would be a chapter 31, book 2. No way would I have imagined the circumstances in which I'd be writing it either. As you will have worked out, I mainly write in the past tense but occasionally present. Not that it'll be the present when you read this but it is as I write it. It was looking like we would be staying in Poland for the foreseeable future. Those pubs would have to wait. Don't worry dear reader, everything is in perspective, in case you were beginning to think that I'm completely devoid of emotions. There's very little that puts me off my determination to fulfil the completion of collections but health of loved ones is certainly number 1 on that very short list.

Some of my friends seemed rather surprised that I went to Millwall v Leeds less than 8 hours after my mum passed. My kids were abroad. My sister at home with her husband. What benefit was there in me sitting at home on my own? I'd been preparing for the inevitable for a few days. Did Leeds winning at the New Den that day make it any easier? No, but it didn't make it any harder either. Life goes on as the saying goes. I'm not sure if it's appropriate in this instance. In my book (not either of these, you understand) so long as you do the best by those you love in their time of need......

So that's what we'll be doing. In the meantime I'm going to see how many stories I think I may have left for you, of relevance to the initial point of the books. Whilst they didn't add any new airports I'm going to start by lightening the mood with a couple of more recent surprises.

However, here's the issue with writing in the present; things can change very quickly. I'm currently in my favourite writing location, just 48 hours after writing the above. On a flight but let's keep the suspense of the routing for now and go back to the previous paragraph. This surprise has a real feelgood factor, I reckon. No new airports but a very happy flight nonetheless. I had a plan to nip down to South Africa for the final test match in 2005. If England could avoid defeat they would win the series. Day 1 was washed out, so I decided I would head down the following evening to catch the final 3 days. Flights were looking pretty busy but it was worth standing by. My son, Callum, 11 at the time, was upset and couldn't understand why I forbade him to go on a sleepover. After all I'd let his elder sister do just that. He grizzled "it's not fair" as I said he had to accompany me with his mum to Heathrow as I was travelling on standby to Paris for work and may need to head to Gatwick if I failed. That was no reason for him not to go on the sleepover but he was less of a fighter than his sister. She would've done more than grizzle.

Off we set to Heathrow, I headed to the BA standby desk while he waited with his mum and little sister, grumbling away at the unfairness of it all. "Good news, I'm on the flight but I'm not going to Paris. I'm going to Johannesburg for the cricket" I announced on my return. "Oh dad! You're so jammy", he moaned. I'd already got him hooked on cricket. "Yeah, but guess what? I've got 2 boarding passes and your name's on the other one!" Cute, eh, dear reader? He was rightly overcome with emotion but through his tears of joy his first words were:" but what about school, dad?". "Don't you worry about that sonny. We've gotta dash, are you coming?" It was a fabulous 3 days; England drew so won the series and I have many happy memories of this trip as I hope he does too.

I could write a whole chapter on trips with my kids, many of which did involve adding to the airport collection but that would be self-indulgent, wouldn't it? You could argue that of all this is anyway. I'm just going to even things up with a quick story on my 2 daughters. Jordan, eldest daughter, had gone to Lanzarote. Her partner, James's parents have a home there. I cleared it with James that we planned a surprise visit. They were going over to Fuerteventura for a night so we timed it that we could meet them off the ferry. I hope it was the shock that Jordan's first words were "What are you doing here?" rather than disappointment at seeing us. If it was the latter at least Aggers got 2 new airports in.

I travelled a lot with my youngest daughter, Molly. The age gap between her and her elder siblings is such that they were doing their own thing and didn't necessarily want holidays with dad; Jordan even turned down a week in Brazil (new airport, Salvador, in case you're wondering) just to go clubbing in London one night! Molly had quite a habit of being sick, particularly on planes, stomach migraines apparently. Now I was a pretty hands-on dad but one thing I'm not great at is sick, particularly other people's. Milky baby sick is fine but once it's got food in it? Molly was very fortunate that on our solo long-haul trips she only knew the business class cabin. I was very lucky that we invariably had the seats facing each other with a divider in between for those not travelling together. I don't have a surprise flight to recount with Molly but what surprised her was my reaction towards the end of a flight to Houston. "Dad, I think I'm going to be sick". I handed her the sick bag and promptly raised the divider. Bad parenting? Well she'd had plenty of practice and what was the point of me joining her on the sick list? I don't think it scarred her but she's not forgotten it 15 years later.

So we're on the descent now, bit bumpy for writing. Or so we were. And now I'm back in my favourite writing place (82 hours later)..... well, not the best example; Aggers is in 8A and I'm in 32F. I'm not sure if the chap in 32E is extra-large, just an experienced space invader or that I'm more than happy to share what space I have with Aggers. Let's just say it's a bit cramped but hey, it's a stunning sunrise, even if for once our refusal to pay to sit together failed. The point of sharing more stories was to fill time while we finished the pubs, not pad out the book. However, there's been some unexpected developments and we have a few days to do as we please.

You're obviously desperate to know where we were going on

that first flight. So a 4-hour train ride took us from Kedzierzyn-Kozle to Poznan. But as the train pulled into (the other) KK (not Kota Kinabalu obviously) where was the buffet carriage!? One of the beauties of Polish trains is that there's no daft fare systems like in UK; rock up on the day and it's the same price as if you book a month in advance. You can even buy the ticket on the train, no threats of massive fines. And I get an old man's discount without paying £30 for a card for the privilege. Win, win, win. Previously we had treated ourselves to first class and ended up sitting in the buffet car. So this time we bought 2nd class but where was the buffet car? Broken down in the engine shed! Aggers seemed more peeved than me which was a sure sign that she certainly did enjoy the experience. No real hardship, let's just upgrade to first class. Well for £6 why wouldn't you? Why am I telling you all this? Because not due to a Ryanair/Wizzair type of policy we ended up sitting in opposite ends of the carriage in separate compartments. Absence makes the heart grow fonder so I was very fond of Aggers when we reunited in Poznan. She had probably been content with the break from me; I was already quite excitable.

Here's another example of why I can't knock Ryanair; they were flying us from Poznan to Leeds(/Bradford to give it its full title) for £13! I've mentioned bonkers Sarah in Leeds as recently as our trip to Harrogate but God love her: "Hi Sarah, we're heading to Leeds unexpectedly tomorrow night. Don't suppose you'd be around for a catch up etc." "Hi A&A, well I'm working til 10pm but if you don't mind making your way from the airport and letting yourselves in, I'll definitely be ready for a glass or 2 by 10.15. Keep your shoes on as Penny is really quite incontinent these days. Be lovely to see you". Our type of person. Barely a 30-minute walk from the airport, we even had time to pop in to Sainsbury's, grab a few bottles, calm Marley down and be in situ for Sarah's arrival; a very welcome bonus to our trip up north.

After a quick 1/2 (pint) for breakfast in Leeds City Station Wetherspoon we were off on the train to Newcastle. Now it would be remiss of me not to mention how fabulous that train journey was, for me. As per usual with the cricket let's just say India v England 1st test, 2024. Actually I'm not sure that'll do in this instance. Of all the amazing test matches England have been involved in, and mainly won, in the last 18 months this one was the most unbelievable. If I wasn't the only one in our carriage listening to the enthralling end to yet another historic test match culminating in the most unexpected, remarkable victory for England, I was the only one displaying any audible emotion. Although Aggers shares one of her nicknames with the BBC's chief cricket correspondent, even though our first date was at the Oval (Surrey v Northamptonshire Pro40 day/night, since you ask, on a glorious August evening in 2011), she still doesn't get the transformation in the England test cricket team. At least she got Marcelo Bielsa.

Obviously that train journey cost twice as much as the Ryanair flight (4 times if not booked in advance! Mental). Naturally I had some anxiety that Luther's Bar in Newcastle University would be unexpectedly closed; staff shortage on a Sunday morning? Unexpected incident Saturday night still under investigation? It's happened before, think Retford. This time our sole purpose of going to Newcastle-upon-Tyne was to chalk off/add Spoon 898. At least we were just passing through Retford and at least 3 others that have been closed due to unforeseen circumstances. I had called the pub before booking the flight to check that they were normally open and allowed non-students but resisted the desire to phone them Sunday morning for a live update. We had to go there anyway and I was a bit sidetracked by events in Hyderabad anyway, to be honest.

Not only were they open, it was actually a pretty nice pub, virtually deserted with a couple of superb beers and still serving haggis in memory of Burns. The only thing missing; carpet! Possibly only the second Spoon we'd visited missing this vital ingredient. Oh by the way, in case you were wondering Penny is a 17-year old dog and there were a few puddles. Aggers wasn't wrong when she described me as hyper. Somehow I'd managed to order myself 3 pints with my haggis and 2 for her. I won't bore you with the details.

A couple of hours later we were speeding our way on Lomo to London. We were off to the planned venue for our 900-celebration party. Understandably we're not likely to be in the mood for a party for a while so there was no need to wonder if any of our long-suffering friends would be prepared to trek to Euston at 48 hours' notice to join us in what would now be 899. Remarkably, Gill the Wetherspoon photographer would be though. Not a bad little pub the Captain Flinders and it had a carpet, back to normal Spoons. As an example of attention to detail the pub manager pointed out to us that if you looked closely there were a few cats' faces woven into the carpet; apparently Captain Flinders took a cat, Frim, on his expeditions. 899! 1 to go.

In order to add some normality to life and not be too weird Monday was a rest day. Clearly it would be slightly odd not to visit loved ones so that's what we did. We did refrain from including Wetherspoon in our adventure when we were let loose with our delightful 2-year-old granddaughter Elodie but don't you worry we'd already taken her for her Spoons debut - in Crowborough - before she reached that age. We know she can't wait to return.

In addition to there not being any attractive flight prices from Heathrow T4, the delightful train drivers were planning their latest strike for the morning of our departure. To be fair it didn't take too long to come up with our return route. There's no way I could bring myself to pay £200 to fly to Paris or Amsterdam. Even more so there's no way I could voluntarily leave us high and dry indefinitely on 899. Good old Malcolm dropped us at Croydon from whence we could cram into a tram to Wimbledon and a couple of tubes to Heathrow T4, the promised land. I had phoned the Star Light on the Friday to see if there was any way they could help us mark our achievement, landmark, whatever you would like to call it. "Oh, if only you'd called a bit earlier I would have made sure but I go on leave in 20 minutes" was the much more welcoming response than I anticipated. "Let me leave a note for my colleagues and hopefully they can do something". That was better than

I expected, even though I couldn't have let them know any earlier. We didn't know ourselves. 48 hours earlier these last 3 pubs seemed like they would be months away.

When we arrived at T4 Aggers said she needed the toilet before we went through security. I didn't need to excuse myself then to check in secret if the pub knew we were coming. I called the Star Light, started to explain myself, "yes we're expecting you" was the most welcome interruption followed by the instructions on where to find them. I played dumb, not difficult for me, in trying to locate the pub but soon enough there it was!

And 9 0 0 in balloons pinned to the wall with an ice bucket containing a couple of bottles of champagne on the table below it. Well done Spoons, well done us! Well done us being Aggers' response to my 'well done Agnieszka' after a good day walking completed. We were both glad we had allowed ourselves a couple of hours to celebrate before our flight, particularly when Kieron told us that breakfast and anything else we fancied was "on the house". Now don't be getting any ideas and go trying to con free drinks and food out of Spoons. We reckon we'd earned it. So, we indulged in a couple of large breakfasts, washed down with a few coffees and a pint of Guinness. The staff were all so friendly and welcoming. We even ended up with a team photo amongst our collection. We have our very own 'Wetherspoon Reserved' sign to stick on the wall as well as our only Wetherspoon menu as an additional souvenir.

We initially had our reservations about finishing our Spoons mission at an airport pub but the staff and the pub's attention to history led us belatedly to realise that really, where better for a couple of airport and Wetherspoon addicts to climax? At least Leeds was a new airport for Agi even if, sadly, as we had hoped we wouldn't be flying off to a new one from Heathrow. If only I hadn't been so kind as to fit Malta (the cheapest flight that day from T4) into our recent plans for Agi, then at least one of us would've been heading off to a new airport. To be honest neither of us cared much. We were way more excited and happier than we anticipated on completion. We agreed that the enthusiasm of the staff on our achievement really enhanced the feelings. If we'd been a day earlier we would have had another £60 and a few more hours to spend in the pub; Air Malta was delayed a few hours and had to offer passengers refreshments. Where better to redeem the vouchers than in a Spoon?

Alright I know we've only visited 900 pubs. No great hardships involved, not everyone's idea of fun or the best use of time and money, no benefit to anybody else except Wetherspoon shareholders (numbering cousin Philip amongst them) but it has been almost 8 years in the making. I don't think either of us felt that slight sadness we felt at the end of a National Trail. A bit of relief that we'd done it. There will be other Spoons and hopefully they won't all be in universities or Haven Holidays parks. I won't feel the urgency to get there as soon as they open. After all, getting back to 92/92 football grounds has often taken many years. For now we're done; 1000/500 airports, 92(155)/92 football league grounds, 15/15 open National Trails and 816 (900)/816 open Wetherspoons.

LET ME FINISH? Well, WE bloody well have and on schedule too.

# EPILOGUE

That last (ever?) writing on a plane was an early morning flight from Malta to Krakow. Hopefully there would be a buffet car on the train to finish our trip off nicely. There was but by golly were the staff miserable or what?

Was that last trip a bit mad? Has the whole journey to get to 900 pubs, 155 football grounds, 1000/500 airports and 15 National Trails been nuts? We think so but in the most positive way. We haven't done anybody any harm in the process (no matter what those dicks who feel we're singlehandedly destroying the planet by travelling on scheduled flights that will operate anyway think).

"What's next?" This was the oft repeated response when we went public with our Wetherspoon finale. I've actually just realised that I asked the very same question in the preface! The answer simply is more of the same without the mania. We certainly have plenty of National Trails walking to keep us going for a few years. We will visit new Wetherspoons as they open and when it is convenient for us. A new football league ground here and there will hopefully not prove beyond me.

Most importantly if our luck prevails we will continue to wander this wonderful planet. A random check the other day on the Ryanair website revealed 2 new destinations in Morocco: Beni Mellal and Errachidia. We will not be short of inspiration to keep exploring but a new, addictive collection? No! Enough! Or should that be: no? Enough? Never say never, eh?

I've decided to spare you any appendices with lists of 1,000+ airports, 155 football grounds, 15 National Trails and 900 Wetherspoon pubs. In the unlikely event that anybody would be slightly interested they may appear on our website one day. They may already be there. I've just got one more story: I'm sure nobody remembers that I said I'd tell you about Kos and the after-pub outing and the fact that I haven't. There's lots of stories particularly relating to airports out of the 4 collections that I haven't told but you've probably had your fill, so just one more.

I'd only been on an aeroplane 12 times when I joined Dan Air; my first flights being when I was 9 years old to Palma and back from Gatwick. I remember nothing of them yet I remember the FA Cup Final just a few weeks earlier (Man City 1 Leicester 0, 1969). It would be 7 years before I set foot on a plane again. My school friend, Mathew Davies, had encouraged me to become interested in airlines and their different aircraft. We were no spotters but we did go over to Heathrow a couple of times so by the time I boarded the British Caledonian Boeing 707-320 to Vancouver via Manchester the journey was most certainly going to be a part of the holiday. I thought it very glamorous but looking back we were squashed in like a modern-day Ryanair equivalent. I didn't love B707s then. I wanted to get on a jumbo (which I did the following year) but 16 years, 736 flights and 393 airports later when I had the opportunity to fly business class on a very old Air Gambia B707 to Banjul I had respect and love for this pioneer of long-haul jet flying. You could argue that the Comet deserves that title and it kind of does. At least I managed a quick flight deck trip on a Comet 4B to Frankfurt and back before Dan Air retired all their ageing Comets.

I know, what's this got to do with Kos? Well you didn't think I was going to finish my writing career without a ruddy good digression did you! It will lead me back to Kos at some point. I knew I liked flying a lot after my 10 pre-Dan Air flights to Canada (2 trips incorporating 10 flights that is) and after my flight deck trip to Bergen and back I really liked it. So much that I took a B707 flight deck trip to Zurich and back on my day off while Jackie was in Menorca and shortly before Dan Air retired their last 2 B707s. After my 'surprise' flight to meet her in Menorca I'd got a taste for it so one evening, a few days, maybe weeks later, after leaving the pub I called the office to see if there were any flights still going out that evening that I could jump on. A slightly bemused supervisor said that there was an 0100 scheduled departure to Kos. Why would I want to fly to Kos and back through the night on my days off?

I asked myself that question several times on that flight but the novelty factor had driven me. It was pretty cool to an 18-year-old, fresh out of school, to leave the pub on a Thursday night and just fly off to Greece at a moment's notice completely free and in the flight deck. We had to make a fuel stop in Athens on the return flight which, if the captain hadn't exercised his discretion, would have been where we stayed for 12 hours due to duty hours limitations. That would've been quite cool on reflection. I'd only really been to Canada at this point with day trips to Seattle. That's the Kos story out of the way, not that exciting really was it, but of course it's got me thinking; the there and backs on the flight deck were quite sparse for the next couple of years (and normally had a purpose; getting duty free fags for the supervisor for example) but in the early 1980s they took off! Dan Air used to run charter flights to several German cities every Monday and Friday for German charterers. Some of the crews started to come into our office post-flight offering crates of German lagers at ridiculous prices; 24 x 330ml cans for anything from £3-5! Mental, even 40+ years ago. We learnt that staff and crew could bring in 10 crates each duty-free!

This practice flourished until one aircraft came back with so many crates of beer in the hold that the Fuel Control Manager questioned the excessive fuel burn, seriously, but not before I had added Hamburg, Hannover, Dusseldorf and Stuttgart to my list and revisited Berlin Tegel, Munich and Frankfurt when it was my turn to take a 3-hour "lunch break" to go get the beers. I enjoyed travelling on the flight deck on these short flights. Landings were always interesting. Although I believe it was common practice to ask other airlines if they would allow a flight deck landing visit I only recall doing it twice; with Cathay Pacific to the notorious old Hong Kong Airport (number 290 on my list) and into Heathrow with the same airline. I'm sure I could have done many more either with Jim the pilot or arranged by him but 9/11 put paid to that unfortunately. I did manage one flight deck landing with him and it was one of my most memorable; Leeds had had a very successful 2000/01 season so we decided we'd have a little celebration trip. BA were flying from Gatwick to Entebbe (number 491) and it just so happened Jim was rostered to fly on a Friday evening and back on a Monday evening (there was also a flight Sunday evening which I could catch - time was a precious commodity for me back then). The approach over Lake Victoria at dawn was simply stunning. Visiting the source of the Nile and randomly catching the end of the Uganda FA Cup Final in Kampala made it a very special weekend. I didn't need a reminder of how fortunate I was but I did get one; our firm had recently moved to an office located within walking distance of Gatwick. Whilst waiting for a security gate to be installed we had a cheerful chap living in a small caravan guarding the entrance. I bade him farewell on Friday evening and when I returned Monday morning he asked me why I was so early and whether I'd had a nice weekend. "Actually it wasn't bad, I've been to Uganda for the weekend". I told him that it cost me about £80, I've always had this thing about people thinking that I'm richer than I am. "Wow, you're so lucky I haven't been home in 10 years", was his still cheerful response. Home being Kenya not Uganda, but you see what I mean?

I would have to settle for the view from my Jim-arranged business or first-class seat of San Francisco (514), Dhaka (518), Beijing (632), Freetown (675) and previously visited Tokyo - Narita, Vancouver, Seattle and Santiago de Chile amongst many others; the views of the Andes on the latter being truly spectacular even from the passenger seats. I really do owe him a few pints in Wetherspoon! Actually one of those free upgrades has a funny story. I don't think there's a ruling on how long an epilogue should be or what it should contain. I'm just slowly saying goodbye to you and writing. Maybe this should be chapter 32? Anyway, it's not and I was going to Panama (5 new airports) via Houston (George Bush). Jim had done the business, "just make yourself known to the cabin crew as usual". I did but was rather shocked by the response: "Ah, so you're the real Alan Forbes!" Pardon? "I've already upgraded one Alan Forbes. I didn't reckon on there being 2 of you". She was almost apologetic. Anyway, luckily the other Alan Forbes hadn't taken the last business class seat, far from it, but she plonked me down next to him, maybe figuring that we'd have more than a name in common. Au contraire, what an utterly miserable, ungrateful sod. By virtue of having the same name as me and me having a ruddy good mate he was going to spend the next 9 hours being wined and dined by BA's finest. I didn't expect him to kiss my feet or whatever but he could've at least raised a smile and acknowledged his good fortune. I raised the divider before he could.

Milestones or memorable airports/flights, pubs, walks, footy grounds? Well I'm going to sign off with a few of the first 2. The milestones can and have occasionally been wrong as you've seen and readjusted but I think the memories are fairly accurate. Houston George Bush had actually been my 100th airport nearly 40 years earlier on that shortened French Polynesia holiday. The first visit to Leeds/Bradford was number 178. I only managed 21 flights to or from Leeds before our recent arrival from Poznan between 1987 and 2011and that was the first non-LUFC related flight. This was primarily because any Gatwick to Leeds service was quite short-lived. It made more sense to fly from Gatwick to Manchester and catch a train to Leeds than schlep over to Heathrow. Once the government decided to slap increased taxes on domestic flights it also became rather expensive!

Pisa would become 200th. The memories are better though. My first visit to the Seychelles brought up number 60 when we landed on the grass strip on Bird Island. Departing from Denis Island some 531 airports and 33 years later was just as much fun even if there had been a fair few idyllic Island airports in between. Flying to Exeter (99) to play cricket at nearby Ottery St Mary. Parma and Forli (569/570) my first of so many into one out of another with Ryanair and latterly Wizzair. Stellenbosch (457): the only airfield where I took off in an aeroplane and didn't land in one!

I have been very lucky to travel business class, and occasionally first, on a very decent number of the 2,200+ flights I've taken so far. Apart from the obvious comfort provided primarily by BA and less frequently Virgin, Malaysia Airlines and Thai International amongst others a few flights stand out for reasons other than airport collecting: KLM, Amsterdam to Bonaire (545), a delightful DC10 flight (although they'd been renamed MD11 by then). Why? 2 reasons; my only flight over central London at cruising altitude on a beautiful clear January morning and the fact that there was the most wonderful guide dog - a White Shepherd - accompanying the only 2 other passengers in the business class cabin. He was impeccably behaved throughout the 9-hour flight and luckily for him had a bit of room to roam around. I hope he enjoyed his holiday in Bonaire. I certainly enjoyed his company. Aruba, Curaçao, Fort Lauderdale, Washington National and Baltimore were also added on that little "work" jaunt.

Luton to Dubai and back on a Silverjet Boeing 767. My only all business class flight. No chance of being downgraded. Malaysia Airlines from Kuala Lumpur to Heathrow on an Airbus A380. The double decker for the non-aircraft enthusiasts. Everything seemed much bigger on this plane so I'll leave it to your imagination as to why the flight was memorable! The connecting flight from Manila to KL was special too for the superb views of Mount Kinabalu in the distance. Apart from pretty shite weather throughout, 4 new airports in Philippines;

Cauayan, Tuguegarao, Legazpi and Naga (732-735) made that trip worthwhile. Finally a special mention for Phuket Air. I don't think they lasted any longer than Silverjet but what a contrast. Their very ancient Jumbo was of the B747/300 variety. Unlike the newer B747/400 it did not have the range to fly non-stop from Bangkok to London so made a fuel stop in Sharjah (already done, number 110, 19 years earlier). Our outbound flight from Gatwick to Bangkok passed without incident in the big old-fashioned style business class seats. Rumours were rife during our 2 weeks in Thailand that they were about to go bust even though they were adding Amsterdam to their network. When we arrived into Bangkok from Krabi (554, Trat had chalked up 553) we were told that our flight was delayed 24 hours. To be fair they put us straight into the airport hotel. The next morning the fun started; just as we were planning to leave the hotel to go sightseeing in Bangkok for the day we received a call in our room that the flight would now be leaving soon (around 1 pm I think) and to make our way back to the airport. We finally pushed back around 4 pm but returned to stand with a technical problem. It was rectified quite swiftly but as we pushed back again a rather panicky-looking stewardess ran into the flight deck. All we heard repeatedly was "but captain she no wanna fly". After a period of time while we can only imagine that the cabin crew were trying to get the passenger to take her seat we returned to stand again.

It was seriously very, very hot in that plane and we were lucky; we were in the spacious upper deck but it was hot enough that Callum stripped down to his boxers, he would've been 11 years old. Jordan and Molly sweated it out fully-clothed but it sounded like there was mutiny downstairs and quite a few passengers were demanding to be let off the plane. Finally we all disembarked as the airline couldn't find any staff to offload the bags belonging to those who'd had enough. There were some fairly angry punters. One particularly large, obnoxious and scary looking Brit was threatening the timid and tiny female Thai staff that if they didn't get him out of there soon he wouldn't be responsible for his behaviour as he had run out of his medication. When we were advised a few hours later that we would be flying to Amsterdam where Phuket Air had arranged a Transavia flight to take us on to Gatwick the very same fat, horrible git was demanding that they arrange a flight for him from Amsterdam 3 days later! I could only assume he thought he could obtain his "medication" in Amsterdam.

We finally took off around 11 pm, some 11 hours after we'd gone back to the airport. What a shambles. To be fair the transit went smoothly in both Sharjah and Amsterdam. About a week later a Phuket Air B747/300 was impounded at Gatwick due to continuous non-payment of fees and the airline was banned from flying to EU countries. I reckon it was about 4 months or so later I received a call from a pal at Gatwick warning me that Phuket Air's old banger would be taking off shortly. Warning me because our office was directly in the Gatwick flightpath around 30 seconds after take-off. It positively screamed over our office never to be seen again.

St. Matthew's Hall in Walsall. Not a bad pub but why so memorable? Well, it was pub 5 (583) on a day where 15 were crammed into a day, our personal best/worst, in Aggers' ultimately doomed attempt to make our wedding night Spoon hotel number 600. Nothing remarkable about that but a 1030 video call from Jordan informing/showing us that our gorgeous granddaughter, Elodie, had decided to arrive 3 weeks early whilst we were nurturing an early half pint in aforementioned establishment meant we were "wetting the baby's head" as soon as absolutely possible. You could argue that there was a fairly high chance we would be in a Wetherspoon when this family first arrival occurred.

When we were first approached by the press to cover our Wetherspoon collection they asked for a top 5 out of 700. Tricky but we had to choose. As our 900 was covered, some local rags in Cumbria picked up that Keswick was number 5 on that list. I think we need a top 10 really. When it comes to footy grounds I only need a top 1, Elland Road obviously. Talking of which I was disappointed to learn that I only saw Leeds at 33 of my original 92. I did manage 38 new grounds with Leeds (including a straight run of 18, followed by another run of 11 making 29/30) out of the 63 taking me to the current 155 total. And.... I've now seen Leeds play at 110 out of those 155 plus a further 20 non-league/European grounds. Quite a variety from Histon to the Camp Nou.

Favourite National Trail? Pennine Way, well it gave us the most satisfaction for sure. Toughest? South West Coast Path. Most enjoyable? Cleveland Way. Most scenic? Pembrokeshire Coast Path. Wettest? Offa's Dyke Path and Glyndwr's Way. Least inspiring? The Ridgeway. Easiest? South Downs Way. Flattest? Thames Path. Least interesting? Peddars Way section of Peddars Way and Norfolk Coast Path. Quickest? Yorkshire Wolds Way. Most underwhelming? Cotswold Way. Most Wetherspoons at the start of the trail? Hadrian's Wall Path. Closest to home trail? North Downs Way. And finally, favourite incomplete and never likely to be finished trail? Pennine Bridleway. But....I....Digress!

Back to memorable Wetherspoons in no particular order and then I promise, I really will shut up. Actually, I'll try and keep to some order. If I don't give a reason, it just means it's a very nice pub. September 2011, 0900, after recently moving our relationship on from friends to a bit more (than friends) I met Agnieszka at The Beehive South Terminal Gatwick to say goodbye to her as she embarked on a business trip to Cuba. "Coffee?". " Actually I'll have a large glass of red wine, please, Alan". Okaayyy. Fair enough, if slightly surprising. "Don't worry, Alan. Not my normal hour to start drinking but I found out yesterday that my ex-husband is on the same flight". We've never been back to this pub so it is officially number 1 on the list. It would be 3 years before we subconsciously added The Oxted Inn (our "local") as number 2. If you'd told us on either of those occasions that we would clock up another 899/898 Wetherspoon pubs what do you reckon the response would be? "Spadaj!" Well, I wouldn't have said that then. My Polish hasn't progressed massively since but that's probably one of my favourite words and it's appropriate here = get lost!

It's appropriate that Wetherspoon Leeds (station) was number 3. Don't worry I'm not going to list all 900 as you'll have worked out anyway as this is the penultimate page. The George in Croydon was number 8. I reckon the first pub we went to, once it became a thing was The Edward Rayne in Raynes Park (since closed), number 13, 31 May 2016. 320 days later we were in pub 100 although I'm not sure we knew it at the time and although I do remember it, it wasn't very memorable, if that's not a complete contradiction; The Old Market Hall, Mexborough, towards the end of our first Spoons bender, 18 pubs in 2 days. 6 months later The Leading Light in Faversham, Kent was privileged to become number 200. Clearly we meant business in 2017. 100-200 consisted predominantly of pubs in and around London and the South East but a trip to South Wales included the very pleasant The King's Head in Monmouth (151), a fine town too. The route to 300 followed a similar pattern but did include our first foray to Scotland and a surprise 40th for Aggers in Stoke Newington (271); The Rochester Castle is a fine old traditional boozer, currently Wetherspoon's oldest but I believe sadly up for sale now (Feb 2024). The Waterend Barn in St Albans (232), The Commercial Rooms in Bristol (266) and The George in Wanstead (293) deserve a mention. As for 300 itself the wonderful The Man in the Moon in Newport, Isle of Wight I hasten to add, not South Wales made our top 5 and was a worthy landmark. If I had to pick 2 between 3 and 400 for the pubs alone it would be The Playhouse in Colchester (367); the name probably provides a clue to the building's original purpose and the fabulous The Samuel Peto in Folkestone (345); probably should've been in the original top 5. However, The Coliseum in Abergavenny (337) has a special memory; Jordan (eldest daughter) was treating Molly (9 years her junior) to a riding weekend for her 18th birthday present in the Brecon Beacons. We just happened to be heading in that direction to start the Pembrokeshire

Coast Path. Jordan and I shared our progress down the M4 and she managed to convince Molly that the Wetherspoon in Abergavenny would be a suitable venue to take breakfast. Surprise!

The Barrel Vault in St Pancras, newly opened at the time, was our last London pub (358) until Greenwich O2 and Euston came along. We were picking up speed, 4 1/2 months for that century. Rushden was a fairly unremarkable 400 but we did celebrate overnight in The Pilgrim's Progress Spoon hotel in Bedford for 401.

We set off on our worldwide travels in March 2019 with 435 pubs under our belts. The Cabot Court Hotel in a very windy Weston-Super-Mare being a pretty decent place to start our first Spoon's sabbatical. Now we didn't have work to consider we powered our way to 500 in 3 months on our return from South America. It was pretty cool that 499 and 500 were 2 fine pubs in Leeds and that a member of the Batty family was with us to celebrate; young but not so small Joe! The Hedley Verity would've been better as 500 than The Cuthbert Brodrick but we didn't know that at the time. Our slow progress from 500-600 was initially self-inflicted - January and February in India or UK? - and then Covid. A gap of 267 days between The Bradley Green in Biddulph (545) and The Wallace Hartley in Colne (546, obviously) threatened our loose plan to complete the Wetherspoon collection within 5 years of leaving our jobs. We were under half way and figured that roughly 100 new pubs per year, bearing in mind we planned to winter abroad and spend much of the summers in Europe, would be achievable. The rest.... is history!

OK, just before I go, I'm sure you worked out why Stellenbosch was different but just in case; the door opened at 12,000 feet and I'd like to say out I jumped, but that would be a lie. I was pushed, fainted pretty soon after, momentarily regained awareness at 5,000 feet when the parachute opened, then slept again until a few seconds before landing... on my feet.

I blame the very alcoholic lunch required to get me to even contemplate a skydive but, bloomin' 'eck I was scared. But I did it and I've done it; I am finished! We've done it and we're finished!

Maybe see you in a Wetherspoon one day?

# AFTERWORD

If you would like to find out more about our travels or are simply desperate to know if I managed to visit the remaining airports on my "list" then www.aatravels.info is the place for you.

# BOOKS BY THIS AUTHOR

## But I Digress

In the unlikely event that you want more and didn't start with this best seller, my best seller that is, you can find out how it all started.

There are a few anecdotes on how our finishing line started to appear on the distant horizon and the occasional attempt to inspire you to follow in some of our footsteps.

## Cured - But It Took 100 Journeys Around The World.

Coming soon (maybe!).

Printed in Great Britain
by Amazon